Women Adrift

Women in Culture and Society
A series edited by Catharine R. Stimpson

Women Adrift

*Independent Wage Earners
in Chicago, 1880–1930*

Joanne J. Meyerowitz

The University of Chicago Press
Chicago and London

The University of Chicago Press, Chicago 60637
The University of Chicago Press, Ltd., London
© 1988 by The University of Chicago
All rights reserved. Published 1988
Paperback edition 1991
Printed in the United States of America

97 96 95 94 93 92 91   5432

Library of Congress Cataloging-in-Publication Data

Meyerowitz, Joanne J. (Joanne Jay)
    Women adrift : independent wage earners in Chicago,
1880–1930 /
    Joanne J. Meyerowitz.
        p.   cm.—(Women in culture and society)
    Bibliography: p.
    Includes index.
    ISBN 0-226-52197-4 (cloth)
    ISBN 0-226-52198-2 (paper)
    I. Women—Employment—Illinois—Chicago—History.
2. Women—Illinois—Chicago—Social conditions.
I. Title. II. Series.
    HD6096.C4M49 1988
331.4'09773'II—dc19   87-22449
                                                      CIP

♾ The paper used in this publication meets the minimum
requirements of the American National Standard for
Information Sciences—Permanence of Paper for Printed
Library Materials, ANSI Z39.48-1984.

To My Parents,
Freda and Irving Meyerowitz

Contents

Tables

Illustrations

Acknowledgments

I am happy to thank the many friends and colleagues who helped me write this book. I owe my greatest debt to Estelle B. Freedman, my adviser, teacher, and friend. She read and reread more versions of every chapter of this work than any sane author could expect. Her high standards and her encouragement improved every page. Leila J. Rupp also strengthened this work greatly through careful reading and gentle criticism of the entire manuscript. I am especially grateful to her for sponsoring me as a postdoctoral fellow at Ohio State University, allowing me the luxury of a year of full-time writing. John Alexander, James Grossman, Susan Hirsch, Christina Simmons, and Catharine Stimpson also provided helpful comments on every chapter. Lois Rita Helmbold not only gave useful suggestions on improving parts of the manuscript; she offered and continues to offer wise counsel on everyday behavior in academe.

This book began as a dissertation. At that stage I benefited from the advice of Carl Degler, Paul Seaver, and Barton Bernstein and from the financial support of the Whiting Foundation and Stanford University. The comments and camaraderie of the Women's History Writing Group sustained me through what might have been a lonely dissertation-writing process. Thanks to Antonia Castañeda, Estelle Freedman, Gary Sue Goodman, Gayle Gullett, Lois Rita Helmbold, Gail Hershatter, Emily Honig, Valerie Matsumoto, Katharine Poss, Vicki Ruiz, and Frances Taylor.

With generosity, friends, colleagues, and even strangers shared their insights, sources, resources, and unpublished manuscripts. I am grateful to Mari Jo Buhle, Dorothy Sue Cobble, John Mack Faragher, Gary Sue Goodman, James Grossman, Rachel Heimovics, Lois Rita Helmbold, Jean Carwile Masteller, and Janice Reiff. I also appreciate the rich life histories shared with me by retired wage-earning women in Chicago, especially Eulalia B., Philiminia P., and Pauline R., and the welcome offered by Eve Mansardo of the Amalgamated Clothing and Textile Workers Union retirement center in Chicago. Friends and relatives opened their homes to me as I buried myself in my research. Thanks to Freda and Irving Meyerowitz, Leon Goldberg, Jeanine Mellinger, and Daniel Victor Rosenberg. On the most practical level, Warren Van Tine helped by loaning his office, replete with photos of John L. Lewis, for an entire year, and Caleb Deupree assisted at the final stage by typing the bibliography.

The librarians and archivists at the University of Illinois at Chicago Manuscript Division, the University of Chicago Manuscript Collections, the Chicago Historical Society, the Newberry Library, the central branch of the Chicago Public Library, the Hull House Association, the Schlesinger Library of Radcliffe College, and the Library of Congress assisted me greatly with my seemingly endless requests for books and documents. In particular, Mary Ann Bamberger of the University of Illinois at Chicago and Archie Motley of the Chicago Historical Society offered invaluable help with locating obscure sources.

Several foundations and institutions supported this work financially. The quantitative research was funded by a Newberry Library Exxon Foundation Fellowship, an American Historical Association Beveridge Grant, and a National Endowment for the Humanities Summer Stipend. As I revised the manuscript, I received generous support from the University Postdoctoral Fellowship Program of Ohio State University and the Charles Phelps Taft Fund of the University of Cincinnati.

Last but not least, I thank Beth Meyerowitz and Pat Swope for their friendship and perspective.

Foreword

The American women who grew up after the Civil War and hammered out careers before World War I were a robust, gritty crew. Think of Gertrude Stein, born in 1874; Mary McLeod Bethune, born in 1875; Helen Keller, born in 1880; or Rose Schneiderman, born in 1882. They helped to construct modern literature, education, and politics.

No matter how singular they might have been, such mettlesome personalities were no more removed from their period than single stars from galaxies. As Stein and Keller were composing their texts, as Bethune was teaching young blacks, as Schneiderman was leading the labor movement, the meanings of "womanhood" were changing. Between 1880 and 1930, more and more women, both black and white, began to live apart from their families and to make money in a burgeoning, nonagricultural, urban labor market. World War I speeded up this process. A popular label for such garment workers and laundresses, saleswomen and clerks, cabaret dancers and day working servants, teachers and nurses, was "women adrift."

Joanne Meyerowitz has now written a solid, meticulous history of these pioneers of social space. Although she focusses on the working-class women of one urban center, Chicago, her lens is broad enough to show a nation. Indeed, she suggests that women in the industrializing Third World today might be rewriting, in their own languages, the story of these Chicago women. Sympathetically, she reveals the drama and dailiness of their lives, the interplay of toil and leisure, workplace and domesticity, isolation and sexuality, rude realities and desire, pocketbooks and books.

Women took on the city for a variety of reasons. Some had an appetite for autonomy that families on a farm could not feed. Others were escaping from families that were poor, abusive, or battering. No matter what the individual motive, women tended to start their quest on the machine that became the symbol of a technological, mobile society: the train. Remember that Dreiser's *Sister Carrie*, in 1900, begins with an image of Caroline Meeber, his woman adrift, boarding the afternoon train for Chicago with her little trunk and tacky handbag. Often an arduous test, the train station became the gateway into a new life.

The enduring challenge of that life was survival. The urban labor market wanted female workers. However, in part, they were desirable because they were cheaper than male workers. Women were pinned into sex-segregated jobs and paid as if their wages were pin money. Often, they could afford only coffee for breakfast, bread for lunch, airless rooms for shelter. Yet, the "women adrift" did survive. Courageous, competent, they created urban subcultures. There, peers and friends replaced the family as a primary support group. Most networks were heterosexual, but some were lesbian.

Boldly, Meyerowitz proposes that these subcultures provided the middle class with a model of rebellion and freedom. "Women adrift" were not mimics of modernity. On the contrary, they charted the waters of modernity for their more affluent, often self-consciously bohemian "sisters." The "women adrift" furnished rooms of their own, even if the furnishings were often rough, even if the rooms were often shared.

Because of their class, gender, and, for blacks their race, these vanguard women were unable to represent and culturally define themselves. In the last part of the nineteenth century, their popular image was that of passive victims in need of rescue. Meyerowitz is both scrupulous and sardonic when she analyzes the YWCA as an institution that the middle-class woman was to manage for the sake of the beleaguered working-class girl. However, during the first part of the twentieth century, the manufacturing of images, and the products themselves, shifted. The emerging discipline of sociology helped to transmit this image to the elite. The "woman adrift" was no longer passive, but active; no longer a victim, but an aggressive and selfish gold-digger. If men had once sexually exploited her, she now went after them.

Like the most supple historians of gender, Meyerowitz realizes that many women are neither totally powerful nor totally powerless, neither totally willful nor totally wiped out. Instead, she pictures modern women who did what they could for themselves and with their time. They patched together choice and compulsion, self-expression and necessity, the open stride of freedom and the pinch of circumstance. Her modern women confronted both "a new set of possibilities" and "a new set of material and ideological constraints." Without cultural power, without much protection from a harsh market, they were resolute. They bought their own bread and grew some roses, too.

Catharine R. Stimpson

Introduction

At the turn of the twentieth century, record numbers of American women began to move beyond the traditional female domestic sphere. Following the lead offered by pioneering women in the half century prior, increasing numbers of women entered universities and professions, formed organizations for social change, experimented with bohemian life-styles, and demanded a voice in the political sphere. The innovations of these middle- and upper-class New Women have attracted the attention of historians, but by far the largest group of women to move beyond traditional domesticity entered the public sphere quietly to work for low pay as wage laborers.[1] From 1880 to 1930, the female labor force increased from 2.6 million to 10.8 million.[2] The number of women gainfully employed grew almost twice as fast as the adult female population.

Among these wage-earning women, a sizable group, known popularly as "women adrift," not only entered the work force but also lived apart from the homes of family, relatives, and employers.[3] In an era when family life all but defined American womanhood, thousands of such women boarded and lodged in the cities. Most were migrants. In a worldwide and still continuing population movement, often from country to city, women moved from their homes in search of available work. In addition to migrants, a few urban women left home lives nearby in the city. In 1900, one in five urban wage-earning women lived "adrift."[4]

These women did not comprise a homogeneous group. While young and single women predominated, the group included older women and separated, divorced, and widowed women. Though largely poor, they came from various social backgrounds. Native-born black and white women migrated from America's farms, towns, and cities, and foreign-born women came from overseas and Canada. Some left home solely for economic reasons. Others left to escape disintegrating family lives, stigma, and abuse, or to pursue ambition, romance, and adventure. Most lived "adrift" briefly, for a few months or years before they married; others lived "adrift" for all or most of their adult lives.

For the historian, these diverse "women adrift" of the turn-of-the-century city offer the opportunity to investigate American womanhood stripped of family and domestic roles. What happened when women without extraordinary wealth or education moved beyond the family? What shaped their experiences? What social, economic, and ideological constraints did they face? In their work and in their leisure, what options were available to them? As they established new lives apart from family, what preferences did they express?

In the classics of sociological theory, lone migrants, usually male, left the protective and restraining influences of family and village for the impersonal individualism of the city. Not so for the "women adrift." Despite their varied motives and backgrounds, these women shared certain experiences that limited the possibility of genuine and comfortable independence. Although they moved apart from family and kin, they continued to live in an economy where employers and others assumed that wage-earning women had wage-earning fathers or husbands to contribute to their support. With the important exceptions of women who had professional training and those who sold their sexual services, "women adrift" supported themselves on low wages intended for dependent daughters or wives. In addition, vulnerable and sexually suspect, lone women often encountered sexual harassment and stigmatization.

Under such circumstances, most "women adrift" did not move from family and community to a life of individualism or, for that matter, to a life of victimization. Instead, they formed social and economic relationships in the city to substitute for the support and companionship of family. They moved from family and community to new urban social networks. In the late nineteenth century, many women joined existing households, living as though they were daughters in the homes where they boarded and lodged. Increasingly, though, women rejected the parental supervision of surrogate families and turned instead to their peers. They created new relationships that were less permanent and more contractual than relationships in the family. In some cases, they cooperated with other women and sometimes men, pooling resources for shared housing, food, and fuel, or joining together in clubs for shared entertainment. In other cases, women came to depend on higher-paid men. Adopting new urban dating patterns, they relied on men for entertainment, luxuries, and sometimes necessities. By the early twentieth century, many "women adrift" belonged to urban subcultures in which women gave men sexual "favors" in return for limited economic support. A few women entered homosexual subcultures, and here too economic dependence was common.

Like the middle- and upper-class New Women, the "women adrift" challenged the dominant Victorian sexual ethos. When they moved away from home, they belied the tenet that all women, single or married, needed the economic and moral protection of family life. When they mingled freely with men in rooming houses, at work, and at places of recreation, they undermined the "separation of spheres" that had segregated women from men by relegating them to the domestic world of the home. And when some of them expressed their sexuality openly, they defied the claims to "passionlessness" that Victorian writers saw as the basis of women's moral superiority to men.

These departures from middle-class mores attracted public notice. At the end of the nineteenth century, observers saw "women adrift" as symbols of moral decay. The more sympathetic writers, often middle-class women, considered wage-earning women the victims of a ruthless urban and industrial society. They feared that women without the anchor of family would starve or drift into prostitution. In popular romance fiction and in reform literature, authors constructed a discourse that portrayed "women adrift" as pure and passive orphans threatened with sexual danger. The interest in women who lived apart from family continued into the 1920s. By that decade, popular and academic writers had developed a radically different discourse. In films, fiction, and the writings of urban sociologists, the "woman adrift" had become a symbol of modern urban individualism, a self-seeking woman who shunned the constraints of family. The new discourse emphasized the sexual experimentation and gold digging of some wage-earning women and neglected the poverty that most continued to face. The "woman adrift," once seen as a passive exploited victim, had become an active opportunistic exploiter.

This change in discourse both reflected and influenced a broader shift in popular conceptions of American women from the Victorian angel to the modern sex symbol. The decline in the older sentimental image of innocent "women adrift" occurred, in part, as social investigators recognized that the women they considered childlike victims were often resourceful, willful, and sexual adults. At the same time, emerging popular culture industries, like movies and cabarets, used a newer image of vibrant, sexual "women adrift" to titillate audiences and sell urban vitality. The change in images corresponded with the waning influence of Victorian moral reformers, often female, and the rise to cultural power of manufacturers of commercial entertainment, often male.

The history of "women adrift," the challenges they posed, and the responses to them are the subjects of this book. Chapter 1 examines the social origins of "women adrift" and their motives for leaving home. Chapter 2 explores the hardships experienced by women alone in the city, and Chapter 3 discusses the discourse on self-supporting women developed by reformers, popular romance novelists, and social investigators in the late nineteenth and early twentieth centuries. Chapters 4 and 5 examine the ways in which women supplemented and pooled their resources in surrogate families and among peers. Chapter 6 discusses the changing popular image of "women adrift" from 1900 to 1930.

While this work draws on a national literature, I chose to examine more closely the experiences and environment of "women adrift" in a single city. I selected Chicago because it approximated the national average in the proportion of wage-earning women who lived "adrift," it had an ethnically and racially diverse population, and it attracted reformers and sociologists interested in wage-earning women. Equally important, Chicago has excellent historical collections. Late-nineteenth and early-twentieth-century investigators, reform organizations, and social scientists left substantial records of their work and of social conditions in the city.

The study spans the years from 1880 to 1930. In these years, concern for "women adrift" reached its peak. Social observers recorded details of the otherwise anonymous lives of wage-earning women. In these years, too, migration of women into cities increased. The population of cities and the female labor force expanded greatly. The influx continued through the 1920s, but, with the onset of the Great Depression, the population movement slowed.

The sources used include the papers, case records, newspaper clipping files, and annual reports of organizations concerned with "women adrift"; the papers of individual reformers and social scientists; published and unpublished social investigations; advice books to working women; contemporary magazine and journal articles; popular romance novels and confession magazines; autobiographies; and oral history interviews. For quantitative data, I drew two systematic samples of "women adrift" from the federal manuscript census for the city of Chicago, 957 women from the census of 1880 and 905 women from the census of 1910.[5] These samples provide rich data on age, race, ethnicity, occupation, place of birth, and housing arrangements. Because the U.S.

Census Bureau keeps census schedules closed to the public for seventy years after collection, I could not draw samples from the census of 1920 or 1930.[6] Whenever possible, I tried to remedy this imbalance with evidence from federal and state surveys, published census reports, and social science research.

In general, this book focuses on what the diverse group of "women adrift" shared and not on what divided them internally. Still, where evidence permits, I discuss the differences in experience and expectation among women of varied ethnicities, races, ages, and class backgrounds. The clause "where evidence permits" has major import here, for, as most social historians know, sources often include a fuller record of white women than of black women, of native-born women than of immigrants. In addition, few sources discuss the women who lived "adrift" after age thirty-five. Finally, in most cases, the sources do not reveal whether a woman came from an urban or rural background. Within these limits, this study explores how some wage-earning women moved beyond the roles of daughter, wife, and mother and experienced life in the city without the mediation of family.

This account of self-supporting women addresses ongoing historiographical debates concerning the meaning of wage work for women. Until recently historians have relied primarily on two models to interpret the history of wage-earning women. The older "liberation" model finds that work for wages disrupted family and ethnic traditions and brought a new economic independence that liberated women from the repressive patriarchal standards of community and kin. As Edward Shorter writes, "Economically independent women have greater liberty than economically dependent ones."[7] In contrast, the more recent "family economy" model minimizes the impact of industrialization, migration, and urbanization on working-class women. This model emphasizes continuity rather than change. Family and ethnic cohesion blunted the negative impact of migration and industrialization. To support their kin and to stave off poverty, poorly paid wage-earning women remained dutiful daughters and wives in the traditional family economy. As Leslie Woodcock Tentler writes, "Neither the emotional nor the economic realities of working-class life prepared [women] to assume a role independent of this [family] loyalty."[8]

The two models lead to contradictory images of the "woman adrift." The liberation model mirrors the 1920s image of the opportunistic urban pioneer. Here the "woman adrift" is the quintessential emancipated woman. The family economy model tends to echo the late-nineteenth- and early-twentieth-century guardians of the family who feared for the safety of women without family nearby. Here the "woman adrift" is a poor, vulnerable, and isolated woman who needed but lacked "the economic protection of family membership."⁹

Another approach, however, emphasizes both the possibilities for change created by wage work and the constraints that limited women wage earners' freedom of action. Focusing on particular historical contexts, historians have begun to explore when, where, and why wage-earning women defied traditional roles and authorities, and when, where, and why they did not.¹⁰ This approach often draws implicitly on studies of nineteenth-century middle-class "women's culture" and sociological studies of informal networks and subcultures.¹¹ Historians of wage-earning women now find extrafamilial "work cultures" in department stores, factories, hospitals, and offices, and peer-oriented leisure-time subcultures in working-class neighborhoods and recreation facilities. They depict these informal networks of friends not simply as support and survival networks but also as potential arenas of change, areas where women sometimes forged new standards of behavior that defied the standards of employers, family, and community leaders.¹²

In this "subcultural" approach, the "women adrift" were neither liberated individuals nor isolated victims. On the one hand, prevailing institutions and ideologies shaped and circumscribed their choices. As the United States industrialized and the service economy developed, a sex-segregated labor market relegated women to the lowest paying jobs. In addition, employers, rooming house keepers, and others discriminated against "women adrift," often because they suspected them of immoral behavior. On the other hand, jobs in the city enabled women to live, however poorly, outside of the family and explore new social networks. Especially in the furnished room districts of the city, urban entrepreneurs invested in restaurants, rooming houses, and recreation facilities where such extrafamilial social networks might grow. In this interpretation, wage work not only oppressed women; it also created the preconditions for new urban subcultures.¹³ In this context, "women adrift," as historical actors, created new social ties to cope with and challenge social and economic conditions over which they had no direct control.

The social ties created by "women adrift" in the new subcultures they formed have meaning beyond the women directly involved. For one, they inform our understanding of the early twentieth-century "revolution in manners and morals." Historians have long treated this shift from Victorian sexual reticence to modern sexual expressiveness as a middle-class phenomenon grounded in a search for pleasure.¹⁴ More recent research, however, points to a working-class component.[15] As seen in the subcultures of "women adrift," this component grew not only out of a search for pleasure, romance, and excitement but also out of economic need and the customary dependence of women on higher-paid men. The "women adrift" who challenged convention most entered subcultures that sanctioned extramarital sex. For these women, a sexual relationship also represented an economic strategy for alleviating poverty. When they rebelled against the sexual conventions of their parents and of middle-class reformers, they pulled female economic dependence outside of the family and into the realms of dating, cohabitation, gold digging, and casual prostitution. In short, the sexual relationships in the subcultures formed by "women adrift" reveal the neglected economic roots of modern sexual expression.

At its most speculative, this work suggests that "women adrift" helped set patterns that other women later followed. In the furnished room districts of the 1910s, middle- and upper-class bohemian intellectuals may have observed and learned from the unconventional behavior of the working-class women who were their neighbors. Middle-class pleasure seekers may have copied the blueprints of "sexy" behavior provided by "women adrift" who worked as cabaret singers and chorus girls. Observant social investigators and reformers who studied the daily actions of self-supporting women gradually rejected earlier images of helpless, passionless womanhood. By the 1920s, young middle-class flappers romanticized and imitated the working-class women who lived on their own and socialized with men. And popular movies and pulp magazines used the overt sexual behavior of some "women adrift" to spread a new stereotype of women as sexual objects. In these ways, the wage-earning women who lived apart from family were a vanguard in the decline of Victorian culture.

The "women adrift," then, stand at a juncture in U.S. women's history. They moved from a female domestic world in predominantly rural societies to a sexually integrated, urban environment. Bereft of family support and confronted with poverty, they created new subcultures, challenged Victorian prescriptions, set patterns for contemporary sex roles, inspired social reformers, and influenced popular culture. Their history links together the history of women, work, sexuality, social reform, and popular culture in the late-nineteenth- and early-twentieth-century city.

Chapter One
Apart from Family

In Theodore Dreiser's novel *Sister Carrie,* published in 1900, eighteen-year-old Caroline Meeber decides to leave her family and kin. The story begins as she moves to Chicago from her small-town home a few hundred miles distant. Dissatisfied with life, Carrie longs to experience the bustle of the city and to indulge in urban consumer pleasures. Yet in Chicago she encounters relentlessly bleak conditions. She boards in the grim home of her sister and brother-in-law, secures grinding work in a shoe factory, and grudgingly gives most of her meager wage to her sister. But the city, a "magnet," still attracts Carrie powerfully. With the aid and encouragement of a wealthier suitor, she soon moves out into rooms of her own.[1]

The fictional Sister Carrie contradicts the model of the "family economy" that social historians have described recently.[2] In this model, members of a household cooperated as one economic unit. They pooled their resources and decided together how best to divide their labor. As part of a strategy for family betterment, a daughter often worked for wages. She lived in the home of her parents or relatives until she married, and turned all or most of her pay in to the family fund. A wife more often worked at home. She maintained the household and sometimes supplemented family income by caring for boarders, taking in laundry, or sewing. In the ideal family economy, women, whether wives, mothers, daughters, or relatives, lived within the protective bounds of the home.

As Dreiser recognized, families did not always function so smoothly. In fact as well as fiction, wage-earning women boarded and lodged in the city without the aid and immediate comfort of family and relatives. Thousands of women left their homes because their parents, husbands, or kin could not or would not contribute to their support; because they needed work and could not find jobs nearby; because death, divorce, or desertion had disrupted their families; because they had ambition;

and because they felt restricted, stigmatized, abused, unwanted, or unhappy at home. Their presence in the city demonstrates that the real
family economy sometimes failed to match the ideal.

From the early years of Anglo-American colonization, some women
lived apart from family and relatives. Widows, divorced and deserted
wives, and "spinsters" sometimes lived on their own and supported
themselves as seamstresses, milliners, spinners, laundresses, nurses, mid-
wives, boarding house keepers, teachers, and shopkeepers. Some lone
women boarded in the homes of their neighbors, while the least fortunate women wandered in poverty from town to town. Indentured
servants and slaves, sometimes severed from family, lived in the households of their employers and owners. In addition, as a form of apprenticeship, rural daughters often moved into neighbors' homes as
hired household help, and some urban daughters lived as servants in
the homes of prominent members of their communities.[3]
 By the early nineteenth century, many women in search of work
left not only their homes but also their hometowns. Rather than working for and living with neighbors, they migrated to the rapidly growing
cities. In some cases, female migration to cities seems to have outpaced
male. Among free blacks in antebellum Southern cities, for example,
the number of women exceeded the number of men. The sex ratio
(men:women) was lower in the cities than in the countryside.[4] Similarly,
among whites in New England, young women outnumbered young
men in the population of cities while young men outnumbered young
women in the population of smaller towns.[5]
 In the city, women who lived apart from family generally had less
freedom than men. By the early nineteenth century, self-supporting men
typically boarded and lodged with private families or in larger commercial boarding and lodging houses. Most led "semiautonomous" lives:
they lodged in households but escaped the restrictions and supervision
of family life.[6] Women typically led more circumscribed lives. The majority of wage-earning women in the early and mid-nineteenth century
lived as servants in the homes of their employers. As late as 1870, over
60 percent of all wage-earning women in nonagricultural occupations
worked as servants.[7] The family setting of domestic service supposedly
protected women from the harsher world of self-support.
 Other women who lived apart from family also found themselves
in institutions that substituted regulation for family supervision and
provided them with food and shelter. In the antebellum South, slave
women, sometimes separated from family, had no choice but to live
restricted lives in the quarters provided by their owners. And in the

North, young women textile workers boarded in company-owned houses under the watchful eyes of company-hired housekeepers. Even some prostitutes stayed sequestered in houses of prostitution. The world of work, like the family economy, limited the independence and public mobility of women.

Some wage-earning women, however, lived and worked in semi-autonomy from family and household.[8] Like their male counterparts, these women concentrated in the larger cities where opportunities for work attracted migrants from small towns and rural regions. It is impossible to say how many working women lived on their own or, for that matter, how many women worked for wages in the first part of the nineteenth century. In 1830, reformer Matthew Carey estimated that a total of eighteen to twenty thousand self-supporting women lived in Boston, New York, Philadelphia, and Baltimore.[9] Later in the century, a heightened concern for self-supporting women suggests a possible increase in their numbers. An editorial in the *New York Tribune* in 1845 stated: "poor girls continually flock to the city from every part of the country, either because their friends are dead and they have no home, or because they have certain vague dreams of the charms of city life."[10] During the 1860s, an increasing number of women supported themselves as their fathers, husbands, and brothers fought and died in the Civil War.[11]

These women often earned abysmally low pay. In fact, we know about them largely from the protests raised regarding their wages. Matthew Carey wrote to publicize the low wages of women, and the *New York Tribune* editorial continued, "Arriving here, they soon find . . . how rashly they have entered a condition where it is almost impossible for them to subsist."[12] Self-supporting women themselves sometimes formed organizations to demand higher wages. During the Civil War, one group of women who made military uniforms in Cincinnati wrote to President Lincoln, "We are unable to sustain life for the price offered by contractors."[13]

In most accounts, the majority of mid-nineteenth-century self-supporting women worked in the needle trades in occupations beset with low wages and irregular work.[14] "Our hearts sicken within us as we read the prices paid needlewomen," wrote Virginia Penny in an 1863 investigation. "The majority of sempstresses [*sic*]," she continued, "have no time they can call their own. Those that sew 12 or 14 out of the 24 hours, *without any relatives or friends even to be protectors for them,* and often in bad health, have no time for mental improvement or social intercourse."[15] A decade later, a seamstress in Chicago reported similar conditions. "Many homeless sewing girls in Chicago, poor like myself," she concluded, ". . . were born in happy homes, but now alone are struggling for an existence."[16] While women factory workers earned somewhat higher wages, women in other major occupations, such as laundry work, could expect to earn little more than needleworkers. For the nineteenth-century woman, extreme poverty often accompanied the semiautonomy of living away from home.

The self-supporting women of the early and middle decades of the nineteenth century were the precursors of a larger group of "women adrift" that emerged in the last decades of the nineteenth century. In 1900, according to a special census report on women at work in twenty-eight cities, 19 percent of urban wage-earning women lived apart from family and relatives.[17] Chicago, ranked eighth in the list of twenty-eight cities, had over twenty-two thousand wage-earning women who lived away from home.[18] These women comprised 21 percent of the wage-earning women in the city (see table 1.1). These figures do not include the large group of domestic servants, the majority of whom continued to lead more circumscribed lives in the homes of their employers.

The expansion of the female labor force accounts for much of the increase in the number of women adrift. In the late nineteenth and early twentieth centuries, the demand for women workers grew tremendously in nonagricultural sectors of the economy. From 1880 to

Table 1.1   Boarders and Lodgers among Adult Working Women, 1900

City	Boarders (%)	City	Boarders (%)
St. Paul, Minn.	33.6	Buffalo, N.Y.	17.3
Lowell, Mass.	31.9	St. Louis, Mo.	16.4
Minneapolis, Minn.	31.2	Baltimore, Md.	16.0
Boston, Mass.	28.0	Cleveland, Ohio	15.7
Kansas City, Mo.	24.9	Fall River, Mass.	13.9
Washington, D.C.	23.3	Milwaukee, Wis.	13.9
Philadelphia, Pa.	21.9	Louisville, Ky.	13.5
Chicago, Ill.	21.1	Atlanta, Ga.	12.9
Detroit, Mich.	20.6	Brooklyn, N.Y.	12.8
Rochester, N.Y.	20.0	New Orleans, La.	12.6
New York, N.Y.	19.7	Paterson, N.J.	12.6
Indianapolis, Ind.	19.1	Newark, N.J.	12.1
Providence, R.I.	18.9	Cincinnati, Ohio	11.7
Pittsburgh, Pa.	18.4	Jersey City, N.J.	10.8

Source: U.S. Bureau of the Census, *Statistics of Women at Work* (Washington, D.C.: Government Printing Office, 1907), p. 29.
Note: Servants and waitresses are excluded from this table.

1930, the female labor force grew by 307 percent while the adult female population increased by only 171 percent.[19] By 1930, one-quarter of all adult women and over half of all single adult women worked in the wage labor force.[20]

At the same time that the demand for women workers rose, the occupational distribution of female workers shifted so that a smaller proportion of wage-earning women lived in the homes of their employers. The rapid growth of corporate bureaucracies and of retail merchandising created new clerical and sales jobs for women. Accordingly, the number of women who worked in "trade and transportation" skyrocketed between 1880 and 1930, increasing from less than sixty thousand to over two million.[21] As new options in other occupations opened, the proportion of women who worked as domestic servants declined from 47 percent in 1880 to 33 percent in 1900 to 22 percent in 1930.[22] In addition, the proportion of domestic servants who lived in their employers' homes decreased markedly in the early twentieth century.[23]

The demand for women workers was especially great in the cities. From 1880 to 1930, the female labor force in Chicago increased from 35,600 to 407,600, or by over 1,000 percent.[24] The rate of increase of the female labor force in Chicago was over three times as great as the rate of increase of the female labor force for the nation as a whole. In 1930, 32 percent of the adult female population and 67 percent of the single women in Chicago were gainfully employed.[25] The data on Chicago indicate more general trends. By 1930, 27 percent of adult women in cities worked for wages while only 15 percent earned wages in the rest of the nation.[26]

As the proportion of urban women who worked for wages increased rapidly, so did the proportion of urban women who lived "adrift." In fact, the number of women adrift grew about as rapidly as the female labor force expanded, ranging roughly between one-fifth and one-sixth of the nonservant female labor force of Chicago. These figures, however, cloak the huge increase in absolute numbers. In 1880, an estimated 3,800 wage-earning women lived apart from family and relatives in Chicago; in 1910, the number had grown to approximately 31,500.[27] The results of several surveys conducted in Chicago and other cities from 1888 to 1925 corroborate these findings.[28] While comparable data are not available after 1925, a rough and conservative estimate places the number of women adrift in Chicago in 1930 at 49,100.[29]

At the turn of the century, the popular stereotype of the woman adrift looked much like Sister Carrie: young, single, native born, and white. Census data, however, reveal a strikingly heterogeneous group. In 1880

Table 1.2   Average Age of Women Adrift by Marital Status, 1880 and 1910

| | Average Age | |
Marital Status	*1880*	*1910*
Single	26.2 (650)	29.0 (613)
Separated and divorced	32.3 (64)	36.9 (95)
Widowed	41.3 (202)	45.2 (185)

Source: Federal Manuscript Census, Chicago, Women Adrift Samples, 1880 and 1910.

Notes: Much of the increase in average age over time is due to increased longevity of the female
   population. It reflects a more general aging of the Chicago female population. See age distribution tables, decennial U.S. Census Bureau reports. Figures in parentheses are base *N*s for
   the adjacent averages.

and 1910, the women adrift of Chicago included black women as well
as white women, separated, divorced, and widowed women as well as
single women. They ranged in age from fourteen to eighty-seven. They
came from Chicago and its midwestern hinterlands, from elsewhere in
the United States and Canada, and also from Europe.

The stereotype, though, reflected a certain reality. The largest
group of women adrift were young, single women who, like the majority of working women at home, expected to support themselves for
only a few years before marriage. In 1880, half of the women adrift
sampled, and in 1910 over two-fifths, were single and under the age of
thirty.[30] For most of these women, self-support was a brief stage in the
life cycle. Around 1890, for example, Ann J., a native-born white woman,
lived on her own for only one month before she married, and in 1913
a newly arrived Polish immigrant boarded in Chicago for only nine
months.[31] More typical, perhaps, was Pauline R., a native-born Jewish
woman, who boarded in Chicago for two years before she moved in
with her aunt.[32]

Put another way, the turnover rate of this group was high. Every
year young women entered the ranks of self-support, while others left
the city, moved in with relatives, or married. Few women lived on their
own in the city at the younger ages of fourteen, fifteen, and sixteen,
ages at which many urban working-class daughters found their first
jobs. Nevertheless, due to high turnover, the average age of single
women adrift remained consistently young (see table 1.2). Given this
high rate of turnover, figures that estimate the number of women adrift
at any one point in time clearly undercount the number of women who
lived apart from family at some point in their lives.

A smaller group of single women lived on their own at later stages
of their life cycles. Whether they chose not to marry or had no op-

portunities, many of these women lived on their own for prolonged periods of their lives. Sarah K., a native-born white woman, lived on her own in Chicago for at least thirty years, and Caroline O., a black woman, lived "adrift" for at least twenty-five.[33] As they aged, other unmarried women who lived in their parents' homes also moved out on their own to provide for themselves. These older women comprised a relatively large proportion of the single women adrift: in 1910, 25 percent of single women adrift in Chicago were thirty-five years or older, while such older women comprised only 11 percent of all single women in the city.[34]

While the majority of women adrift were single, the daily support and companionship of family and relatives was not assured to women of any marital status. In 1880 and in 1910, widows comprised slightly over one-fifth of the population of women adrift in Chicago. A few separated, deserted, and divorced women also lived apart from family and relatives. This group of women grew as divorce rates increased in the late nineteenth and early twentieth centuries. Some of these women reentered family life through the return of their husbands or, as with widows, through remarriage.

Compared to the female population of the city of Chicago, the distribution by nativity and race of women adrift was weighted heavily toward native-born daughters of native-born parents (see table 1.3). In Chicago, in 1900, over one-third of white native-born wage-earning

Table 1.3   Nativity and Race of Women Adrift, 1880 and 1910, and Adult Female Population of Chicago, 1910

Race and Nativity	1880 Women Adrift (%)	1910	
		Women Adrift (%)	*Female Population of Chicago Aged 15 and Over (%)*
Black	4.1	5.9	2.4
Foreign-born white	41.2	40.5	43.7
Native-born white with foreign-born parent(s)	19.3	26.2	35.3
Native-born white with native-born parents	35.4	27.4	18.7
N	957	905	

Sources: Federal Manuscript Census, Chicago, Women Adrift Samples, 1880 and 1910; U.S. Bureau of the Census, *Thirteenth Census, 1910, Population*, vol. 1, p. 619.
Note: Comparable figures for the adult female population of Chicago are not available for 1880.

Table 1.4   Women Adrift and Chicago Population Born Outside of
Illinois, 1880 and 1910

	Women Adrift	Chicago Population
1880	84.5% (957)	60.7%
1910	80.0 (905)	53.2

Sources: Federal Manuscript Census, Chicago, Women Adrift Samples, 1880 and 1910; U.S. Bureau
of the Census, *Tenth Census, 1880, Population,* vol. 1, pp. 536, 537; idem, *Thirteenth Census, 1910,
Population,* vol. 1, pp. 772, 774, 776, 778.
Note: Figures in parentheses are base *N*s for the adjacent percentages.

women with native-born parents and over one-fourth of black wage-
earning women lived apart from family and relatives. A smaller proportion of immigrant wage-earning women in Chicago, about one-
fifth, lived "adrift." Least represented among the women who lived
apart from family were the native-born daughters of foreign-born parents. Only 13 percent of these working women lived on their own in
Chicago.[35] Because their families often lived in the city, these women
had less need to migrate from family in order to find work. And those
who did migrate often moved in with urban kin.

   This distribution was not peculiar to Chicago. In each of twenty-
eight cities studied in the 1900 special census report, the proportion of
women adrift among native-born white wage-earning women with native-born parents was higher than the proportion adrift among all working women in the city. In most northern cities studied, black women,
too, lived on their own more frequently than other women. The proportion adrift among single black women was strikingly high in the
largest northern cities. In Chicago, Philadelphia, Boston, and New York,
over 40 percent of single black working women, servants excluded,
lived on their own. In contrast, in each of the twenty-eight cities, the
proportion of women adrift among white native-born working women
with foreign-born parents was smaller than the proportion of women
adrift among all wage-earning women.[36]

Whether black, white, single, widowed, separated, or divorced, most
of the women adrift were migrants to the city. In 1880, five-sixths and,
in 1910, four-fifths of the women sampled listed birthplaces outside of
the state of Illinois (see table 1.4). In addition, many of the women
born in Illinois had also migrated from Peoria, Rockford, Joliet, and
other Illinois cities, towns, and rural regions.

   Demographers of the United States, Europe, Asia, and Latin
America have long noted that young women predominated in certain

streams of migration, especially short-distance migrations from country to city.[37] Studies of American rural regions in the late nineteenth and early twentieth centuries indicate that women left the countryside at a faster rate than men. A recent study of farming communities in Iowa, Minnesota, and northern Illinois, for example, found a "defeminization" of the rural population between 1870 and 1900. Especially on smaller farms, but also on larger farms and in nonfarm rural households, daughters were the first to leave home.[38] In a national study of the farm population in 1920, the U.S. Census Bureau reported: "the farmer's daughter is more likely to leave the farm and go to the city than is the farmer's son."[39] Studies conducted in New York, Minnesota, Kentucky, and Michigan found that more daughters than sons migrated during the 1920s as well.[40]

Among the native-born migrants to Chicago in the late nineteenth and early twentieth centuries, young women seem to have outnumbered young men. The changing sex ratio in Chicago among young adult blacks and native-born whites suggests the predominance of women. Between 1890 and 1930, the number of young women tended to grow at a faster rate than the number of young men. In the later years, a consistently low sex ratio suggests that the influx of young women continued to exceed the influx of young men (see table 1.5).

The native-born white migrants to Chicago came from two major pools of population. In the late nineteenth century, the majority of native-born white women poured into Chicago from the Northeast. These women traveled westward primarily from the overcrowded cities and depleted farmlands of New York. By 1910, this stream of migrants had diminished, and a larger and growing group of white women

Table 1.5   Sex Ratios (Men:Women) of Blacks and Native-born Whites, Chicago, 1890–1930

	Blacks		Native-born Whites	
Year	*Ages* 15–24	*Ages* 15–29	*Ages* 15–24	*Ages* 15–29
1890	1.191	1.289	.947	.978
1900	1.015	1.077	.922	.950
1910	.893	.962	.919	.928
1920	.900	.923	.902	.906
1930	.806	.848	.931	.942

Sources: Derived from U.S. Bureau of the Census, *Eleventh Census, 1890, Population,* vol. 2, p. 117; idem, *Twelfth Census, 1900, Population,* vol. 2, p. 126; idem, *Thirteenth Census, 1910, Population,* vol. 1, p. 439; idem, *Fourteenth Census, 1920, Population,* vol. 2, p. 291; idem, *Fifteenth Census, 1930, Population,* vol. 2, p. 954.

converged on the city from its more recently populated midwestern hinterlands, from outlying areas of Illinois and from Wisconsin, Indiana, Ohio, Michigan, Iowa, and Missouri.[41] By 1910 almost two-thirds of the native-born white women adrift born outside of Illinois came from the Midwest (see table 1.6). The proportion of white migrants from the Midwest seems to have increased further in the 1910s and 1920s. A survey of 962 native-born, young, white women adrift conducted in 1931 revealed that over 90 percent had migrated to Chicago from farms, towns, and cities in Illinois, Iowa, Wisconsin, Michigan, and Ohio.[42] For the most part, these patterns of migration mirrored the migrations of native-born Chicagoans as a whole. Because women adrift were on average considerably younger than most adult Chicagoans, however, they tended to have arrived in the more recent migrations from Chicago's hinterlands (see table 1.7).

Black women followed different paths of migration to Chicago. In 1880 and in 1910, the largest group of black women adrift in Chicago, almost half, came from the Upper South states of Kentucky, Tennessee, and Missouri. A smaller group of migrants listed birthplaces elsewhere in the South. In 1880, one-fourth of black women adrift came from the states of the Deep and Atlantic Coastal South; in 1910, almost one-third. During and after World War I, the stream of migrants from Mississippi, Alabama, Georgia, and other parts of the Deep South swelled to a flood.[43]

As native-born women arrived in Chicago from the South, Midwest, and East, foreign-born women migrated from Europe and Canada. In 1880, over two-thirds of the foreign-born women adrift in Chicago came from Ireland, Germany, Sweden, and Norway. Somewhat smaller groups came to Chicago from Canada and England. The foreign-born population of women adrift changed, however, with the early twentieth-century influx of eastern European immigrants. By 1910 the Scandi-

Table 1.6   Region of Birth of White Native-born Women Adrift, 1880 and 1910

Region of Birth	1880	1910
Midwest	39.6%	63.3%
Northeast	55.7	22.1
South	4.2	8.1
West	.5	6.5
N	379	308

Source: Federal Manuscript Census, Chicago, Women Adrift Samples, 1880 and 1910.
Note: Women born in Illinois are excluded from this table.

Table 1.7   Region of Birth of Black and White Native-born Women Adrift and the Native-born Population of Chicago, 1880 and 1910

Region of Birth	1880		1910	
	Women Adrift	*Chicago Population*	*Women Adrift*	*Chicago Population*
Midwest	38.8%	32.1%	358.0%	51.0%
Northeast	51.6	57.1	20.3	27.7
South	9.2	8.7	15.8	13.9
West	.5	2.1	5.9	7.4
N	15		355	

Sources: Federal Manuscript Census, Chicago, Women Adrift Samples, 1880 and 1910; U.S. Bureau of the Census, *Tenth Census, 1880, Population,* vol. 1, pp. 536, 537; idem, *Thirteenth Census, 1910, Population,* vol. 1, pp. 772, 774, 776, 778.
Note: Persons born in Illinois are excluded from this table.

navians, Germans, and Irish comprised only two-fifths of the foreign-born "adrift" population, and the proportions of Canadian and English women adrift had also diminished. By far the largest group of foreign-born women adrift in 1910 were Polish women. They were joined by smaller groups of Lithuanian, Bohemian, and Russian Jewish women.

The ethnic distribution of women adrift did not match the ethnic distribution of the Chicago population. German women, Italian women, and, to a lesser extent, Russian-Jewish women were underrepresented in the adrift population. In 1880 the proportion of foreign-born women adrift who came from Norway, Sweden, and Canada exceeded the proportions of Norwegians, Swedes, and Canadians in the foreign-born population of Chicago as a whole. In 1910, Polish women were highly overrepresented. Twenty-nine percent of foreign-born women adrift were native Polish speakers, while only 16 percent of the Chicago foreign-born population listed Polish as their mother tongue.[44] To a lesser extent, Norwegian, Swedish, Canadian, Irish, and Lithuanian women were also overrepresented in 1910 (see table 1.8). The limited available evidence makes it difficult to explain this ethnic variation. On the one hand, the ethnic distribution of women adrift in New York or even in Chicago in, say, 1900 may have been different. On the other hand, the distribution presented here may represent cultural patterns. Historical studies show that Italians and eastern European Jews constructed especially strong family and kin networks.[45] Women in these groups may well have remained with kin more often than other women.

Different streams of migration to Chicago peaked in different decades. The native-born white population of Chicago increased most rapidly in the 1890s and in the years after 1910. The black migration to Chicago increased dramatically when the First World War and, later, immigration quotas curtailed the number of newcomers from overseas. The influx of immigrants peaked in the 1880s and 1900s (see table 1.9). After the onset of World War I, the rate of increase of the foreign-born population of Chicago gradually diminished.

In general, though, the number of migrants to Chicago, female and male, fluctuated as perceptions of availability of work in the city changed. Migration peaked in periods of urban prosperity and plummeted in times of depression. During the World's Columbian Exposition of 1893 and during World War I, observers noted that large numbers of women lived apart from family in Chicago. During periods of high unemployment, such as the 1894 depression, the number of newcomers declined, and some unemployed migrants moved to other cities or returned to the homes of their relatives.

In an era when the majority of women lived with family or kin, why did these women leave their homes? The most obvious reason and the reason most often cited by historians is the need for work. According

Table 1.8   Ethnicity of Foreign-born Women Adrift and Foreign-born
Population of Chicago, 1880 and 1910

	1880		1910	
Ethnicity	Women Adrift	Chicago Population	Women Adrift	Chicago Population
Canadian	10.4%	6.5%	5.5%	4.0%
English	8.1	6.4	3.9	3.6
German[a]	18.8	36.7	13.8	23.3
Irish	22.1	21.7	11.6	8.4
Italian	—	.7	.3	5.8
Lithuanian[b]	—[c]	—[c]	5.0	2.6
Norwegian	14.0	4.8	7.5	3.0
Polish[b]	1.5	2.7	29.0	16.1
East European Jewish[b]	—[c]	—[c]	3.9	8.8
Swedish	14.2	6.3	10.2	8.0
All other	10.9	14.2	9.3	16.4
N	393		362	

Sources: Federal Manuscript Census, Chicago, Women Adrift Samples, 1880 and 1910; U.S. Bureau of the Census, *Tenth Census, 1880, Population,* vol. 1, pp. 538–41; idem, *Thirteenth Census, 1910, Population,* pp. 854, 855, 989.
[a]For 1910, these figures exclude German-Polish immigrants who are categorized here as Polish.
[b]For 1910, these figures are (of necessity) drawn from the census category "mother tongue."
[c]Figures not available for 1880.

Table 1.9   Sources of Increase of Population, Chicago, 1870–1930

Decade	Total Increase in Population	Increase in Foreign-born Population	Increase in Black Population	Increase in White Population from Elsewhere in U.S.	Increase in Births over Deaths
1870–80	205,108	60,302	—	95,000	50,000
1880–90	496,665	244,769	7,791	144,106	100,000
1890–1900	588,725	137,584	15,879	265,262	170,000
1900–1910	468,708	194,105	13,953	48,650	212,000
1910–20	525,422	24,165	65,000	236,257	200,000
1920–30	674,733	36,575	146,000	259,158	233,000

Source: Homer Hoyt, *One Hundred Years of Land Values in Chicago: The Relationship of the Growth of Chicago to the Rise in Its Land Values, 1830–1930* (Chicago: University of Chicago Press, 1933), p. 284.

to many demographers as well, the primary "push" for large-scale migration during industrialization was economic hardship at home and the primary "pull" was the availability of work in the cities.[46] Most of the women adrift left their families, as men did, in search of work.

The geography of the female labor market compelled many women who needed work to go to a large city like Chicago to find it. Aside from a limited number of positions as servants and a handful of jobs as teachers, job-seeking women found few occupations open to them in rural areas and small towns. As one student of migration wrote in 1924, "Fewer women than men are needed on the farm. One woman, ordinarily, does the work of the family. . . . Practically the only alternatives to marriage for country girls are teaching school and leaving home to go to the city."[47] Similarly, in some smaller industrial cities like Gary, Indiana, and Youngstown, Ohio, where traditionally male heavy industries such as steel predominated, jobs for women were scarce.[48]

Information about the availability of work in Chicago often traveled by word of mouth and personal correspondence. In cities as well as in rural regions, overseas and within the United States, women learned from friends and relatives of jobs available in Chicago. In one case, a young woman from Wisconsin traveled alone to Chicago when "a girl, a chance acquaintance from Chicago, wrote her about a fine position."[49] In another case, a Polish woman living in Pittsburgh migrated after relatives told her that "wages were much better" in Chicago.[50]

Popular literature, too, informed women about available jobs. Women who lived in the outlying regions of Illinois read advertisements for work printed in the Chicago daily newspapers.[51] Ads for work in Chicago also appeared in other newspapers and magazines. A woman in St. Paul, Minnesota, for example, read of job openings in a Chicago theatrical company.[52] The nationally distributed black newspaper, the *Chicago Defender,* played an especially influential role in the migration of black women from the South. Advertisements for work in Chicago, such as the following, appeared during World War I: "Wanted—25 girls for dishwashing. Salary $7 a week and board. John R. Thompson, Restaurant, 314 S. State St. Call between 7 and 8 A.M. Ask for Mr. Brown."[53] Feature articles in the *Defender* also promoted northward migration. In fact, in 1917 the newspaper conducted "The Great Northern Drive," a campaign aimed explicitly at attracting migrants to Chicago. "I am a reader of the Defender," wrote one woman from New Orleans, "and I am asked so much about the great Northern drive. . . . So many women here are wanting to go that day."[54]

Especially in working-class, tenant farm, and small farm families, daughters often migrated in search of work when the income earned by the father did not suffice to support the entire family. As home manufacturing declined, an unemployed daughter who lived at home drew on the family resources for food, clothing, and shelter, and offered little in return. In short, unless she worked for wages, a single daughter burdened her family. "I have a mother and a father my father do all he can for me but it is so hard," a black woman from Alexandria, Louisiana, wrote to the *Chicago Defender.* "A child with any respect about herself or hisself wouldn't like to see there mother and father work so hard and earn nothing. I feel it my duty to help."[55]

Other women moved on their own after death or divorce further disrupted the family economy. In some cases, the death of a primary breadwinner, a relatively common occurrence, threw women wholly on their own resources. Ann J., a long-term resident of Chicago, lived adrift first as an orphan and then again, twenty-two years later, when her husband died.[56] Other orphans and widows who did not live in large cities often migrated in search of work. One white woman from Wisconsin, for example, moved to Chicago for work after the death of her parents because "there was nothing to be found in the little country town where she lived."[57] A smaller group of women entered the labor force and moved on their own when divorce removed their customary male source of support.

In fatherless families, daughters often felt a pressing need to earn wages. Mary Kenney, later a labor leader, supported her invalid, widowed mother. She came to Chicago in the late nineteenth century when she lost her job in a bindery in Hannibal, Missouri. "I was told there was plenty of business in Chicago," she wrote later, "If I could not get work in a bindery, I'd work at anything, even at washing dishes in a hotel."[58] A fifteen-year-old black woman in New Orleans sought work without success for three months. She then decided to move to Chicago. "The only help I have is my mother . . . ," she wrote, "and she have four children young then me . . . and she have such a hard time tell she is willing for me to go."[59]

Some women had jobs or economic support at home but came to Chicago in search of more rewarding or better-paying work. Black women (and men) from the South expected to find higher-paying jobs and less overt employment discrimination in northern cities. The sister of one black woman sent her to Chicago at age fourteen "because it was said to be a place where colored people had 'a chance.' "[60] A widow in New Orleans who sought a position in Chicago wrote, "I read and hear daily of the great chance that a colored parson has in Chicago of making a living with all the privileg that the whites have." It was hard, she continued, for a lone black woman to earn a living in New Orleans because "everything is gone up but the poor colored peple wages."[61]

Women who desired careers also came to the city with hopes of finding greater opportunities for upward mobility. One white office worker, for example, left a dead-end job in her home town when a friend told her of better opportunities in Chicago.[62] Another woman ran away from home to pursue a career on the stage.[63] Like men, these women saw the city as a place to pursue their ambitions.

While the search for employment is the most obvious motive for migration, it fails to explain fully why many women left their families. In the personal accounts of women adrift and in the case records of social investigators, other explanations appear with frequency. It is impossible to quantify these motives, and it is equally difficult to assign priorities when women listed several different reasons for leaving home. Nonetheless, these additional motives point to a private side of the female migration experience often neglected by demographers and historians.[64]

For example, in some cases, parents or guardians expelled daughters from their homes. They simply chose to terminate their economic obligations. A case record published in 1916 recounted the story of an eighteen-year-old woman who "arrived in Chicago from Joliet on a cold spring Saturday morning." The record continued tersely: "Her aunt had given her a ticket to Chicago and one dollar and told her to go to the city and find a job."[65] Another such woman came from a troubled home in a city in Indiana. Her mother was dead; her father drank and gambled; her stepmother disliked her. When she was seventeen, "her father refused to clothe her and in an awful fit of anger swore that he would do nothing more for her."[66] In this case, the cooperative family economy collapsed in irreconcilable conflict.

In other cases, adult daughters returned to their parents' homes only to find their parents unwilling to care for them. When her husband died in 1916, Philiminia P., a twenty-two-year-old black woman, returned to her parents' home in Denver, Colorado. "They treated me so rotten," she said, "I come back [to Chicago]. . . . My family put me and my three brothers out."[67] The family economy did not always provide adult daughters and sons with cushions in times of crisis.

Extended kin networks sometimes proved equally unreliable. Young women adrift spoke frequently of unhappy and abusive relationships with stepparents, aunts, uncles, and other guardians. They often left home when one parent died and the other remarried.[68] In some cases, women resented the grudging support of their relatives. One woman from a western state moved to a nearby town because she could not get along with her stepmother. She worked for her uncle as a receptionist but received no pay. She decided that "she would prefer to take care of herself among strangers to the poor-relation treatment she was then receiving," and she moved to Chicago.[69]

Some married women left their homes when their husbands refused to continue support. A woman from Shreveport, Louisiana, came to Chicago after her husband left her and her baby died.[70] Another woman left Wisconsin when her husband, in love with another woman, expelled her from their home. She arrived in Chicago with a dollar and a half in her purse.[71] Other women, who had lived with their husbands in Chicago, found themselves adrift when their husbands deserted them.[72] In the family economy, married women, like children, held a vulnerable position, dependent on men who could withdraw their support.

Several motives for leaving home point to specifically female concerns. Some women left their homes to escape the stigma attached by family and community to unmarried women suspected of sexual activity. Raped, pregnant, and "seduced and abandoned" women sought the anonymity of life in a city where no one knew them. One such woman came to Chicago in 1888 after a farmer in a nearby county had seduced and impregnated her.[73] Another woman worked as a live-in domestic servant until she met a young man who "ruined and deserted" her. After an attempted suicide, she too fled to Chicago.[74]

In other cases, parents and guardians expelled daughters for sexual behavior deemed unacceptable. A young Jewish woman came to the attention of Hull House in 1898 when she attempted suicide. She was eight months' pregnant and had lived and worked in a sweatshop after her brother had turned her out of his house. The investigator who helped her verified that "her relatives will have nothing to do with her."[75] An investigator of prostitution in 1911 found a woman whose parents "made her leave home because she went out at night." She told the investigator that she was " 'going to hell proper' now."[76] The sexual double standard led these parents and guardians to punish their daughters more harshly than they might have punished their sons.

Just as blacks and Jews often migrated in family groups to escape racial oppression and religious persecution, so some women who lived in patriarchal families moved out on their own to escape oppressive male relatives. Some women left home because fathers, stepfathers, uncles, or husbands battered them. In one such case, a twenty-year-old woman "had lived with an uncle in Pennsylvania, who demanded her wages, and upon her refusal beat her." According to the charity worker who interviewed her, "She arrived at our terminal still carrying the bruises."[77] In another case, a Hungarian immigrant came to Chicago from New York to escape her violent and alcoholic husband.[78]

In other cases, sexual abuse at home prompted female migration. Several cases of incest and attempted incest appeared in the case records of social and charity workers. The Travelers' Aid Society of the Young Women's Christian Association reported a case in 1912 in which a young woman "arrived in the city at midnight without hat or coat, seeking protection." In this case, a stepfather "had been making improper advances." The woman had "resisted," but "her life was threatened if she told her mother." Eventually, the stepfather became "so insistent that the girl was afraid to remain longer and she fled."[79]

Women adrift, however, were not simply the victims of poverty, stigma, and abuse. Increasingly in the early twentieth century, women actively chose to leave home to escape the restrictions routinely imposed upon daughters in the family economy. Parents, fearful for their daughters' chastity, often restricted their daughters' nightlife, and, in addition, parents often required daughters (and less often required sons) to turn their entire wage into the common family fund.[80] Some daughters protested by leaving home.

Some moved away when parents or guardians refused to let them spend their evenings as they chose. One woman ran away from home after her parents threatened to send her away for "go[ing] out with fellows," and an Italian woman moved from her home in Chicago in part because "her father would not allow her to go out evenings into the street."[81] In the early 1920s, another woman came to Chicago from Michigan after her stepfather attempted to whip her for staying out late on a date. "We kept having fights back and forth about the boys I went out with and the hours that I kept," she explained, "He even accused me of wanting to do things which I'd not even thought of doing up to that time." After one "big fight," she told her stepfather that she "wouldn't stand" for a whipping and "would leave home." "I was always willing," she concluded, "to stand up for my rights."[82]

A job in the city and a room of one's own offered women a degree of freedom from such parental supervision. It also offered a chance to experiment with openly sexual life-styles. In 1899 a fifteen-year-old woman told investigators that she left her home in Savannah, Illinois, when a "girl who used to live there . . . induced her to come back with her to Chicago and 'live off the men.' "[83]

Other daughters left home because they resented their lack of economic independence. One woman ran away from home because her father, an alcoholic, demanded her wages.[84] In a letter to the *Farmer's Voice*, Miss Alta Hooper warned farm parents that their daughters would leave home unless accorded greater economic freedom: "She isn't going to 'stay put,' but will get out where she can earn some money of her very own, to buy the little things so dear to the hearts of girls; and she will not be questioned and scolded over every little expenditure."[85]

The new possibilities for urban consumer pleasure attracted some of these women. The new urban nightlife—movies, dance halls, cabarets—offered women entertainment and the chance to mingle with their peers. And advertising broadcast the possibility for consumerism in department and other retail stores. Like Sister Carrie, many young women seemed especially eager to spend a greater share of their wages on attractive clothing. One eighteen-year-old Danish woman ran away from her cousin's home in Michigan in part "because she could not have the clothes she wanted."[86] As another woman explained bluntly, "I wanted more money for clothes than my mother would give me. . . . We were always fighting over my pay check. Then I wanted to be out late and they wouldn't stand for that. So I finally left home."[87]

After 1915 a few women began to identify the desire for adventure and travel or the lure of the city as their primary motive for leaving home. They simply found their home environments "dull." They came to Chicago "just to see the sights"; they wanted "experiences" or a "fling."[88] A black woman from Birmingham, Alabama, an orphan, said, "Well, I got to running around over the world like young folks will do, you know. Just packed up and got to travelling."[89] Most likely, the language these women chose to explain their migration reflected changing norms of acceptable behavior. It probably also reflected an era of relative urban prosperity. In 1931, as Chicago's economy collapsed, only

2.5 percent of a group of white women surveyed said they came to Chicago for "new experiences."[90]

Anecdotal accounts of migration do not permit finely tuned assessments of how the motives of women from various ethnic and racial groups differed. It would, of course, make sense that black women from the sharecropping South would cite poverty more often than white women from midwestern family-owned farms. Evidence from black rural communities also suggests that sexually active women there had less need to leave home because they were less severely stigmatized than women in native- and foreign-born white communities.[91] Further, it seems plausible that shorter-distance migrants, who might return home easily, would make the decision to leave home more lightly than women who came to Chicago from overseas. In general, though, most of the motives for migration—death in the family, conflict with relatives, desire for independence, desertion, ambition, poverty, abuse—cut across racial and ethnic lines.

In some ways, Sister Carrie represents the women adrift of turn-of-the-century Chicago. For Carrie and for the women adrift, the decision to leave home expressed the difficulties and dissatisfaction women experienced as members of the family economy. Recent historical writings tend to depict the family during the era of industrialization as a flexible and resilient institution, but, in some cases, the family split under the disruptive impact of poverty, death, and desertion.[92] Historians of European women have argued that women migrated as part of a "family strategy," an economic calculation based on the needs and decisions of the entire family unit.[93] In the case of Sister Carrie and of the women adrift of Chicago, this approach provides only partial explanation and often obscures the conflicting interests of individual family members.[94] Stigma and abuse sometimes overshadowed cooperation, and increasing urban opportunities for self-indulgence sometimes appealed to women weary of self-abnegation in the family interest. By choice and out of necessity, then, thousands of daughters, wives, and widows, like Sister Carrie, moved outside the family's compass.

In other ways, Sister Carrie's unique adventures hardly represent the diverse experiences of the growing group of women adrift. In the fictional world of Theodore Dreiser, Carrie, liberated from family and "glad of her release," steps into the city "full of the swirl of life."[95] Supported comfortably by salesman Charles Drouet, she shops in downtown department stores, dines in elegant restaurants, and attends the latest shows. Eventually, she leaves Drouet for the wealthier George

Hurstwood and rises incredibly to stardom on the New York stage. As the story ends, Hurstwood, abandoned and poor, commits suicide, and Carrie, alone and still vaguely dissatisfied, rocks herself in a rocker. Her success is bittersweet, but her independence is genuine. Once she leaves her sister's home, she never returns and never looks back.

In the real world of Chicago, such spectacular material success was, not surprisingly, highly unusual. Most women adrift could not leave the family economy behind as easily as Sister Carrie. Just as urbanization and industrialization shaped the life of the family, so, conversely, the family economy reached into urban and industrial institutions. Once in the city, a woman adrift sought a home and a job, yet both housing and job markets operated on the assumption that women lived with kin. In addition, employers, neighbors, and acquaintances looked askance at the woman alone. Sister Carrie sidestepped the hardships of living apart from family; most women adrift did not.

Chapter Two
"A Lone Woman Can't Be Too Careful"

In 1880 the Chicago encountered by a "woman adrift" was a substantial city of almost thirty-six square miles, the home of over a half million people.[1] By 1930 it sprawled across more than two hundred square miles and housed almost 3.4 million.[2] Throughout this fifty-year period, the downtown area held some of the nation's largest retail stores and finest hotels, much of the Midwest's commerce, and many of the transient, down-and-out, unemployed men of the city. Streetcar lines and, by the 1890s, elevated railways radiated outward from the city center. On the South Side of the city, most of Chicago's growing black population gradually trickled into a district surrounded by wealthier neighbors and interspersed with some of the world's most notorious brothels. On the Southwest Side, the stockyards exuded a thick odor of blood and decay that, by the twentieth century, permeated the poorly constructed wooden homes of eastern European immigrants. Farther to the north, on the West Side, Jews, Greeks, Italians, Jane Addams's Hull House, warehouses and factories gradually pushed the elite citizens of the city into the suburbs. And, on the North Side, Poles and Italians joined native-born Americans and German immigrants in a jagged patchwork of overlapping neighborhoods.[3]

In many respects, this was a harsh environment for the typical woman adrift. From her first arrival in Chicago through years of self-support, she learned to mistrust strangers who might see her as an especially easy mark for exploitation, and she learned too that strangers often mistrusted her, reading her lone status as a badge of sexual misbehavior. She found that she had little access to the cushions that family and community provided for daughters, wives, and mothers. And she discovered further that employers paid her the low wages of a dependent daughter or wife.

These hardships persisted through the years from 1880 to 1930. They do not encompass or define the experience of women adrift, but they do represent an important facet of these women's lives. Leaving home did not "liberate" oppressed women to lives of self-seeking and self-satisfied individualism. Instead, life "adrift" presented not only a new set of possibilities but also a new set of material and ideological constraints.

A woman adrift usually first viewed Chicago through the window of a train and first entered the city through the railroad station. The bright lights in the station, the clattering noise of the trains, and the bustling crowd greeted her as she stepped onto the platform. She probably saw most of her fellow passengers rush to meet friends and relatives or head purposefully for home or hotel. Porters accosted her, asking to carry her luggage, and cabmen vied with each other for the privilege of transporting her through the city.

Women who came to Chicago with sufficient amounts of money, ambition, and self-confidence usually had joyous first impressions. "Never shall I forget the time of the night that I arrived at the Northwestern Station," one migrant remembered, "my purse clutched tightly in one hand, and my bag in the other, shaking my head at redcaps, confused and dazzled by the glare of the lights—but my heart singing, my ambition aflame."[4] This woman came from Emporia, Kansas, with over fifty dollars in her purse, determined to work by day and take music lessons at night.

Women who arrived naïve and timid more likely experienced anxiety. For Pauline G., arrival in Chicago in 1912 was simply another episode in a long and harrowing journey from Poland. When her mother died and her father remarried, Pauline's brother sent her money to come to the United States. The journey took her about one month and, through it all, Pauline remained a fearful observer, highly aware of her inexperience. "When I was a young girl," she recounted, "I never go no place. I don't know nothing." So timid was she that, at first, she felt embarrassed to eat publicly on the train traveling through Germany. In New York, on Ellis Island, she sat alone "quiet and look. . . . They watched you—watch you—every step you make." And, one week later, on arrival in Chicago, she sat again in the train station. "So I sat in the branch. I waiting. Well, I didn't know much."[5]

Arrival was probably frightening to many women (and men) who traveled alone and came to the city without friends or relatives to greet them. It may have been especially frightening to women who had been warned of crime in the city, who arrived without any knowledge of how to obtain housing and employment, who spoke no English, and who had naïve expectations of finding relatives or friends for whom they had no addresses. Some of these women came to Chicago penniless and others with inadequate sums for initial room and board. A black woman came to Chicago from Alabama, for example, "without money, hat, or anyone to meet her," and a white woman came from Wisconsin "with only one cent in her purse."[6] These women often depended on the kindness of strangers, and some of them found their way quickly to charity organizations and social workers.

Other women had more dismal experiences. A seventeen-year-old Polish woman without any money had an incorrect address for her sister's home: "The woman who lived there angrily refused to let her stay until morning. . . . [And] the expressman told her 'nobody could find her sister if nobody knew her address and that he wasn't going to take her back for nothing.' "[7] A German-Hungarian woman without money slept out of doors while she looked for work during the day. The police arrested her, and the judge sent her to prison because "she had no friends and needed cleaning up."[8] Another woman, a native-born American, spent her only dollar on one night's lodging and one meal. She then sat quietly for the next two days in the railroad station and in the waiting room of a downtown store.[9]

The least fortunate women were accosted by criminals who betrayed the trust of newcomers. Thieves sometimes chose railroad stations as the most likely locations in which to find vulnerable prey. Dishonest cabmen overcharged migrants and sometimes stole their baggage. A fourteen-year-old girl from Cleveland "was taken" to a hotel where "her money $2.00 and her satchel and her bag were taken from her."[10] Thieves and con men may well have cheated and robbed naïve male migrants as often as they cheated and robbed naïve female migrants. Rapists, panderers, and mashers, however, chose women newcomers as their primary targets for sexual exploitation. One woman, in search of a hotel room, accepted the help of a man she met outside the Dearborn Street Railway Station. He took her to a nearby hotel "where she was outraged and detained for weeks."[11] Other newcomers encountered procurers who attempted to entice them with offers of high pay in brothels. More often, migrants encountered city slickers who simply hoped to seduce them.[12]

Aware of the potential trials of newcomers, some women avoided arriving in Chicago alone. One woman said, "I was afraid to come to the city alone and so [my sister] came out and got me."[13] Before they left home, other women tried to make arrangements for friends to meet them at the train and for temporary housing.[14] One Bohemian woman wrote from Missouri to the Immigrants' Protective League asking for "any place or somebody where I could go for a few days before I will work. . . . I do not want to go to a hotel when I am a stranger in Chicago."[15]

Rather than remain outside of a family setting, numerous migrants and some of the women with family nearby chose to become live-in domestic servants. Although the proportion of women working as live-in servants dropped in the second half of the nineteenth century and continued to drop in the twentieth, many women still accepted this work. Penniless migrants who needed immediate room and board but could not afford to buy them often entered live-in service. Also women who were afraid of the city chose to become live-in domestics. A young black widow from New Orleans tried to arrange a live-in position in Chicago in a "good home with good people" because, she wrote, "its very trying for a good girl to be out in a large city by self among strangers."[16] Some of these women rejoined the ranks of women adrift once they had earned some money or felt more comfortable in the city.

The structure of available housing compelled other newcomers to place themselves in household settings. Until World War I, housing in Chicago consisted largely of two-, three- , and four-bedroom houses and flats. Small apartments, constructed for one or two occupants, were virtually nonexistent. In 1880 and in 1910, fewer than one in seven women adrift lived alone, and the majority of those who did live alone were separated, divorced, and widowed women, many of whom probably lived in the homes or with the furnishings they had shared with their husbands.[17] Most of the newcomers who did not become live-in servants and who had no friends or relatives with whom to stay had little choice but to fit themselves into the available space in others' dwellings.

A woman who rented a room could expect to live in a tiny and stark hall bedroom with, perhaps, one window that looked out onto the air shaft or the alley between two buildings. Her room would have a bed, a wardrobe or closet, some drawers, and maybe a chair or nightstand. Her landlady—a wife, widow, or older single woman—would probably ask her to use as little light and heat as possible since the cost of fuel was high. She would share a bathroom with the landlady's family and with other lodgers. And, if she boarded as well as lodged, she would eat meals of varying quantity and quality prepared by the landlady at specified times.

Women began to search for these rooms immediately after arrival. "Upon reaching Chicago," one account reads, "she immediately bought a daily paper and looked at the boarding house advertisements."[18] White women looked for rooms in the classified advertisements of the Chicago daily papers; black women often turned to the columns of ads published in black newspapers like the *Chicago Defender*. Answering such ads could be risky, though, for occasionally advertised homes were found to be fronts for brothels.

Not all rooms were advertised in the papers. In most neighborhoods, a Room for Rent sign in the window or over the door of the home provided sufficient advertisement (see fig. 2.1). Women in search of housing often walked through neighborhoods and knocked on the doors of homes with signs in the windows. In the era before the telephone, a migrant would walk from address to address, sometimes with luggage in hand. According to the Chicago Commission on Race Relations, in the years between 1915 and 1920, when black migration to Chicago was high, "hundreds of unattached men and women could be seen on the streets as late as one or two o'clock in the morning, seeking rooms shortly after their arrival in Chicago."[19]

Other rooms were rented by word of mouth. Bessie Van Vorst, a middle-class woman who posed as a factory worker, sought the guidance of Hull House upon her arrival in Chicago in 1902. She walked the streets of the neighborhood at dusk searching for the addresses given her. "There were no names on the corner lamps," she wrote, "and the house numbers were dull and needed repainting. It was already late in the afternoon: I had but an hour or two before dark to find a lodging."[20] By the twentieth century, room registries, managed by churches and charities, also provided newcomers with addresses where they might find suitable housing.[21]

With directions from friends, relatives, police, and charity workers, the women adrift quickly sorted themselves into different neighborhoods. Black women searched for housing in black neighborhoods, and white women searched in white neighborhoods. Most immigrants rented rooms in households with foreign-born heads; most native-born women with native-born parents moved into the homes of the native born (see table 2.1). Newcomers whose mother tongue was not English usually found their way into homes where their native language was spoken. For example, in 1880, over 70 percent of the Scandinavian women adrift moved into homes where the household heads were Scandinavian, and, in 1910, over 90 percent of the Polish women adrift lived in homes with Polish household heads.

In many households—immigrant, black, and native-born white— men found rooms more easily than did women. Landladies preferred male lodgers whom they considered less demanding. They complained that female lodgers used the bathroom too often and broke house rules that prohibited cooking and laundering in the rooms. According to one study of the black population of Chicago, "[families] sometimes complained of lodgers and declared that they would prefer not to take them at all, especially women lodgers. The objection to married couples and unattached men was not so pronounced."[22]

Fig. 2.1. Furnished rooming house, Chicago, c. 1928. (Source: Regenstein Library, University of Chicago)

Table 2.1   Race and Nativity of Women Adrift by Race and Nativity
of Household Heads with Whom They Lodged, Chicago,
1880 and 1910

Household Heads	Women Adrift			
	Black	*Foreign-born White*	*Native-born White w/ Foreign-born Parent(s)*	*Native-born White w/ Native-born Parents*
1880				
Black	100%	0%	0%	0%
Foreign-born white	0	70	56	24
Native-born white	0	30	44	76
N	39	281	140	244
1910				
Black	100	0	0	0
Foreign-born white	0	83	41	20
Native-born white	0	17	59	81
N	53	252	157	174

Source: Federal Manuscript Census, Chicago, Women Adrift Samples, 1880 and 1910.

In addition, landladies and neighbors sometimes suspected women adrift of what they considered immoral sexual behavior. Recalling her youth in Chicago, one working-class woman who had lived in her parents' home said, "If a girl didn't live at home, we thought she was bad."[23] The few women who rented their own apartments or flats also encountered the same stigmatization. A Chicago waitress said, "I was afraid on account of what people would say about a girl living alone. . . . The landlord didn't want to rent to me, either. This is a respectable building and they have to be careful."[24] In contrast, men who lived on their own found their independent status accepted without suspicion.

Most women adrift began to look for work immediately after they had found housing. As in the housing search, a woman answered newspaper advertisements, went into factories, restaurants, and stores with Help Wanted signs in the windows, and found jobs through word of mouth. Women also registered at employment agencies, some of which specialized in clerical work, hotel jobs, nursing, or domestic service.[25]

The process of finding work could be grueling and disappointing. Most women adrift did not have the economic security of assured food and housing that sustained a woman who lived at home through a prolonged job search. And many women came to Chicago with misinformation about the ease with which work could be obtained. In addition, some prospective employers took advantage of a lone woman's vulnerable position by propositioning and otherwise sexually harassing her.[26]

Women adrift may also have had greater difficulty finding work than women who lived at home because employers sometimes discriminated against lone women in hiring. Like landladies and neighbors, some employers suspected the woman who lived away from home of immoral behavior. Others knew that the wages they paid did not suffice for independent living. In 1894, Edward Hillman of the Boston Store, an employer of about nineteen hundred women in Chicago, articulated this position. "A girl who boards out cannot support herself on a low wage," he said, "We have to enforce the rule as to living with the family or with friends to insure the moral character of our employe[e]s."[27] Similarly, in the 1920s, the American Telephone and Telegraph Company had a hiring policy that favored "girls who live at home, who are American, and who are 'respectable.' "[28] Some women adrift probably learned that their job applications were considered more seriously when they lied about their housing arrangements.

As women exhausted themselves pounding the pavements and as their money ran out, they sometimes despaired. Especially in years of recession, records of charity organizations and sensational newspaper articles reported accounts of great misery and failure. In 1895, for example, a charity worker found a young woman crying in the Northwestern railroad depot. The woman, she learned, came from the South "and went to a hotel until she could find work, which she supposed an easy thing to do." She searched for work "until she was exhausted, and tried in every way she knew to obtain employment, but without success." Finally, her money ran out. "She could not stay at the hotel, she had no work and no friends."[29] Thirty years later the *Chicago Tribune* carried a story about a woman from Wisconsin who swallowed poison after an unsuccessful job search. According to the article, "She could find [no work], her hotel bill was due, she was too proud to write to her parents." This woman recovered, and, like many other women unable to find work, she returned to the home she had left because of conflict with her parents.[30]

Other unsuccessful job seekers turned less dramatically to live-in domestic service. The long hours, restricted independence, and personal subservience of domestic work repelled many wage-earning women. But the continuing demand for domestic servants led some women to accept such positions when they could find no others.[31] Like the migrants who entered service immediately upon arrival, these unsuccessful job seekers could work for a time as domestics and then try again to find other work.

The more successful job seekers found work in a large variety of occupations. In 1880, almost half of the women adrift in Chicago worked in the needle trades, holding such jobs as dressmaker, seamstress, and tailoress, and almost one-fifth held service jobs, most often domestic day work and laundering. Other women adrift worked in a number of occupations including sales work, teaching, boarding or rooming house keeping, and office work. In 1910 the proportion of women adrift who worked in the needle trades dropped to one-fifth while the proportions of women adrift in most other occupational categories rose. Clerical and service work showed especially large increases (see table 2.2). Within occupational categories, the largest specific occupations of women adrift in 1910 were dressmaker, laundress, nurse, stenographer, day-working servant, seamstress, and saleswoman (see table 2.3).

In most respects, the occupational distribution of women adrift reflected the larger occupational patterns of all wage-earning women in Chicago. In the total female labor force, as among women adrift, the proportion of women who worked in the needle trades declined after 1880, and the proportion of women in clerical jobs rose. In both groups, the proportion of women who owned or managed small businesses and the proportion of women who worked in semiprofessional

Table 2.2 Occupational Categories of Women Adrift in Chicago, 1880 and 1910

Occupational Categories	1880	1910
Needle trades	48%	20%
Other manufacturing	4	9
Service	19	28
Clerical	4	14
Sales	6	7
Entrepreneurial/managerial	5	8
Semiprofessional	9	12
Professional	1	1
Other[a]	5	1
N	951	904

Source: Federal Manuscript Census, Chicago, Women Adrift Samples, 1880 and 1910.

[a] "Other" includes fortune-tellers, ragpickers, women who "worked out," etc. It is high in 1880 because, in that year, it includes several women who listed themselves as prostitutes. (Prostitution was not listed as an occupation in the 1910 census.)

jobs, such as teaching and trained nursing, increased only slightly (see table 2.4).

The stratification of jobs by nativity and race among women adrift reflected the larger class divisions in the Chicago female labor force. Native-born white women, who often had better education and usually came from less impoverished backgrounds, worked at the more prestigious jobs that required grammatical English and middle-class dress. They were more likely than others to work in clerical, sales, and semi-professional jobs. By 1930, over one-half of the native-born white working women in Chicago worked as "clerks and kindred workers."[32] Black women, excluded from most clerical, sales, manufacturing, and semi-professional jobs, worked in a variety of service jobs, most often as laundresses and day-working servants. A few black women worked as dressmakers, seamstresses, and rooming house keepers. During and after World War I, an increasing number of black women worked in factories, and a few worked in offices.[33] Foreign-born women who did not work as live-in domestics worked most often in other service jobs and in

Table 2.3   Major Specific Occupations of Women Adrift in Chicago, 1880 and 1910

1880		1910	
Dressmaker	20%	Dressmaker	9%
Seamstress	14	Laundress	8
Tailoress	9	Nurse	6
Servant[a]	7	Stenographer	6
Laundress	6	Servant	5
Saleswoman	5	Seamstress	5
Prostitute[b]	4	Saleswoman	5
Schoolteacher	4	Rooming house keeper	4
Rooming house keeper	3	Dishwasher	3
Clerk	2	Clerk	3
		Waitress	2
		Milliner	2
		Schoolteacher	2
		Bookkeeper	2
		Cook	2
		Tailoress	2
All others	26	All others	34
N	951	N	904

Source: Federal Manuscript Census, Chicago, Women Adrift Samples, 1880 and 1910.
Note: The specific occupations included here are all those listed in the manuscript census in which at least 2 percent of women adrift worked.
[a]The servants listed here include only those who did not live with their employers.
[b]Prostitution was not listed as an occupation in the 1910 manuscript census.

Table 2.4   Occupational Categories of Women Adrift and the Female
              Labor Force, Chicago, 1880 and 1910

	1880		1910	
	Women Adrift	*Chicago Female Labor Force*	*Women Adrift*	*Chicago Female Labor Force*
Needle trades	51%	54%	21%	22%
Other manufacturing	4	13	10	6
Service	13	12	24	11
Clerical	4	1	15	24
Sales	6	6	8	11
Entrepreneurial/ managerial	5	4	8	5
Semiprofessional	10	6	13	10
Professional	1	0	1	0
Other/unknown	6	4	1	11
N	885		858	

Source: Federal Manuscript Census, Chicago, Women Adrift Samples, 1880 and 1910; U.S. Bureau
of the Census, *Tenth Census, 1880, Population,* vol. 1, p. 870; idem, *Thirteenth Census, 1910, Population,* vol. 4, pp. 546, 547.
Note: Domestic servants are excluded from this table.

manufacturing jobs, such as in the garment trade and meat-packing
plants. The increasing percentage of foreign-born women who worked
in stores and offices in Chicago was greater than the percentage of black
women in these jobs but always much smaller than the percentage of
native-born whites (see table 2.5).[34]

Ethnic distinctions in the occupations of women adrift, strongest
among newcomers, also mirrored the patterns seen in the female labor
force as a whole. In 1880, 80 percent of Scandinavian women adrift
sewed for a living, while Irish women adrift were more likely than
others to become day-working servants. In 1910, most Russian-Jewish
women adrift worked in the garment industries, and the vast majority
of Polish women adrift worked in other manufacturing industries and
in service jobs.[35]

In some respects, however, women adrift deviated from the occupational distribution of the Chicago female labor force. In 1910, white
women adrift were less likely than white wage-earning women who
lived at home to work in clerical jobs and more likely than women who
lived at home to work in factories, a reversal of the pattern seen in 1880
(see table 2.4). This new distribution was not due to changes in the
nativity distribution, for it appeared among both foreign- and native-
born women. Nor was it a function of the changing age distribution,
for both clerical and factory workers were young. Perhaps, by the early

Table 2.5   Occupational Categories of Women Adrift by Race and
Nativity, Chicago, 1880 and 1910

	1880			1910		
	Black	Foreign-born White	Native-born White	Black	Foreign-born White	Native-born White
Needle trades	5%	54%	46%	19%	23%	18%
Other manufacturing	0	3	5	0	15	6
Service	68	25	10	76	37	16
Clerical	0	1	7	0	5	22
Sales	3	2	8	0	4	10
Entrepreneurial/ managerial	8	6	4	2	8	9
Semiprofessional	3	4	13	4	8	17
Professional	0	0	1	0	0	1
Other[a]	13	4	6	0	1	1
N	38	387	521	53	362	478

Source: Federal Manuscript Census, Chicago, Women Adrift Samples, 1880 and 1910.
[a]"Other" includes fortune-tellers, ragpickers, women who "worked out," etc. It is high among
   black women in 1880 because it includes 4 women who "worked out" (probably day-working
   servants).

twentieth century, employers, more concerned about propriety than
factory managers, hesitated to hire women adrift. Or perhaps more
young white women adrift of the early twentieth century came from
poorer working-class backgrounds in which they had few opportunities
to receive the training increasingly required for clerical jobs.

   Most of the other ways in which women adrift deviated from the
more general occupational patterns of the Chicago female labor force
can be explained by their tendency to accept jobs that supplied them
with meals or helped them pay rent. For example, the large number of
rooming house keepers accounts for most of the slight overrepresentation of women adrift in entrepreneurial jobs. A rooming house keeper
had the rent on her house paid by the roomers who subletted rooms,
and, if she kept boarders, the time she spent preparing their food
provided her meals as well. Other women adrift readily accepted jobs
where employers served meals at the workplace. Nurses, trained and
untrained, often ate their meals in the hospitals and with the private
families where they worked. Similarly, dishwashers, waitresses, and
kitchen help ate at the restaurants that employed them. Nurses account
for much of the slight overrepresentation of women adrift in semi-
professional jobs, and restaurant workers account for much of the overrepresentation in service occupations in 1910. The only other major

occupational group overrepresented in 1910 was laundresses, especially operatives in commercial laundries.[36]

The detailed occupational distribution should not obscure the overall picture. Women adrift worked in traditional female-dominated jobs. While they moved beyond traditional family roles, they did not escape the sex-segregated labor market. This had profound implications: the low wages paid in female-dominated occupations undermined the independence of women who tried to support themselves.

Men who lived apart from family usually earned wages intended for self and sometimes family support; in contrast, many women earned below-subsistence wages. Employers assumed that all working women lived in families where working males provided them with partial support. It profited employers to use this idealized version of the family economy to determine women's wages. Thus, a completed job search was a dubious success for many women adrift, for they continued to encounter the hardships of poverty after they had found jobs.

Virtually no one denied the inadequacy of the average woman's wages. Since early in the nineteenth century, wage-earning women and reformers had called perenially for higher pay. Even conservative writers who disparaged women adrift acknowledged that the average wage-earning woman did not earn enough for self-support. In 1888, one such writer, "J," responded to an exposé of Chicago sweatshops, arguing that wage-earning women, "if they were good for anything," should live in families as servants instead of working for "the pittances they are getting at the places you write of and boarding themselves." Blaming women for their own poverty, the writer claimed, "They do not deserve pity. They desire to be 'ladies,' 'salesladies,' etc." Still, the writer admitted, "All know they can not board and clothe themselves on the pay you say they are getting."[37]

Even employers conceded readily that they did not expect women workers to live solely on their wages. They often stated that women received free or cheap room and board in the homes of their parents, and, if pressed, they claimed to hire only women who lived with family or friends. In 1913 an Illinois State Senate Investigating Committee found that over half of the 13,610 women employed in five of the largest stores in Chicago earned less than a living wage. "With a few exceptions," the report stated, "the employers maintained that the girls lived at home, or said they did, and that the burden of their support fell upon the fathers."[38] Comments of this kind became common enough that one social investigator in Chicago referred simply to " 'the living at home' excuse [given by] the employer who is questioned about his wage scale."[39]

A survey of store and factory workers, conducted by the federal government in 1908, found that over half of the women adrift in Chicago earned less than eight dollars a week, the widely acknowledged subsistence wage. The survey revealed that women department store workers who lived "adrift" earned an average of $8.17 per week, and 66 percent earned less than this average. The same study found an average wage of $7.23 per week among Chicago women factory workers who lived away from home. This figure did not include eighty-four self-supporting packing house workers who reported an average of $4.55 per week, with only three of the eighty-four earning over six dollars.[40] These figures reflected a nationwide pattern. A study of working women in Boston, published in 1911, showed average wages ranging from $6.50 per week for kitchen workers to $9.61 per week for clerical workers.[41] In 1914, women in twenty-four manufacturing industries nationwide earned on average $7.75 per week; in the same industries, men earned on average $13.92.[42]

The low wages of many women adrift would not cover the necessary expenditures for independent living. Before the period of rapid inflation beginning in 1915, numerous social investigators found that a woman needed a minimum of eight to twelve dollars per week to cover her cost of living. One budget based on the cost of living in Chicago in 1907 and 1908 totaled $9.70 per week, excluding items such as soap, medicine, newspapers, and books.[43] A Boston study, based on the actual expenditures of 450 wage-earning women, reported the same figure, $9.70, as the minimum weekly living wage.[44] In 1913 the Illinois Senate investigation produced another minimum budget accepted as sound by "employers as well as employees." The budget of $8.00 allotted $3.00 for room rent, $2.70 for meals, 60 cents for carfare, and $1.70 for clothing, laundry, and all other expenses.[45] Margaret Dreier Robins of the Women's Trade Union League considered twelve dollars the minimum. "If her wages fall below that amount," Robins said, "she merely exists. She is obliged to deny herself proper food and suitable clothing."[46]

Middle-class women reformers, one might argue, used middle-class standards in calculating these budgets. In fact, a woman adrift might buy room and board for considerably less than the $5.70 listed in the above itemized budget. For that price, a woman could rent a private bedroom in a residential neighborhood and eat three ample meals a day. For less money, a woman might rent a bed in a room shared with the landlady's children, a cot set up in a kitchen, or a poorly heated and ill-ventilated room. In order to buy cheaper board, she might eat only coffee and bread for breakfast and lunch, or she might skip supper a few nights a week.

The budgets calculated by middle-class reformers do not seem inflated, though, for wage-earning women themselves made similar calculations. "I'm getting $9 a week," one woman reported, "and I don't believe I'll ever have a new dress or hat again."[47] Another woman, a bookkeeper who earned the relatively high wage of twelve dollars a week, found that "even $12 a week is a very small salary." When spending five dollars a week for room and board, she wrote, a woman had little money for car fare, shoes, clothes, and laundry. "Each week brings in an extra expense item. . . . How can she save a little for the rainy days?"[48] A twenty-eight-year-old prostitute, who had worked in the office of a Chicago laundry, said, "it is impossible for [a woman] to live on less than $12 to $15 a week." This woman found that "decently furnished rooms, kept properly warmed, and fairly clean" cost at least three dollars a week. And, she continued, "you cannot eat a meal that has any nourishment for less than twenty cents to twenty-five cents."[49]

Those women at the bottom of the wage scale lived in abject poverty. In 1910 a seventeen-year-old native-born white woman worked as an inspector in a retail store for four dollars a week. She lived in an ill-ventilated room, ate poorly, and sewed her clothes from fabric she bought on credit.[50] In 1913 a Russian woman whose husband had left her worked in a garment factory for four dollars a week. Her interpreter said, "She says when she has more money she eats better and if she has less she eats less. . . . She wears one [dress] until she cannot wear it, and then she gets another one."[51]

The poverty of many women adrift continued after 1915, although it was somewhat alleviated in the 1920s by an increase in women's real wages. Between 1914 and 1920, both the average weekly wages of women workers and the cost of living rose rapidly. During the 1920s, when wages and prices stabilized, one set of figures indicates that women's real wages (in twenty-four manufacturing industries nationwide) fluctuated from 20 percent to 40 percent above their prewar level.[52] This increase should not be overemphasized, however. The figures do not identify the regions or sizes of cities where the increase was greatest, nor do they include most occupations. More important, the increase in wages did not bring the average woman's earnings high enough to cover the cost of independent living. In 1930, for example, the average female clerical worker in Chicago earned twenty-four dollars per week, and the average female manufacturing worker earned twenty-two dollars.[53] In the same year, sample budgets gave twenty dollars as the minimum sum necessary for a working woman who lived in a subsidized boarding home in Chicago and twenty-five dollars for a Chicago working woman who lived in a commercial rooming house, providing she had "a boyfriend who takes her out to dinner occasionally."[54]

The drag of racism pulled the wages of black women lower still. Black women routinely earned less than white women for the same jobs, and, additionally, they were excluded from a wide range of "women's" jobs, especially those considered most desirable. In laundries and kitchens, black women often received one dollar less per week than white women. The records of a Chicago employment agency showed that "where the white cooks received eight dollars per week the Negro cooks were paid seven dollars."[55] Almost no black women held jobs in offices and stores in Chicago in the late nineteenth and early twentieth centuries. The Chicago Urban League considered it a major breakthrough when, in 1919, at the League's urging, Sears, Roebuck, and Company hired twelve hundred black women as office workers.[56] Employers also excluded black women from many manufacturing jobs. The growing number of black women who found work in industry frequently found themselves with the work that white women refused to accept. By the 1920s, for example, black women had secured a foothold in Chicago's slaughtering and meat-packing industry. But "they worked at the lowest paid 'blind-alley' jobs in the yards" and were excluded openly from the jobs with better work conditions.[57]

The irregular and seasonal nature of much of women's work compounded the problem of inadequate wages. Workers paid by piece rates, as in the clothing and meat-packing industries, often received work irregularly even during the heavy seasons. Without a steady distribution of work, a high piece-rate payment could result in low weekly wages. In 1888 a Chicago woman who boarded at the Home for Self-Supporting Women earned only $4.21 in two weeks because "the work was given out to her slowly." She had to quit her job and find another which would pay enough to cover her $2.25 weekly expense for room and board.[58] In many industries, women expected to be without work for a portion of every year. A 1908 investigation of the Chicago stockyards found that 255 of 333 long-term women workers surveyed worked for less than fifty-two weeks in the year. Of the 255, 182 reported "no work" available as the cause of their unemployment.[59] In years of depression, of course, unemployment was more severe.

Wage-earning women who came to the city with hopes of sending money home to their families often found that they did not earn enough to contribute substantially to their relatives' support. Most studies that itemized the expenditures of women adrift made no mention of money sent home. One 1908 survey, however, found that less than 25 percent of the women adrift surveyed in each of seven cities contributed to "needy relatives." This figure is high because the survey included a small, though unspecified, number of widows and "deserted" women who supported dependent children.[60]

Some women adrift did move up a limited occupational ladder: their wages increased, at least minimally, as they gained experience in a particular job. In a 1908 survey of over thirty-four hundred women factory workers in seven cities, the average wage increased slowly but steadily from $4.62 per week for women with less than a year of experience to a peak of $8.54 per week for women with sixteen to twenty years of experience. The average wages of almost fourteen hundred retail store workers increased more dramatically, from $4.69 for women with less than a year of experience to $13.33 for women with sixteen to twenty years.[61]

In addition to those women whose wages increased with experience, a few women moved into semiprofessional and professional careers. An extraordinary example is Mary Anderson, the factory worker who later became director of the U.S. Women's Bureau.[62] In a somewhat more typical mobility pattern, women moved from positions as saleswomen to more professional jobs as buyers.[63] In 1880 and in 1910, almost one-fourth of the single women adrift in Chicago over the age of thirty-five held semiprofessional and professional jobs. In 1880, most of these women worked as teachers; in 1910, half of them worked as nurses. These women may have moved up an occupational ladder. More likely, perhaps, some of the women with better jobs remained adrift at older ages because, as self-supporting women, they felt less compelled to marry.

The economic security of older woman adrift, however, should not be overstated. Most faced increasing difficulties as they aged. Employers discriminated against older women, especially in hiring for jobs in offices, factories, and restaurants where biases in favor of youthful sexual attractiveness gave young women and conventionally pretty women a competitive advantage. One older kitchen worker in a restaurant explained to a younger woman why she would not leave her low-paying job: "You are young, girlie, you can afford to be independent, but I am old. If I give up this job, where can I get another?"[64] A self-supporting widow, Ann J., who had worked in several Chicago factories also found that she could not compete with younger women. She was laid off frequently, she explained, "because she was not attractive, or because she was old. She sees that an old woman does not have a chance."[65]

Moreover, older women often earned lower wages despite their years of experience. In the same survey cited above, the average wage of women factory workers dropped after a peak of $8.54 per week for women with sixteen to twenty years of experience. Women with over twenty years of experience earned on average $7.64 per week, and the few women with over thirty years of experience earned on average only $6.51. Similarly, the average weekly wages of women who worked in retail stores declined from a peak of $13.33 to $11.52 for women with over twenty years of experience.[66]

Most older women, however, did not work in factories, restaurants, offices, or stores. As they aged, many women adrift moved into occupations considered appropriate for older women. These jobs were not necessarily higher paying, but they often accorded a small degree of independence from employers. After nearly thirty years as a live-in nurse and servant in Chicago, Caroline O., a black woman, turned to jobs where she lived on her own, washing and cleaning by the day.[67] Rather than work in factories and commercial laundries, other older women worked in their homes as dressmakers and hand laundresses. Some older women gained a measure of independence as rooming house keepers. Cora J., a white woman, worked as a stenographer in Chicago for seven years and as a general office worker for three years. She then rented two houses, furnished them, and sublet the bedrooms.[68] Another white woman, Sarah K., supported herself as a hairdresser and waitress for eighteen years before she too rented and ran a rooming house.[69]

Ann J., laid off from factory work, secured employment, room, and board as a chambermaid in a hotel. She saved her earnings and eventually managed to purchase a rooming house. As her interviewer wrote, "It was the only way she knew of by which she might become independent." Independence, though, did not allay her anxiety. Cheated of $150 and suspicious of her male roomers, she said, "a lone woman can't take any chances, because if she doesn't look out for herself in this world, no one else will." She could afford neither "the time nor the money to keep [friends]," and she worried "for hours" about her future, wondering "how much longer she [would] be able to work." She feared that her final years would "be spent in the poorhouse." According to Ann J., "a lone woman can't be too careful."[70]

The poverty of many women adrift and the long hours of hard work took their toll. Women complained of exhaustion. "I do not have time to make acquaintances," wrote one woman who worked for $5.50 per week in the basement of a large department store. "I love to read, but I have no chance to get library books; all I see is an occasional paper. I get home so late that I am too tired to go out at night and, besides, I have to wash and mend my clothes."[71]

Without family nearby to offer support, women worried about sickness and unemployment. Many had little or no savings available for use during emergencies. For some of these women, life seemed especially bleak. When one woman "without home and money" slipped on the ice and broke her ankle, she found herself committed for months to the county hospital.[72] A few days of illness could lead to the loss of a job which could lead in turn to eviction. In 1919 a Chicago policeman rescued an ill, unemployed, and evicted woman adrift as she tried to drown herself in Lake Michigan.[73] Another woman adrift left the following message before she committed suicide: "I have worked until I can work no longer, and I am disgusted with life."[74]

To avoid poverty, some women adrift, especially young women, chose to work in the one sector of the female labor force where an unskilled woman earned adequate wages—what might be called the sexual service sector. The most obvious form of sexual service work is, and was, prostitution. In 1880, 4 percent of the sampled women adrift listed their occupation as prostitute. This figure may well be low since many prostitutes probably hid their occupation from census takers. In fact, by 1910, census schedules no longer listed prostitution at all. A 1911 municipal investigation, however, reviewed the cases of 2,420 prostitutes and estimated that 5,000 "professional" prostitutes worked in Chicago.[75]

Some women adrift turned to prostitution specifically because they needed or wanted money. One such woman became a prostitute after six months of unemployment. "I found that it was almost impossible for an inexperienced girl to get employment, even at $5 per week," she wrote. "Finally I had no money left with which to pay my way. By this I don't mean that I had only a few dollars left; I had not one penny in my shabby little purse."[76] Another prostitute, who had worked for four years in Chicago, also testified that she chose prostitution because she "needed money." She had worked in a shoe factory in Cincinnati for five dollars a week; at the time of her testimony she earned from twenty-five to thirty dollars weekly.[77]

The profits of prostitution, though, often did not accrue to the women who performed the work. Various forms of subjugation—to pimps, madames, and police—made prostitution a low-paying job, and sometimes slavery, for many women. Furthermore, the ever-present threats of venereal disease and physical abuse made prostitution a dangerous occupation.[78]

Newer forms of sexual service work, emerging in the late-nineteenth- and early-twentieth-century cities, placed women in less personal, more contractual relations with those who managed their work. The growth of urban commercialized recreation industries created these "modernized" sexual service jobs for women. In cabarets, dance halls, and restaurants, owners hired women to attract men in order to increase the profits of their enterprises. A guide for male "pleasure seekers" in Chicago that appeared in 1892 reported that a company needed a "number of shapely women in the cast" to secure an engagement at the bawdy Madison Street Opera House.[79] Two decades later a reporter in Chicago described a similar situation in a cabaret with all black performers where "personal charms" were "apparently better recommendations than singing ability."[80]

Chorus girls, masseuses, and, later, cabaret dancers, taxi dancers, and cocktail waitresses all earned the higher wages of sexual service without necessarily selling themselves for intercourse.[81] In 1891 a woman working in a massage parlor justified her sexual service work by the higher wages she received. "I wasn't able to make enough money at bookkeeping (from six to seven dollars a week) to pay my way," she wrote. "Here I get from ten to twelve dollars a week."[82] In 1913 a black woman dancer at a "notorious" Chicago café testified that she earned her living by dancing for only three minutes every night. Her employer stated that he paid performers from twenty-five to thirty-five dollars a week.[83] A later investigation found that cabaret entertainers in Chicago earned from eighteen to seventy-five dollars a week, enormous wages to an unskilled woman worker.[84]

Although historians often neglect the sexual service sector, it is central in defining the female labor market. Of the unskilled women adrift, only the sexual service workers were not paid as dependent daughters. They probably escaped the assumptions of the family economy because the demand for their work outreached the supply. Or perhaps because employers and others distinguished so sharply between "dutiful daughters" and "fallen women," they could not assume that a sexual service worker had support from her family.

Although the sexual service worker escaped the poverty of other women adrift, she paid the price of more severe stigma. As sexual service work expanded beyond prostitution into legitimate commercial institutions, it did not necessarily gain in respectability. In the mid-1920s, for example, a hostess in a Chicago cabaret, who earned from thirty-five to fifty dollars per week, suffered from her mother's disapproval: "I'm not doing anything wrong. . . . I could sent [*sic*] [my mother] ten dollars every week but I know she won't take it. . . . If I'm making a fair living this way why should anyone object. . . . I'm not doing anything really wrong, really."[85]

In fact, any woman adrift without professional training who did not suffer from visible hardship risked accusations of immorality. As a 1908 advice book to self-supporting office workers stated, "A girl who is obliged to earn her own living, cannot afford to do anything that will cause talk, and nothing generates gossip quicker than the fact that a girl apparently spends more than she is known to make."[86] The unskilled woman adrift lived poorly, or else she was damned.

Outside of the family as well as within it, American womanhood was defined in terms of family membership. Although she moved apart from kin, a typical woman adrift could expect to earn the wages of a dependent daughter or wife. She faced stigmatization and discrimination because she was not visibly dutiful to parents, husband, or children. And she was vulnerable to sexual exploitation by criminals and mashers who saw her lack of nearby kin as a weakness. These hardships—low wages, stigmatization, sexual exploitation—distinguish the woman adrift from her male counterparts who also boarded and lodged in the city.

The hardships, of course, tell only part of the story. While some women adrift were genuine victims, most were not. Many women practiced severe personal economy, but few starved or committed suicide. Some women earned adequate wages for modest self-support, and even the poorest women often had ways to reenter families if life "adrift" became intolerable. They entered live-in domestic service, returned to the homes of their kin, or married. Furthermore, poverty and stigmatization are relative. For a black woman from the rural South or a peasant woman from Poland, wages earned in Chicago, though below the poverty level, were usually higher than wages they had earned earlier. For a sexually active woman, occasional suspicious glances from strangers may have seemed preferable to daily ostracism by family and friends. Equally important, as later chapters show, women adrift found resourceful ways to live in the city. They created substitutes for family life, and they cooperated with and depended on their peers, stretching, pooling and supplementing their wages.

The hardships are important, though, not only because they point to the constraints faced by women adrift, but also because they captured public notice in the late nineteenth and early twentieth centuries. The combination of independence from family, naïveté, low wages, and sexual service work sparked the imaginations of Victorian and, later,

Progressive writers. The woman adrift became a symbol of the threats that industrialization and urbanization posed to womanhood and the family. Conservatives condemned the women who left their homes and cast aspersions on their morals. A few reformers and radicals predicted a future economic independence for women. But the writers who attracted the most public notice sympathized with the poverty of wage-earning women, worried about their chastity, and sought to provide them with protective surrogate families.

Chapter Three
Orphans and Innocents

In Chicago, "women adrift" came before the public eye at least as early as 1873. In September of that year, a man who signed himself "Edgardus" wrote a letter to the *Chicago Daily Tribune* asking wealthy men to donate funds for a boarding house for working women. Edgardus wrote "with feelings of sympathy and sorrow" for "the deserving homeless girls" of Chicago whose small wages kept them impoverished. Pleasant boarding homes with low fees, he argued, would save the "discouraged and desponding one" from turning to the temporary and ruinous embraces of "some heartless man."[1] In the two weeks that followed Edgardus's letter, a handful of writers submitted letters in support. At this point, the attention paid to women adrift might have subsided had not a letter from "Paterfamilias" introduced an opposing view. Paterfamilias advised poor working women to enter domestic service in private homes where they could receive room and board. He implied that women adrift had only themselves to blame for their poverty since they might easily choose to live in a more homelike and secure setting.[2] Paterfamilias's letter launched a debate that continued for over two months. All told, the *Daily Tribune* published fifty-seven letters and two lengthier articles.

While a few maverick writers took up novel themes, the bulk of letters argued for one of two opposing views of women adrift. On one side stood the majority of letter writers, including Edgardus, who sympathized with wage-earning women and called for low-cost boarding homes to protect them from poverty and prostitution. Several of these writers contended that some women lacked the strength to engage in domestic service. Others lauded women for aspiring to labor higher than drudgery. They portrayed women adrift as "delicately reared" women struggling "nobly" against a "fate they were powerless to control."[3] The more sentimental writers described them as innocent children or, as Edgardus wrote in a later letter, "girls around whom poverty has thrown its dark mantle, but in whose souls, as yet, the pure heavenly light of childhood glows radiantly and bright."[4]

On the other side, Paterfamilias and his followers took a dimmer view of women adrift. They denied that domestic service was in any way degrading. A woman who considered herself above domestic labor, they claimed, had "false notions of pride," tended toward laziness, longed for finery.[5] "The young women who seek employment as clerks, sewing girls, etc.," one writer stated, "have such exalted notions of themselves that they all aspire to be young ladies and occupy a false position."[6] The problem these writers saw was not simply poverty or its pitfalls but the willfulness of women who stepped beyond "those departments of labor which naturally, and therefore legitimately, belong to them."[7] They portrayed women adrift as ill-bred idlers who refused their womanly calling.

The interest in women adrift continued into the first decades of the twentieth century. In subsequent literature, though, the conservative views of Paterfamilias and his followers dwindled. Those who sympathized with women adrift created the dominant public image of a pure woman in a sullied environment.[8] At its simplest, this image signaled the failure of the forces of good to resist the forces of evil. The family, the haven of love, had not protected its daughters, and the city, with its cruel competition and designing men, threatened to ruin them. Torn from the protective shelter of family and exposed to the muscle of the city, the woman adrift, in her symbolic role, was isolated, vulnerable, and bereft. She represented the victimization of the innocent and weak in an urban world without moral standards.

Four groups of writers played instrumental roles in disseminating the dominant public image of women adrift. The middle-class women reformers of the organized boarding home movement, especially women in the Young Women's Christian Association, elaborated the image. In the decades after the Civil War and continuing into the twentieth century, these reformers established scores of subsidized boarding homes and other services for self-supporting women. In promotional literature, annual reports, and national reform periodicals, they portrayed women adrift as endangered women in need of maternal protection. Second, popular romance novels and story papers, written largely by women, featured the woman adrift as the heroine of urban adventure tales. Peaking in the 1880s and 1890s, this literature presented a caricature of the woman adrift as helpless victim. Third, writers in the campaign against prostitution, primarily journalists and reformers, male and female, combined the caricatures of the romance stories with the reformist concerns of the organized boarding home movement. Although they gained momentum in the 1890s, their most sensational writings, on "white slavery," appeared in highly popular books, magazines, newspapers, and films in the years between 1900 and 1915. Finally, a new generation of reformers, drawn from the ranks of social workers and journalists, recast the Victorian sentimental discourse on women adrift into Progressive social science form. In the early twentieth century, their investigations substantiated the image of the helpless woman adrift by emphasizing the determinism of her bleak environment.

The organized boarding home movement emerged from a decades-long female reform tradition. Beginning early in the nineteenth century, middle- and upper-class women banded together in a variety of organizations to promote benevolence and moral reform. These women transferred the religious ideals of mission and charity, along with the maternal role of guardianship, into new areas outside of the church and the home. Motivated by a sense of female solidarity and a middle-class version of morality, they focused much of their work on aiding needy women who seemed in sexual danger.[9]

Early in their efforts, reformers discovered the homeless working woman. They deplored her destitution and feared that, out of desperation, she would turn to prostitution, an occupation many considered a fate worse than death. After 1830, reformers in several cities organized associations to rescue prostitutes and employ impoverished women.[10] The Female Benevolent Society of New York, for example, helped prostitutes and aided the "friendless female orphan, when no way [was] left for her to obtain a livelihood but that of prostitution."[11] In 1847 the American Female Guardian Society of New York opened the first Home for the Friendless, providing free shelter to poor and homeless women.[12] Similar homes soon appeared in other cities. Chicago's Home for the Friendless opened in 1858, accepting women without regard to race, religion, or nationality, "so long as the applicant seemed to be overborne in the fierce struggle for life."[13] As the word *friendless* suggests, these early institutions focused their efforts on female outcast and charity cases, the prostitutes and the poorest of poor women.

Around midcentury, some female reformers expanded their work to include the average wage-earning woman.[14] These reformers saw that any woman who had no training in marketable skills, who depended economically on a husband or father, might find herself without support. Through an unfortunate twist of fate, they or their daughters might join the ranks of the friendless poor. In the 1850s, reformers advocated that "every girl should have . . . some honorable and useful way of gaining a livelihood."[15] They opened employment bureaus and "houses of industry" to train and place women in remunerative work. The hardships of wage-earning women during the depression of the late 1850s and the low wages of seamstresses during the Civil War underscored the precariousness of women's economic position. In the years after the Civil War, as increasing numbers of women arrived in the cities for work, reformers identified not only the victims of poverty but the potential victims as well. They shifted their emphasis from rescuing the desperate to preventive efforts on behalf of the vulnerable, and they pointed to women adrift as those women most endangered.

New organizations in several cities specifically aimed to aid women adrift. The first such organization, the Ladies' Christian Association, appeared in New York in 1858. A Boston organization, formed in 1866, was the first to call itself the Young Women's Christian Association. Lucretia Boyd, a Boston missionary, initiated the work when she "became greatly distressed by the serious situation that confronted self-supporting girls." By 1875, twenty-eight local YWCAs had over eight thousand members and operated thirteen subsidized boarding homes for working women.[16] In 1876, women in Chicago organized the Women's Christian Association (later renamed the Young Women's Christian Association) "to seek out women taking up their residence in Chicago, and endeavor to bring them under moral and religious influences."[17] The Chicago YWCA first adopted an older nonprofit employment bureau that had been formed "so that amidst the manifold temptations of a large city none might fall from want of a steady occupation," and shortly after established a boarding home where wage-earning women could "find good living and the comforts and blessings of a Christian home."[18]

The YWCA was the largest but not the only organization formed to aid women adrift. In the same decades that the YWCA emerged, other groups organized similar low-cost boarding homes for self-supporting women. In 1888 a federal report on wage-earning women in large cities listed 24 organized (nonprofit) boarding homes for working women in addition to the 15 Women's Christian Association homes.[19] Ten years later, another federal report counted a total of 90 homes.[20] In Chicago, the Woman's Home, a short-lived institution, preceded the YWCA by four years in providing low-cost room and board for wage-earning women.[21] By the end of the century, Chicago had at least eight homes that replicated the work of the YWCA.[22] In 1914 a study found 31 organized homes in Chicago, and in 1921 another investigation found 45.[23] By 1928, Chicago had around 65 organized homes for self-supporting women.[24]

The movement did not reflect the mentality of white, Protestant, native-born women only. In Chicago, Afro-American, Catholic, Jewish, German, Swedish, Polish, and Norwegian-Danish women also established homes for women adrift of their racial, religious, and ethnic groups. By 1914 these women managed at least fourteen homes in Chicago, including four for Jewish women and four for Catholic women.[25] By 1921, at least four such homes housed black working women in Chicago, and by 1928 six.[26] These homes were, in part, a response to the exclusivity of the YWCA. In 1877 the Chicago YWCA voted to deny black women admission to its home.[27] (Eventually black women joined the YWCA and managed a "colored branch" boarding home, but this home remained notoriously underfunded.)[28] Through more subtle deterrents, such as language barriers and Protestant "family worship," the YWCA also discouraged immigrants, Jews, and Catholics. Women from these groups, however, formed their own homes not simply because the YWCA excluded them but because they too believed that women adrift needed special care.

The homes in Chicago operated under a variety of auspices, including churches, religious groups and orders, and secular women's clubs. The Moody Church managed a home for working women as did the black Olivet Baptist Church. The Salvation Army, the Volunteers of America, and the Sunshine Gospel Mission also established homes. Church-affiliated women's groups, such as the Ladies' Benevolent Society of the New First Congregational Church, opened residences in Chicago. The Sisters of Mercy managed the Mercy Home, and Franciscan Sisters managed the House of Providence and the Guardian Angel Day Nursery and Home for Working Girls. Black club women organized the long-lived Phyllis Wheatley Home, and Jewish club women organized the Josephine Club, the Ruth Club, and the Miriam Clubs. A few individual women also established homes: Melissia Ann Elam, an ex-slave, owned and managed the Elam Club Home for Colored Girls, and Ina Law Robertson founded the still-extant Eleanor Clubs.[29]

Other reform organizations offered additional protective services to women adrift. In Chicago, wealthier women joined together to provide inexpensive and wholesome recreation and food through vacation homes in the country, working women's social clubs, and subsidized lunch rooms.[30] The Chicago Woman's Club managed a lodging house for temporarily stranded women, and, for at least a few years, the Home for Self-Supporting Women ran the Provident Laundry which provided temporary employment for unemployed women.[31] In 1907 the Women's Trade Union League of Chicago met lone women immigrants at the train stations and visited them in their homes.³² In addition, the YWCA and, later, the Woman's Church Federation Protectorate and the Olivet Baptist Church, among others, conducted free employment bureaus as well as room registries where women adrift applied to rent rooms in private families.³³

This outpouring of interest and effort on behalf of self-supporting women was based on an image of the woman adrift as endangered orphan. Our clearest sense of this image comes from the annual reports of the YWCA, the only such organization in Chicago to leave detailed historical records. What recurs time and again in these reports is the notion that wage-earning women needed "protection." The reports describe the women adrift who came to the YWCA as "young women . . . who have no natural guardian in the city," "unprotected young girls," and young women and girls "who need the protection and encouragement of Christian surroundings."³⁴ Following in the footsteps of earlier female reformers, the women of the YWCA appointed themselves as protectors. "What could be more worthwhile," asked one report, "than to safeguard and to save the young women who come to our great metropolis from all parts of the world?"³⁵

Why did a woman need protection? The YWCA gave the same answers that female reformers had given for decades. She needed protection because she faced a life of low wages, long hours, seasonal unemployment, and loneliness, or what reformers referred to in shorthand as "the struggle for existence." Protection would offer food and shelter in times of poverty and comfort in times of loneliness.

The concern for economic privation, however, cloaked an overriding concern for sexual morality. To the middle-class women of the YWCA, the "temptation" to virginal women to sell or give away their sexual purity was more dangerous than the "struggle for existence." "We fear unless they are better remunerated," stated Mrs. Leander Stone, an early president, "they will be left the coming winter to freeze in attics, or starve in cellars, or what (god forbid) is worse than death, sacrifice their honor to secure food and warmth."³⁶ The women of the YWCA showed little interest in protecting needy but nonvirginal widows, deserted wives, and unwed mothers.

A young, single woman needed protection, then, not simply to ease material hardships but also to guide and restrain her sexual behavior. Protection included supervision and training in morality. The women of the YWCA wanted to exercise a "kindly guardianship over [working women's] moral and religious interests."³⁷ In an "unprotected" urban setting, "poor country girls" might "drift" into "situations of demoralizing tendency and . . . make acquaintances of doubtful character."[38] The reformers occasionally hinted that protection required the restraint of women who lacked sufficient self-control. As one report stated, "Even the strong and self-reliant flag without some sympathetic interest in their work and welfare—how much more those weaker ones, whose unbalanced characters and morbid passion for dress render them but too easily tempted to folly, and perhaps to a darker end."[39] In Mrs. Leander Stone's words, "There is a tendency, we fear, of our working girls to drift away from sweet and tender home influences which they may have enjoyed in childhood, so soon as they go out into the world for self-support."[40] The women of the YWCA disliked and feared the possibilities for sexual activity that freedom from family seemed to create.

Yet the ultimate blame for going astray rarely rested on the wage-earning woman herself. If some women drifted from home influences, they were likely drawn by scheming men. The Travelers' Aid Committee of the Chicago YWCA, formed in 1888, focused on the struggle between unwitting women and designing men. The committee hired "matrons" to protect women newcomers to Chicago as they arrived alone at railroad stations. It denounced the false newspaper advertisements that lured unsuspecting women job seekers to brothels and the procurers and mashers who met women migrants as they deboarded the incoming trains. The committee stressed the naïveté of women immigrants and rural migrants, claiming as its first purpose "to outwit evil agents, who would deceive the innocent."[41] Like the earlier reformers who worked with prostitutes, the Travelers' Aid Committee shifted the responsibility for sexual activity away from the tempted women to the men (and occasionally women) who had active designs against them.

The cast of characters in a typical scenario reported by the Travelers' Aid Committee included a YWCA matron, an innocent young woman, and a predatory man. In one such scenario, the matron protected a sixteen-year-old woman "who had no knowledge of life and believed everybody" including a young man whose business was to "find innocent victims who were traveling alone."[42] In another case, the woman from the Travelers' Aid Committee pitted herself against a married man who had persuaded a seventeen-year-old waitress to join him in Chicago.[43] The women of the YWCA saw themselves as fighting evil on behalf of women unable to fend for themselves. While some young women adrift were indeed exploited sexually, the women of the YWCA treated all young women adrift as if they were weak-willed victims.

This view of women was not unique to the YWCA. A stereotype of women as the weaker sex had existed for centuries, and a newer stereotype of women as passionless, innocent, and sexually pure had prevailed since at least the end of the eighteenth century.[44] Throughout the nineteenth century, middle-class women used this newer stereotype routinely to assert their moral superiority to lustful men. The female reformers of the first half of the nineteenth century had used these same stereotypes to defend prostitutes. A woman who was no longer sexually pure, they had argued, must have fallen victim to the deceptions or force of a man. These reformers had expressed their anger at male sexual license by claiming the stigmatized "fallen woman" as their innocent, weak, and victimized sister.[45] In the late nineteenth century, the women of the YWCA extended the view held by earlier reformers and used it to protect young wage-earning women who did not live at home. They asserted their own strength and moral superiority, but they adopted stereotypes of female weakness and innocence in order to absolve the woman adrift of any responsibility for her sexual behavior.

To solve the problem of female victimization, the women of the early YWCA did not attempt to raise women's wages or rescue prostitutes or change male sexual behavior. They acquiesced to the social ills that they identified and sought as an antidote to resurrect home life. Their solution rested on the growing importance placed on family by nineteenth-century middle-class Americans. As urbanization and industrialization eroded the small-town community, the family (and especially the mother) was elevated and idealized as the guardian of moral standards. The idealized domestic sphere stood in contrast to the seemingly immoral urban world of corrupt politics, ruthless competition, and rampant commercialized sex.[46] Accordingly, the women of the YWCA, like other nineteenth-century female reformers, saw the family home as the missing "natural" shelter that could protect the innocent woman from an inevitably cruel environment.[47]

The women of the YWCA wanted to provide a "home in every sense of the word," "a house where [women] might come and feel at home in a city of strangers" (see fig. 3.1).[48] They called the residents and managers of their boarding home "the family." This family, as idealized, provided warmth and companionship, moral and religious guidance, support in times of unemployment, and protection from designing men. A female-dominated private sphere would shield the woman adrift from a perilous male-dominated public sphere. "What this world wants is homes. . . . If there is any one who needs a home it : the girl," the Rev. P. S. Henson stated the intention bluntly at an 1895 groundbreaking ceremony for a new, larger YWCA boarding home. "Many times, as a result of desperate straits to which she is reduced, that young life is wrecked and ruined. Here provision is made for her. Pleasant surroundings, congenial companionship, in fact, all the blessings of a home."[49]

The Travelers' Aid Committee, too, attempted to place women in families. The Travelers' Aid workers saw themselves as "missionaries,"

Fig. 3.1. Young Women's Christian Association Home, 288 Michigan Avenue, 1902. (Source: University of Illinois at Chicago, University Library, Young Women's Christian Association Records)

"gently leading back to mother and home the girl about to take the first step downward."[50] They considered a case resolved when they returned a runaway teenager or lost traveler to her family, placed a penniless migrant in a private family as a domestic servant, or sent a self-supporting working woman to live in the YWCA boarding home. Once she saw a wage-earning woman ensconced safely in a home, the Travelers' Aid matron had fulfilled her duty.

As the title "matron" indicates, the women of the YWCA envisioned their own role as that of mothers in their newly created families. In fact, they often referred to themselves and to the superintendents of their boarding homes as "mothers." For example, Mrs. Leander Stone lauded the women of the YWCA as "mothers full of love for our foster children."[51] In an era when the emotional potency of motherhood was at its prime, the YWCA women, like other female reformers in this period, used their status as mothers to further social and charitable programs.

It is not surprising that middle-class women took on this role. Their status and power in society rested to a large extent on their role as keepers of the home. When a daughter moved beyond the reach of the home, duty demanded that a mother follow, extending the home's protective boundaries into the public sphere. In one sense, middle-class women expanded their roles as an offensive move. With a firm belief in female moral superiority, women reformers entered the public sphere assured of their right to be there. As reformer Frances Willard wrote in 1887, "If I were asked the mission of the ideal woman, I would reply: *it is to make the whole world homelike.*"[52] And, by supporting the wage-earning woman, reformers affirmed that she too had a legitimate public role.

In another sense, however, the women of the YWCA may have moved defensively. By the late nineteenth century, a declining birth rate and a rising divorce rate seemed to threaten traditional family life.[53] At the same time, commercialization encroached on women's traditional home roles. The high visibility of prostitutes in the cities lured husbands away from their wives and threatened to pollute domestic love with diseases spread through commercialized passion. Furthermore, the growth of industry eroded women's productive functions in the home. The death of husbands and fathers during the Civil War and, in Chicago, the literal destruction of homes in the fire of 1871 must have further impressed women with the fragility of their family status. Women tried to defend their domain. Thousands of women in the Women's Christian Temperance Union adopted the slogan "Home Protection."[54] In the YWCA, this home protection assumed special importance because the objects of concern were young and female. If young women expressed their sexuality in public, then all women might lose their status as passionless and therefore morally superior to men. The middle-class women of the YWCA formed surrogate families in which they helped young women whom fate, choice, or a changing economy had left without family support; at the same time, they flexed their moral muscle and bolstered the importance of their own role as moral guardians.

By adopting the role of mother, the women of the YWCA may also have tried to mask the class barrier between themselves and the younger working-class women they hoped to protect. They may have veiled their assumptions of middle-class superiority with the softer language of maternal love, obscuring the hierarchy of class with the hierarchy of parent and child. This mother-daughter bond that the YWCA hoped to cultivate encouraged the infantilization of women adrift. The stereotypes of women as weak, innocent, and passionless invested women with the childlike qualities of dependence, naïveté, and inexperience. Of newcomers to the city, one report wrote, "the poor things wander from place to place, not knowing where to go or what to do."[55] Mrs. Leander Stone frequently chose the image of the orphan to describe the woman adrift. "In Chicago, as in every city the world over, there are thousands of girls, orphaned, so far as natural protectors are concerned," she stated in one address, "but as lofty in sentiment, as pure and ambitious in motive, and as deserving of friends and education as our own loved and more favored daughters."[56] While some wage-earning women came to the city after their parents had died, most left living families behind. The orphan metaphor, rather than describing a reality, conjured an image of vulnerable waifs as almost no other metaphor could. Although the women adrift were old enough to be mothers themselves, the women of the YWCA depicted them as the motherless children of the city.

This picture of women adrift differed from the picture of working men drawn by the Young Men's Christian Association. Founded in 1851, the YMCA pioneered in constructing low-cost familylike boarding homes for single self-supporting men. Like the YWCA, the YMCA stressed the moral guidance that the young migrant to the city needed. But the YMCA did not portray working men as passive orphans. It also did not suggest that young men should return to their parental homes. The YMCA exhorted the young man to control his sexual urges and develop his character toward independent adulthood. The most common metaphor used in midcentury advice literature to self-supporting men was "the youth as the sole navigator of a ship heading out to sea."[57] In contrast, the YWCA did not expect the working woman to steer her own ship. The working woman should never make the journey to adulthood alone. She needed protection from parents or other guardians until she took harbor in a home with a husband. At the first founding of the YWCA in Boston, one speaker made a telling comparison: "The considerations that have led to the formation of a Young Men's Christian Association apply, if possible, with increasing force in the case of young women, who from their position and sex are more unprotected and more helpless."[58]

In the few records available, the managers of the other organized homes in Chicago echoed the language of the YWCA. They aimed to give "protection from the dangers of a city," "safe harbor," or a "wholesome home" to working women "having no home nor protector" in Chicago.[59] Like the YWCA, the other homes hoped to protect women adrift from sexual danger. The homes supplied protection not only to prevent economic hardship but also to "help" working-class women "spiritually and morally."[60]

Middle-class black club women who organized homes were especially concerned with the issue of morality. Derogated by stereotypes of black women as promiscuous and appalled by the vulnerability of young black women to the advances of white men, they sought to defend the "moral integrity" of working-class black women.[61] As Elizabeth Lindsay Davis, a club woman who helped found the Phyllis Wheatley Home, wrote, "Many of these girls were going astray by being led unawares into disreputable homes, entertainment and employment because of lack of protection that strange girls of the other Races enjoy."[62] Drawing on a tradition of mutual aid, other women, like ex-slave Melissia Ann Elam, also opened homes to keep black women "from wandering into [an] immoral atmosphere."[63]

As the number of reform organizations and institutions rose, the interest in women adrift swelled beyond local reform circles. Since early in the nineteenth century, publicists, male and female, had written sporadically of the self-supporting working woman, from reformer Matthew Carey in the late 1820s to feminist Caroline Dall in the 1860s to such lesser-known letter writers as Edgardus in Chicago in 1873.[64] By the 1880s, these reports appeared more frequently in publications intended for national readership. Writers described the difficulties faced by women adrift, related the work of reformers, and called for further action. They defended the homes from critics who claimed that subsidized boarding homes would encourage employers to lower wages, promote female idleness, and discourage women from marriage.[65]

In this national literature, too, writers depicted women in need of moral protection. In an 1899 article, for example, Annie Marion

MacLean found that organized homes were "powerful factors in saving working girls from the glare of cheap entertainments and the dangers of the street." The homes, she concluded, were "veritable virtue-saving stations."[66] Another publicist contrasted the organized homes that supplied "protection when protection is most needed" to the commercial lodging house "with its perilous freedom from all restraint."[67] At least one author found utopian possibilities in the organized home movement. In an overblown article published in 1898, Robert Stein imagined a future in which every city had a "Woman's Hotel." As he envisioned it, this hotel would not only house, employ, and train women adrift, it would also protect them. In fact, "girls of the whole city [would be] from childhood affiliated with it in a vast confederation, and turn to it as their Guardian Power in difficulties." With its "pleasant" homelike atmosphere, the hotel, Stein prophesied, would become "a potent force for 'the debrutalization of man' " because women would no longer feel compelled to marry unless they fell in love.[68]

In general, the reformers and publicists of the organized boarding home movement had more modest aims. They did not hope to change the city, only to protect women from its harsher aspects. To this end, they developed a discourse that portrayed women adrift as vulnerable and passive. They recognized the genuine hardships that a low-income, self-supporting woman faced. But the image of danger they stressed derived less from the economic plight of wage-earning women than from a concern for working-class women's sexual behavior. Because they accepted traditional stereotypes of women as weak and innocent, they read expressions of sexuality by women adrift as female victimization. Furthermore, their vision of themselves as maternal guardians encouraged them to view wage-earning women as children. By the end of the nineteenth century, these reformers and publicists had made the orphaned and innocent woman adrift a recognized figure in local and national reform circles.

The reformers' image of women adrift appeared in fictional form in at least one extraordinary novel. In 1873, the same year that Edgardus wrote to the *Chicago Daily Tribune*, Louisa May Alcott published *Work: A Story of Experience*. Here she tells the story of Christie, an orphan, who leaves the country home of her aunt and uncle to seek work and independence. Once in the city, Christie tries a variety of jobs. Unusually strong and determined, she manages capably, overcoming a number of trials and temptations. But then she despairs, overwhelmed by poverty, isolation, and the apparent emptiness of her life. As in the reports of the YWCA, the orphaned woman adrift, alone in the harsh world, sinks inevitably into crisis. Christie attempts suicide. At this point, her "fallen" but pure-hearted friend Rachel comes to the rescue and leads her to the home of friends. In a domestic setting, Christie regains self-confidence. In the view of both Alcott and women reformers, good women rescue the despairing orphan, and the home protects and heals her. At the end of the novel, Alcott acknowledges the virtue of reform. After marriage, the birth of a child, and the death of a husband, Christie becomes a reformer herself, organizing women to demand higher pay.[69]

But Alcott's story is unusual. The reformers' image of women adrift did not dominate in popular culture. In the late nineteenth century, a somewhat different version of the woman adrift, as stock heroine of thrilling urban adventure tales, appeared frequently in inexpensive "working girl" romance novels.[70] Following in the tradition of eighteenth-century novels of seduction and resistance, these long-neglected romance stories provide a female variant of the Horatio Alger–type stories of male adventure and uplift. Through virtue and luck, an impoverished heroine marries the wealthy man she loves and thereby rises from rags to riches. In more modern form, these novels exist today as Harlequin romances. Highly popular in the 1880s and 1890s, they were printed in serial form in magazines and weekly story papers and as inexpensive books, sometimes paperbound, that sold for ten to fifty cents a copy. Publishers geared the novels to working-class as well as middle-class women readers. The authors, usually female and sometimes pseudonymous, often churned out dozens of romances, plugging minor variations into set formulas.[71]

In these novels, the heroines, like Christie, suffered trials when "adrift" and usually triumphed in the end. Unlike Christie, however, the romance heroines proved themselves utterly helpless. Aside from protecting their honor, they could not care for themselves. Their efforts at self-support were rarely portrayed in more than a page. In fact, many romance heroines never worked at all. Instead, while adrift, they simply endured countless man-made agonies and occasional natural disasters. At the novel's end, the heroines, rescued at last, married happily, or, if they had broken the moral code, they died.

In romance novels, the heroines' experiences as women adrift were usually brief and always dismal. The author often stepped in to lament the situation. In "Violet, the Beautiful Street Singer; Or, an Ill-Starred Betrothal," author Charlotte M. Stanley asks, "Oh, what cruel fate was it that had so suddenly altered the safe, smooth current of her young existence and cast her adrift in this frightful, seething whirlpool of vice and crime?"[72] And, in *A Woman Scorned,* author Effie Adelaide Rowlands bemoans, "She was alone in this cold northern town without friend, without a penny. What was to be done? What was to become of her? Which way should she turn for help?"[73] In the romance novels, life adrift represented catastrophic misfortune and impending doom.

Take the case of Korleen Moore, the heroine of "Her Own Way; Or, Reaping the Harvest." Korleen, a blacksmith's daughter, grows up in Tarrytown, a quiet country village a short distance from New York City. Like all story-paper heroines, Korleen is a "vision of loveliness." But she is also a "poor, foolish, little girl." Her country home seems dull to her; she wants to "see the world." As the author explains, "her heart was not bad; she was only a bit vain and willful." And, the author forewarns, she knows nothing "of the snares and pitfalls" of the world.[74] When the villainous Guy Ruthven arrives in Tarrytown from New York, innocent Korleen succumbs to his attentions and agrees to run off with him to the city. She soon discovers his evil character and begins to pay for her willful ways.

Typically, the plot twists and turns, but, eventually, Korleen, still virginal, finds herself alone in New York. Despite her earlier spunk, she does not now court adventure, nor does she seek a room or a job. Instead, she rues her former willfulness and says simply, "I am alone and adrift; I know not which way to turn, and there is no one to hold forth a helping hand. I wish I could die and be at rest."[75] She sits in the train station, and at dusk she falls asleep in Central Park. When she awakens, she finds herself again in the cruel clutches of Guy Ruthven, a man who looks "upon all women as mere toys for his own amusement."[76] She escapes and then attempts suicide. Predictably, a wealthy man, Ernest Atheldare, rescues her. After numerous additional complications and another suicide attempt, Korleen ends up happily married to Ernest. As the story closes, "His strong arm encircled her, shielding her forever from the storms that might beset her pathway."[77]

Like the reformers of the organized boarding home movement, the romance authors pictured the city as a perilous place for women. But the romance stories sensationalized the dangers, most likely in an attempt to excite readers. One subtitle announces explicitly that the story provides "A Thrilling Portrayal of the Dangers and Pitfalls of the Metropolis."[78] In this story and others, villains—seducers, procurers, thieves, jealous women, and greedy relatives—humiliated, accosted, and abducted the heroines. In other menacing situations, fires and train accidents threatened them. In several stories, illness debilitated them temporarily. When a woman adrift managed to support herself, her employer dismissed her, or jealous co-workers plotted against her, or a customer accused her of theft. The urban world offered no freedom, no opportunity, and little comfort.

In the romance novels, as in the reports of the YWCA, the gravest dangers faced by a woman adrift were threats to her sexual purity. A woman might recover from illness, accidents, or hunger, but if she lost her virginity outside of marriage, her life was "ruined" forever. Here, too, the stories sensationalized the danger. In several novels, heroines, like Korleen Moore, discovered in the nick of time that a seemingly good man was in fact a cad. In one story, a villain convinces the heroine Junie that her missing husband has not really married her. "How was she to face the shame and the terrible disgrace?" In this case, she wanders the streets until she is "faint, hungry, and weary." Then a stranger makes advances, and another tries to force her into prostitution.[79] In other stories, women as well as men threatened the heroine's virginity. In one macabre twist, a seemingly kind woman approaches the helpless heroine, claiming to work for "the Association for the Protection of Strangers in the City." As the heroine prepares to join her, a prostitute, "haggard, painted-cheek, hollow-eyed," warns that the woman will sell her into prostitution. As the heroine flees, the evil woman's sidekick attempts to drug and abduct her.[80]

The novels presented a caricature of the orphaned and innocent woman adrift. The heroines, of course, were always good at heart and sexually pure. They were young, white, native born, and naïve. The stories exaggerated their childlike qualities. In fact, the authors often described them as prepubescent. In one story, "pretty little Bab" is a "poor, innocent, artless child" with the "prettiest promise of a figure."[81] In another story, "Little Sunshine" is a "fairy-like little creature" with "short boyish curls of golden hair," a "sweet girlish voice," and a "sunny disposition."[82] In addition, the heroines were well bred. They came from the wholesome country or from wealthy families. Even the urban working-class heroines turned out in the end to be heiresses, the unknowing daughters of long-lost wealthy parents.

In the city, these women adrift invited pity. Little Sunshine faints from hunger and despair. Pretty little Bab cries, "What shall I do? Where shall I go?" Shortly after, she succumbs to illness and entreats her rescuer, "I have no friends, no home, no place to rest in this great, bad city, and I shall die if you leave me now!"[83] These childlike heroines could not help themselves; instead, they relied on strangers and friends.

In the annual reports of the YWCA, wealthier women, maternal and good, attempted to rescue endangered women adrift. In the romance novels, wealthier women, often evil incarnate, attempted to harm, even kill, them. In "Alice, the Candy Girl: Or a Million of Money," wealthy Verona Clyde, a bigamist and liar, accuses orphan Alice of theft and has her sent to jail.[84] In *Junie's Love Test*, wealthy Mrs. Markham and her two sisters drug beautiful Junie and commit her to a private hospital.[85] The romance authors portrayed wealthy women as greedy, jealous, and vain more often than they portrayed them as caring and kindly. In these novels, unmarried wealthy men rescued women adrift, thus providing the setting for romance and upwardly mobile marriage.

The queen of the romance novels was probably Laura Jean Libbey, the author of over sixty novels in the last two decades of the nineteenth century. Her novels appeared first in serials and then later as inexpensive paperbound books. New novels and reprints of old ones continued to sell into the 1920s.[86] Her books were highly popular, especially among working-class women.[87] In fact, one early-twentieth-century observer of working women referred to the entire genre of romance novels as the "Laura Jean Libbey school of fiction."[88]

Libbey created especially innocent heroines who endured unusually excruciating agonies. As Libbey writes of one heroine, "She was like an infant torn from its mother's breast and thrust out upon the cold mercies of the pitiless world."[89] In *Little Leafy, the Cloakmaker's Beautiful Daughter,* Leafy Clifton, a seventeen-year-old orphan with "a dimpled, saucy, girlish face," endures loneliness, poverty, fire, humiliation, abductions, forced marriage, and attempted suicide.[90] Her most persistent enemy attempts at various points to drown her, gas her, and poison her. She survives it all, virtue intact, to learn that she is the heiress of a wealthy colonel and that her forced marriage was illegal. Needless to say, she marries the wealthy man she loves. In *Ione: A Broken Love Dream,* an orphaned "working girl" with "the grace of a dainty princess" finds herself "friendless and alone, to the mercies of the bitter world."[91] She promptly gets ill and loses her job, then the factory collapses around her, and then she almost succumbs to the attentions of a drunkard and gambler. At this point, she learns that she is an heiress. But, before she marries happily, she faces blackmail, abduction, and a bout of insanity.

The unrelieved agony of life "adrift" heightened the meaning of romance. The trials faced by a woman alone made marriage all the more imperative, for marriage brought salvation as well as love and support. Next to the hell of living adrift, marriage was heaven. In addition, the perils endured by women adrift highlighted the heroines' virtue. They proved their worth by remaining pure in a wicked environment with no one to protect or restrain them. Their virtue was tested, as the title *Junie's Love Test* implies. They deserved to win a wealthy man whom they loved, because, in romance fiction, virtue was rewarded.

To the late-nineteenth- and early-twentieth-century working women who read romances, the novels must have carried positive messages as well as thrilling tales. In an era when women adrift and wage-earning women in general were often portrayed as vulgar and immoral, the stories proclaimed their purity and goodness. Laura Jean Libbey depicted working women as "superior to those gilded butterflies of fashion."[92] One wealthy hero proclaims, "My respect for those honorable young ladies who earn their own bread by honest work is profound."[93] And another hero says, "When a young girl works for a living, she is pure and good."[94] In addition, the novels offered hope in times of adversity. Most heroines survived the struggle for existence, and the comfort they found in the end proved the struggle worthwhile.

Furthermore, in secondary characters, some of the novels did present capable and courageous women adrift, usually of working-class origins. These characters loved and helped their helpless sisters. Mag, an ex-prostitute, and Dinah, a black servant, take care of themselves, each other, and pretty little Bab. Nettie, a consumptive factory worker, finds Little Sunshine a job and shares her rented room with her. Margaret, of "humble origin," vows to protect helpless Agnes Manning in *A Woman Scorned*. "I am strong enough," she claims, "to fight all the world for your sake."[95] A working-class sisterhood replaced the maternal guardianship of middle-class reform organizations.

Still, despite their redeeming qualities, the romance novels presented heroines who seem, to a modern reader, vapid and spineless. The reformers of the organized boarding home movement described childlike, passive women adrift who needed maternal care to protect them from urban dangers. The romance novels went further. The heroines were not only passive; they were wholly incapable of self-support. They might rouse themselves momentarily, but only to protect their virtue. The novels suggested that helplessness enhanced appeal and that independence from family spelled not only danger but also disaster. To save the woman adrift, they offered upwardly mobile marrige as the only viable solution. While the reformers offered help to the woman who supported herself, the novels discouraged self-support. In the romance novels, a woman could obtain steady companionship and security only when she relinquished her independence to a wealthy man.

The sensationalism of the popular romance novels and the reform goals of the organized boarding home movement merged in the campaign to abolish prostitution. This national mass movement against commercialized vice emerged in the 1890s, culminating decades of work by local reformers on behalf of prostitutes. While the organized boarding home movement and the romance novels presented an array of urban perils, the "social purity" crusaders focused their attention almost wholly on sexual danger. As the United States changed gradually from a rural and relatively homogeneous society to an urban, industrial, multiethnic, and class-stratified one, some middle-class citizens feared accompanying changes in moral values and sexual behavior. The highly visible urban vice districts came to symbolize the moral decay they feared, and the abolition of these districts came to represent renewed moral order.[96] Far more popular than the organized boarding home movement, the antiprostitution campaign attracted prominent clergymen, business-men, and politicians as well as reformers and social investigators. Typical of Progressive era social movements, these crusaders turned to the state for reform rather than to individual moral uplift or private institutions. In Chicago, the campaign against prostitution prompted municipal and state investigations, antivice legislation, and closing of the segregated red-light district. After the turn of the century, newspaper and magazine editors, book publishers, and filmmakers publicized the movement in an unprecedented outpouring of exposés. The movement peaked in the years between 1908 and 1915.

Interestingly, the prostitute herself was not the most evocative image in this campaign. She remained an ambiguous figure, defended by sympathizers but also tainted as depraved. In some accounts, she was the victim of evil, in other accounts the cause of it. Her body was polluted by invasive social forces, but at the same time she was the "sinister polluter" of the social body.[97]

The literature of the campaign against prostitution focused instead on the woman adrift as a symbol of purity and naïveté in the evil and sophisticated city. Like the romance novelists, the antiprostitution re-formers embellished the image that the organized boarding home move-ment had developed. In their writings, a woman adrift was endangered in the city, more childlike and innocent than a self-supporting man, and desperately in need of protection. She was the innocent bystander about to be forced or lured to prostitution.

Two pioneering exposés of vice in Chicago, written in the early 1890s, set the themes for later publications. An investigation by the Women's Christian Temperance Union, *Chicago's Dark Places* (1891), and a better-known book by British journalist William T. Stead, *If Christ Came to Chicago!* (1894), featured the self-supporting woman who earned low wages and the "green" newcomer to the city.[98] Em-ployers brought working women to unbearable poverty, and procurers and dishonest cabmen abducted newcomers and sent them to houses of prostitution. These exposés sympathized with the woman whose fate was beyond her own control. "Can it be possible," asked *Chicago's Dark Places,* "to conceive a more awful fate for a girl who wishes to be pure?"⁹⁹ The authors condemned the employers, the procurers, and the men who paid for sexual intercourse.

By the early twentieth century, the homeless working woman appeared, alone and helpless, in tract after tract. Some of the writings echoed the reformers in the organized home movement. Many writers treated women adrift as daughters. According to several writers, the root of the problem was the woman's separation from family. As one author stated, "The danger begins the moment a girl leaves the protection of Home and Mother."¹⁰⁰ Another wrote more bluntly, "Independence has been the cause of the ruin of many girls."¹⁰¹ If necessity compelled a young woman to leave her home, then a surrogate mother might save her. Edward Sims, a U.S. district attorney in Chicago, told parents, "no girl can safely go to a great city to make her own way who is not under the eye of a trustworthy woman who knows the ways and dangers of city life."¹⁰²

Like the women of the YWCA and some romance novelists, these authors occasionally complained that vanity, willfulness, and lack of self-restraint led women to cross the boundaries of propriety. An unusually harsh tract stated, "We know that many young females fall victims to their own improper conduct."¹⁰³ But most of the authors who blamed women adrift concluded that even here innocent, though foolish, women were lured and coaxed by evils they did not fully comprehend. Anti-prostitution writers did not admit readily that unmarried women without major character flaws might engage willingly in sexual intercourse. Instead they blamed moral decay in the city for tempting naïve, weak women and eventually corrupting them. "If your daughter in the future is to make her living in the big city, prepare her for the temptations that will beset her," warned one exposé. "Teach her that it is not the White Slave Traffic she must dread alone. Teach her that it is the place of amusement that seems innocent, the drinking of pleasant drinks, the association with characterless men."¹⁰⁴

Like the romance novels, however, much of the literature of the movement to abolish prostitution had an exaggerated urgency surpassing that of the organized boarding home movement. The sensational tracts written in overblown language have led some observers to refer to the movement as a "panic" or an "hysteria." Especially in the early-twentieth-century exposés of "white slavery," the name given to the abduction and selling of women of all races for sexual purposes, the bitter laments of fictional romance characters passed as social description. "Whether foreign born or native [the girls] all come seeking fame or fortune, burning with high hope and filled with great resolves," wrote Leona Prall Groetzinger in *The City's Perils*, "but the remorseless city takes them, grinds them, crushes them, and at last deposits them in unknown graves."[105] And another writer cried, "Think of all the years these vampires have been trapping poor, innocent little girls and condemning them to fate far worse than death."[106] The more the writers condemned the undeniable evils of sexual slavery, the more they rendered women adrift helpless, pure, and childlike.

As in the romance novels, the homeless working woman provided the contrast to the ills perceived in the city. In its well-known report of 1911, *The Social Evil in Chicago,* the Chicago Vice Commission found that poverty made women adrift weak when tempted by easy money. With less reticence than the women of the YWCA, the commission identified culprits. In a way characteristic of much of the literature against prostitution, it vilified men. The woman adrift gained in innocence as man, "the greatest menace," gained in villainy. The commission denounced "the advances of men without either a spark of bravery or honor who hunt as their unlawful prey this impoverished girl, this defenseless *child* of poverty, unprotected, unloved and uncared for as she is plunged into the swirling seething stream of humanity."[107] Even without culprits the woman adrift could not resist the evil around her. "Every year," one tract claimed, "hundreds of young girls, undefiled and pure, drift into the wickedest city in the world, and are carried away by the glare of the 'Great White Way' and the sensuous lures of the dazzling cafe and the Bohemian pleasures, and become unconsciously the recruits of the great absorbing Vice Trust."[108] Where the city was relentless, women were passive. Where men were vile, women were pure. In short, much of the literature used women adrift as foils.

In the early 1910s, the same contrasts furnished the plots for plays and films about white slavery. The first such play, *Little Lost Sister,* opened to sold-out audiences in 1913.[109] In the book version, a sinister white slaver lures the spirited small-town protagonist, Elsie Welcome, away from her poor family with false promises of a high-paying job and marriage in Chicago. Eventually a crusader against vice rescues her from the Cafe Sinister. But the rescue comes too late, and Elsie returns home to die. The book concludes with a word of warning: "As long as mothers do not know who the young men are with whom their daughters spend evenings away from home so long will there be a troop of Little Lost Sisters tripping, stumbling down the trail that leads hellward."[110] The films, reaching a wider audience still, were highly popular from 1913 to

1915, probably because of their introduction of titillating sexual themes. One of the first white slavery films, *Traffic in Souls,* attracted thirty thousand viewers in its opening week in New York.[111]

By the 1910s, then, the woman adrift of the romance novels, the helpless child bound for disaster, was standard cultural fare. Without direct evidence, one cannot say with certainty that antiprostitution writers borrowed their images from romance fiction. One can say, though, that, despite the scientific fact-gathering surveys of some investigators, the antiprostitution crusaders used the same sensational and sentimental language found in popular fiction to create a sympathetic caricature of the woman adrift. In the campaign to end commercialized vice, this caricature of the helpless woman adrift was not used simply to entertain, but also to promote social change. While the romance novels suggested that upwardly mobile marriage would save the victimized woman adrift, the white slavery literature called for government action.

At the same time as men and women crusaded against vice, another group of reformers, with a smaller contemporary audience, publicized the plight of women adrift more dispassionately in the less judgmental languages of "objective" journalism and academic social science. From the end of the nineteenth century into the 1920s, these reformers, usually female, investigated and wrote about the work and living conditions of wage-earning women. Unlike the women in the organized boarding home movement, most of them did not work through churches or women's clubs. They worked for secular reform organizations, such as the Women's Trade Union League and the Juvenile Protective Association, and for settlement houses, universities, and government agencies. They included a new generation of self-supporting professional women trained in universities as social investigators, as well as middle-class women who volunteered their efforts. As social welfare reformers, they followed in the footsteps of the women of the organized boarding home movement, joined the ranks of well-known community activists like Jane Addams, and foreshadowed the female social welfare policymakers of the New Deal.

These researchers and journalists neither defended women's place in the family nor sought to resurrect the home in surrogate form in the public arena. They also did not try to turn the clock back to the seemingly simple life of the small town or village.[112] Yet, like the earlier reformers, these writers wanted to protect women adrift who seemed to epitomize the problems of urban poverty. Along with the antiprostitution writers, they preferred state intervention to individual moral uplift. They asked the city to station police matrons in public parks and dance halls. They worked for reforms in housing laws, protective labor legislation, and by the 1910s, minimum wage laws for women. Missionary work and private institutions, they argued, could aid only a few, while legislation would cover all wage-earning women. In fact, some of them denounced the organized boarding home movement on the grounds that subsidized homes encouraged employers to pay below-subsistence wages.[113]

The label "woman adrift" captures the tone of this literature. Popularized by a federal investigation published in 1910, the label incorporates an image that appeared frequently in earlier reform and romance literature.[114] The image connoted a lonely rootlessness. Its concomitants were the anchor of family and the turbulent currents of life in the city. Without an anchor, the woman adrift was buffeted hither and yon by currents beyond her control. Specifically, she was buffeted by economic competition and scheming men. In a 1905 article on black women migrants from the South, sociologist Frances Kellor stated, "the cities thus get a group of strangers often without resources, and who must find . . . employment, or drift into immorality, for there are always sharks watching women who are placed in such helpless conditions."[115] With unusually florid language, an article on destitute women, written in 1911, elaborated the image: "there are thousands of homeless women in our great City of Chicago who are like flotsam and jetsam on the ocean of life. They have been cast onto the sea of misfortune and are like shipwrecked beings not knowing how to save themselves."[116]

Reformers used the image of drifting primarily to describe women. They did not use the label "men adrift" to identify the men who lived in YMCA dormitories and in commercial lodging houses. In fact, by the early twentieth century, they paid little attention to the male counterparts of women adrift. The advice literature to working men who lived apart from family had peaked in the years between 1830 and 1860.[117] A woman drifted without a navigator; a man, with proper training, determined his own course. A 1908 article in a popular magazine, *Harper's Bazaar*, restated the older theme: "Adrift in the city, she is far more helpless and in peril than a man in the same straits."[118]

In the late nineteenth and early twentieth centuries, the lone men who attracted public notice, the down-and-out unemployed men, received the telling name "floating population." While low-income women drifted helplessly, these impoverished men floated atop the currents of city life with parasitic ease. The language that some writers used to describe them had no parallel in even the most unsympathetic writings about women. For example, the Chicago Bureau of Charities wrote, with evident distaste, of the "evil of permitting this great army of non-resident idle men to infest the city."[119] The "army" of idle men contributed to the evil in the city that the passive woman adrift suffered.

The social investigators rarely wrote of women adrift as children or orphans; rather, they dwelled on the harsh circumstances of poverty and withheld comment on the women involved. Or, using the contemporary metaphor, they emphasized the swiftness of the currents and played down the ways in which women anchored themselves. They exposed the practices of dishonest employment agencies and discussed the problems of long hours, seasonal work, and unemployment. They compiled statistics on low wages, described dingy commercial lodgings, and investigated the poor fare served in cheap cafeterias and restaurants. Typical titles of studies are *The Living Wage of Women Workers,* "The Housing Problem as It Affects Girls," and *The Food of Working Women in Boston.*[120] The description of the woman adrift dwindled to a description of the inadequacy of her wage, her lodging, and her food. For these researchers and journalists, the women adrift were, as an early and famous exposé was titled, "prisoners of poverty."

The emphasis these writers placed on poverty sometimes hid their concern with sexual behavior. Like the women of the YWCA, the romance novelists, and the antiprostitution campaigners, many of these reformers feared the poverty of women adrift because they associated it with immoral sexual behavior. Rather than drawing a stark picture in which a woman chose between death and dishonor, though, these writers drew more subtle connections between poverty and immorality. Instead of blaming evil men, they focused on the woman's impoverished environment. They identified two specific moral dangers that living adrift posed to women: "the lodger evil" and "the furnished room problem."

The lodger evil referred to the crowding of male and female lodgers, usually immigrants, into one or two small rooms. When men and women lived together in close quarters, reformers feared, women would engage in sexual acts with men to whom they were not married. In Chicago, Louise DeKoven Bowen, head of the Juvenile Protective Association, found that Polish women adrift often boarded in close quarters with men and lost, "in their confined quarters, their sense of what is decent and proper, and soon become demoralized."[121] In the often-quoted words of housing reformer Lawrence Veiller, the lodging evil "frequently leads to the breaking up of homes and families, to the downfall and subsequent degraded career of young women, to grave immoralities—in a word, to the profanation of the home."[122]

In contrast, the furnished room problem usually referred to the isolation of lodgers in drab commercial rooming houses. Here reformers feared that loneliness and poverty would lead unmarried women to imitate the all-too-visible immoralities that provided their neighbors with companions, gifts, and money. Or, drab food, uncomfortable rooms, and lack of companionship might lead a young woman to search for overly stimulating entertainments. New businesses, such as restaurants, dance halls, and cabarets, attracted weary women to mingle with men and indulge in sexual amusements. "With cold rooms, with no opportunities to receive guests and without the privacy even of a single room," wrote an investigator for the Boston-based Women's Educational and Industrial Union, "fully 35 percent of our working girls, if those proportions may be considered typical, are in danger of overstepping social and moral law."[123] Another investigator asked, "Can we not see the relationship between the unsanitary, overcrowded homes, the loneliness and often vicious environment of many lodging houses, and human waste and immorality?"[124]

As they attempted to sway public opinion and to influence legislators, the reformers published exhaustive investigations of the details and consequences of poverty. And they underscored the dangers involved by portraying wage-earning women who could not fend for themselves. Along with other social scientists of their day, some of them adopted an environmentalism so deterministic that it led to the neglect of any resourceful responses wage-earning women may have made to alleviate their own poverty.[125] Despite their objective tone, they maintained the image of female passivity and helplessness conveyed by the women of the organized boarding home movement, the romance novelists, and the antivice crusaders.

When researchers and journalists observed closely the everyday lives of women adrift, however, their research belied the image. While most wage-earning women were more impoverished than wage-earning men and more vulnerable to sexual assault and stigma, they were not necessarily more helpless or more passive. Investigators found numerous examples of women whose resourcefulness removed them from the category of "little lost sisters." Some investigators decided two types of women adrift existed: "the one is self-reliant, self-respecting, and perfectly able from a moral and social point of view to stand alone, while to the other belong the young, the inexperienced, the morally weak, the stranger within our city doors, the discouraged, and perhaps the tempted."[126] Others began to recognize the assertive behavior of many wage-earning women. Reformer Jane Addams, a self-supporting woman herself, wrote, "thru the huge hat, with its wilderness of bedraggled feathers, the [working] girl announces to the world that she is here. She demands attention to the fact of her existence, she states that she is ready to live, to take her place in the world."[127] In the 1900s, this image of assertive women appeared only sporadically; in the 1920s, it would replace the image of orphaned and innocent women adrift.

As wage-earning women left traditional home roles, who would protect them from the hardships of urban life? The women of the organized boarding homes, the campaigners against vice, and the social investigators volunteered. In phrasing the question and attempting to answer it, they criticized the employers who paid low wages and the men who bought and sold women's bodies. They identified genuine problems and helped countless women in need of support. They refused to condemn the women who challenged conventional mores concerning woman's proper place; instead, they broadcast a sympathetic public image.

Their approach to women adrift changed over time. By the 1890s, calls for state intervention supplanted calls for private institutions and moral uplift. In the early twentieth century, the more neutral voice of social science began to replace the sensationalism and sentimentalism of romance novelists and Victorian reformers.

Yet in both reform circles and popular media, stereotypes of female weakness and innocence persisted. Writers elevated helplessness to a virtue and obscured, even obstructed, the actions that self-supporting women took on their own behalf. From a heterogeneous group of women, they chose to focus on the young, and usually on the white and native born. The women who organized homes, the romance novelists, the antivice crusaders, and the social investigators dwelled on urban hardships because they seemed to threaten the chastity of passive women adrift. A "respectable," unmarried woman without a family triggered their fears of moral decline and female victimization.

Historians today often base their studies of wage-earning women on the descriptions of wages, housing, and food supplied by the reformers of the late nineteenth and early twentieth centuries, and sometimes they conclude, as did the reformers, that women adrift were simply the victims of poverty.[128] The poverty of self-supporting women was, unfortunately, real. But the history of women adrift goes further. Out of the research and journalism, the case records of social workers, and the personal accounts of wage-earning women emerge a number of options that women chose and created to stretch and supplement their meager wages. Some of these options indicate a competence, an assertion of independence from supervision, and a sexuality that reformers, novelists, and researchers only gradually and grudgingly recognized.

Chapter Four
Surrogate Families

The daily life of a typical "woman adrift," drawn from the data published by investigators in the early twentieth century, might read as follows. At six in the morning, Cora, age twenty-five, wakes up in the small room she rents for two dollars per week and fixes herself a cup of coffee on a gas plate by the wall. She dresses, wraps a piece of bread in newspaper for her lunch, and leaves for work by seven. At half past seven she places herself in front of a mangle in a small commercial laundry and begins to feed clean, damp sheets between the hot rollers of the machine. Except for a break for lunch, she works continuously until half past five. She earns seven dollars for six days of work. Back at her rooming house by six, she waits her turn to use the bathroom and wash up. Then she walks down the street to the cheap cafeteria where she eats her supper. She eats stew with potatoes and a small hunk of meat, bread, a piece of apple pie, and a cup of coffee. She returns to her room by seven and mends an old shirtwaist, or she washes her clothes and hangs them to dry. If she has time, she writes a short letter to her mother and reads a newspaper or dime novel. She goes to bed at ten.[1]

Such accounts of lonely, scrimping wage-earning women reflect certain realities of poverty. Since many women adrift could not support themselves comfortably, they found ways to stretch their low wages. They rented tiny and unattractive rooms, skipped meals, and ate food of poor quality. They walked to work in order to save money on streetcar fare and worked long hours to increase their earnings. After a full day's work, they sewed and mended their clothes, repaired their shoes and hats, and did their own laundry. They spent little money and time on entertainment or luxuries.

This picture, however, is one-sided. Women were not necessarily isolated simply because they lived apart from family. As social beings in crowded urban environments, many women found others with whom to socialize and to pool and supplement their incomes. In the years before 1915, most women entered living situations that imitated the family, surrogate homes where they might live "like daughters." A small percentage of women adrift lived in the organized boarding homes managed by women in organizations like the YWCA. More women, though, moved into private homes where the family mother took in roomers or into larger commercial houses where women keepers provided room and sometimes board.

Between 1880 and 1930, these surrogate families declined. The old-fashioned boarding home gave way to the more impersonal furnished rooming house and, later, small apartments. Lodging in private families also declined as increasing numbers of women adrift chose to live in furnished rooms, head their own households, or share homes with roommates. In the same period, the managers of the organized boarding homes shifted from an earlier emphasis on maternal supervision to a new emphasis on cooperation with peers.

Working women's desire for independence from supervision promoted these changes. Many women disliked the protection that reformers insisted they needed. In some cases, even women who wrote despairingly of their poverty disdained the parental supervision in families, the guardianship of employers in live-in domestic service, and the condescending charity of reformers in organized homes. As wage-earning women moved away from the domesticity of dutiful daughters and wives, then, many of them did not lead isolated and passive lives despite their poverty. In contrast, they entered new social networks and chose among social options. Increasingly, they rejected imitations of family life and reshaped their social lives among their peers.

In the years before 1930, the majority of women adrift joined preexisting households rather than forming their own. They boarded or lodged in private families or in larger commercial boarding and rooming houses (see table 4.1).[2] In some cases, these rentals provided the kind of family support that reformers promoted. Some families accepted their boarders or lodgers more as daughters than as tenants. In larger lodging houses, too, women keepers might choose to provide some maternal care, especially in the more personal boarding homes where the keepers served family meals and maintained parlors for common use.

Boarding or lodging in a family setting, whether in a boarding home or a private family, could offer benefits to all involved. In many American cities, families supplemented their incomes by taking in boarders, and wives or widows who cared for boarders brought in earnings without leaving the often-preferred domestic sphere.[3] Less

Table 4.1   Housing Arrangements of Women Adrift in Chicago,
1880 and 1910

	1880	1910
Boarding or lodging in family[a]	48%	39%
Boarding or lodging in boarding or rooming house[b]	25	28
Living alone[c]	11	13
Heading household[d]	5	13
Living with roommates[e]	12	8
N	936	897

Source: Federal Manuscript Census, Chicago, Women Adrift Samples, 1880 and 1910.

[a]This category includes households with less than four adult boarders and lodgers in which the listed household head lived with at least one relative. Almost all of these homes were headed by one- or two-parent families.

[b]This category includes households with listed household heads and with four or more adult lodgers or boarders.

[c]This category represents one-person households.

[d]The women adrift in this category were heads of household who took in one or more boarders, lodgers, or friends.

[e]This category includes women adrift who lived in households of unrelated individuals. In some cases, the household had no listed head; in other cases, the listed household head (who was not the woman adrift) had no kin living with him or her. This category is high in 1880 because it included a number of prostitutes who lived together as roommates in households without heads.

often noted are the advantages that boarding and lodging offered the renter. The personal relationship that sometimes developed between landlady and renter translated into subsidies that a working woman or man would not have obtained in a purely commercial transaction.[4]

In some cases, subsidies came from generous landladies who volunteered discounts, food, or services. An investigator in 1908 wrote of a Chicago landlady who cut the rent of a poorly paid tenant. The tenant, a seventeen-year-old department store inspector, earned only four dollars a week. "She rented a poor, ill-ventilated room for $1.25 a week," the report stated, "until the kindhearted landlady, seeing her need, reduced the price to $1."[5] During the 1910 garment workers' strike in Chicago, some landladies allowed their striking tenants to stay on for months without paying rent.[6] Another "generous landlady" story came firsthand from a cashier, who, in 1913, earned seven dollars a week and paid four-and-a-half dollars for room and board. "My landlady is kind," she told the interviewer, "and does my laundry work because she feels sorry for me and I have so little time."[7] Reports like these led some reformers to look to landladies as surrogate mothers who provided material services. One crusader against vice went so far as to claim that "in nine cases out of ten the [landlady] will tide the poor girl lodging in her house over a crisis."[8]

Subsidies might also come from the unequal contributions of men and women to a single "family" fund. In a private home where a woman boarded, the higher wage of the family father might contribute to better quality food and furniture. Or, in larger households, especially in the immigrant neighborhoods of Chicago, a landlady might require her higher-paid male lodgers to contribute a greater share to the household resource pool. A census of Chicago's east European immigrant Back of the Yards community, conducted in 1905, for example, showed that in most homes with both male and female lodgers, men paid more rent than women. In fact, in almost half of the homes, men paid at least twice as much as women.[9] In return for the lower rent, women probably helped with household chores.

In some cases, boarding and lodging offered the tenant less tangible benefits, such as warm family sentiments. Philiminia P., a young black widow, remembered the Reverend and Mrs. Lucas with whom she lodged: "They were just like a mother and father to me."[10] The age difference between the household head and the lodger probably encouraged this imitation of parent-child relationships. In most cases, boarders and lodgers were at least ten years younger than their household heads. In 1880, women adrift in Chicago were on average fourteen years younger than their household heads; in 1910, thirteen years.[11]

Reformers and researchers who investigated housing expected the social interaction between landlady and tenant to generate a homelike atmosphere. For this reason, they preferred smaller private homes where landladies interacted frequently with their tenants. Many of the same church and women's groups that organized semicharitable boarding homes also established room registries that referred wage-earning women to available rooms in private homes.[12] Reformers also preferred boarding, with both room and food provided, to lodging, where a working woman bought or cooked her own meals. They expected the interactions at mealtime to encourage familial bonds.[13]

When the potential advantages of homelike rentals did in fact materialize, women found comfortable, warm, and secure homes. A clerk in a Chicago department store, for example, had come to the city from an "ideal home" on a farm in Illinois. She wrote happily of the newfound home which met her high expectations: "I had been most fortunate at the very beginning of my experience, having found board in a lovely home, where I had all the comforts and a very reasonable board to pay."[14]

Despite these possible advantages, the forms of housing most conducive to family living declined in the years between 1880 and 1930. New forms, with fewer obligations on both landladies and tenants, emerged. Early in the period, the rooming houses replaced the more familial boarding home. While a keeper of a boarding home served communal meals to all of her boarders, the rooming house keeper furnished her sleeping rooms with gas plates for cooking, allowed her roomers to use her kitchen, or let them buy their meals in the numerous cheap cafeterias and restaurants that sprang up in what came to be called the "furnished room districts." In the early twentieth century, writers in several cities noted, and usually lamented, the change. By the mid-1920s, the shift seemed complete. "The boarding-house has passed out of existence in the modern city," an investigator of Chicago's Near North Side wrote in 1925. "The rooming-house which has replaced it has no dining-room or parlor, no common meeting place. The roomers do not know one another."[15]

In Chicago, the shift from boarding to rooming occurred most notably at the end of the nineteenth century. The rapid growth of rooming houses began in the 1880s. In that decade, the number of furnished rooms listed in the Chicago city directory increased almost tenfold, from 58 to 579. In 1893, the year of the World's Columbian Exposition in Chicago, the number of furnished rooms listed first surpassed the number of boarding homes and, after 1897, continued to rise rapidly. In the same years, the number of boarding homes listed in the city directory began a long and gradual decline. By 1917, the last year that such listings appeared, the number of boarding homes had diminished to 131 and the number of furnished rooms had risen to 2,922 (see figure 4.1).

Among the women adrift of Chicago, the shift from boarding to lodging occurred both in larger commercial houses and in private families. In 1880, 77 percent of the women adrift who rented rooms in commercial lodgings were boarders; by 1910, only 32 percent were. In private families, the change was equally dramatic. From 1880 to 1910, the proportion of women adrift in private families listed as boarders declined from 92 percent to 52 percent.[16]

Black women were a vanguard in the decline of boarding. In 1880, only 36 percent of black women adrift in Chicago boarded; by 1910, only 11 percent did so. During the height of black migration, the classified advertisements in the *Chicago Defender* included numerous listings for furnished rooms and only a few for boarding.[17] Several studies noted that black families and the keepers of rooming houses in black neigh-

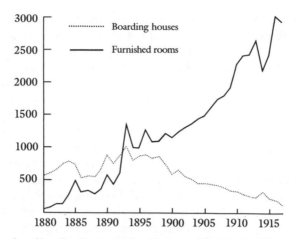

Fig. 4.1. Number of boarding houses and furnished rooms listed in the Chicago city directories, 1880–1917. (Source: Lakeside Directory of Chicago, *1880–1917)*

borhoods tended to share their kitchens with their lodgers rather than prepare meals for them.[18] Because most black women adrift worked in service occupations, many probably received meals in the private homes, hotels, and restaurants where they worked and, therefore, had little need to buy board.

Even among immigrants, who by the early twentieth century chose boarding more often than did native-born women, boarding was a temporary choice. While they adjusted to the city, newcomers placed themselves in family situations with room and board provided. In 1910, three-quarters of the foreign-born women-adrift newcomers to Chicago were boarders.[19] But once they learned the ways of the city, they rented rooms only and bought or cooked their meals on their own. Among immigrant women adrift who had lived in the United States for longer than five years, only one-quarter boarded.

A more gradual decline in the percentage of women adrift who lived in private families accompanied the decline of boarding. From 1880 to 1910, the proportion of women adrift boarding or lodging in private families decreased from 48 percent to 39 percent. In this early period, living in private families dropped most precipitously among older women adrift.[20] After World War I, the descent continued. In her study of housing in Chicago, Edith Abbott reported the results of a series of house-to-house canvases of immigrant residential neighborhoods in Chicago conducted from 1908 to 1916 and recanvases of the same areas conducted from 1923 to 1927. In each neighborhood, the proportion of lodgers dropped between the two investigations.[21] The most obvious source of decline here was the end of large-scale immigration from Europe during and after World War I.

The decline of lodging in private families, however, was more widespread. While the greatest period of black migration to Chicago took place during and after World War I, the percentage of lodgers living in black families was lower in the 1920s than before the war. In two black residential neighborhoods in Chicago, canvased in 1912 and recanvased in the mid-1920s, the proportion of lodgers in the total population declined, from 31 percent to 22 percent in one neighborhood and from 14 percent to 11 percent in the other.[22] The decline of lodging with private families continued also among native-born white women after World War I, even though new migrants continued to arrive in the city. In 1921 a report on the housing of "nonfamily" women in Chicago stated that more women lived in commercial rooming houses than in private families, a reversal of earlier patterns.[23] And in 1928 the Chicago YWCA room registry reported a steady five-year decline in the number of women looking for rooms in private homes.[24]

Why did these changes occur? Some explanations stress the changing needs of families and landladies. In the late nineteenth century, providing for lodgers may have proved more profitable and less time consuming than cooking for boarders, and, ultimately, in the twentieth century, married and widowed women found other avenues for income than taking in boarders and lodgers. Another explanation points to changing standards of privacy within the family. By the mid-twentieth century, families no longer accepted strangers in the home.[25]

The preferences of lodgers, however, were at least as important as the preferences of landladies and their families.[26] Wage-earning women and men seem to have preferred contractual tenant relations over the more personal imitations of family. Early-twentieth-century social scientists who investigated the shift from boarding homes to rooming houses claimed that lodgers preferred the freedom of eating where, when, and what they chose.[27] A Chicago woman stated her preference for lodging in different terms. For a working woman, she wrote, "[boarding] has its drawbacks because she may never have any privacy."[28] Similarly, a woman who lodged in a private family could expect to be watched and sometimes judged by the family she lived with.[29] Some evidence indicates that the demand for living in private families in Chicago dwindled before the supply. The Chicago YWCA room registry found that the number of housekeepers offering rooms continued to grow as the number of women seeking them dropped. "The housekeepers all tell of the difficulty they now have to get roomers," the report stated, ". . . advertising in the newspapers, cards in the windows and listing rooms with agencies all seem ineffective."[30]

While reformers expected the greater interaction between landladies and boarders to generate familial bonds, in fact the forced intimacy of living in private families and of boarding sometimes embittered relationships. Recently a Polish immigrant recounted her experiences as a boarder in a private home in Chicago in the early 1910s. For twelve dollars a month, her landlady let her sleep on a couch in an unheated room. "I was working ten hours—nights—and come home in the morning," she said. "When you're young, you feel hungry. You want to eat. She give me a cup of coffee and a piece of bread in the morning. That's all you get if you board with someone." She found her fare for dinner, pig snout soup, equally unappealing. She supplemented her diet, though, by sneaking food from the pantry, an act that may have satisfied her resentment as well as her hunger.[31]

In the mid-nineteenth century, a migrant to the city had few options in choosing room and board. By the end of the century, though, entrepreneurs had created new urban institutions that catered to the desires of lodgers. These institutions competed successfully with the traditional forms of boarding and lodging. Cheap restaurants and cafeterias offered a woman the chance to maintain her privacy, skip meals without paying for them, eat at irregular hours, and choose the amount and kind of food she wanted to buy. Dance halls, inexpensive theaters, and, later, cabarets and movies provided some nightlife to a woman who might otherwise have spent her evenings in the kitchen or parlor of the boarding home or private family.

Also in the late nineteenth century, new forms of housing appeared. As wealthy residents moved to the suburbs and to more fashionable neighborhoods, entrepreneurs converted mansions in certain districts of Chicago into furnished rooming houses. They divided the large rooms into smaller ones and often furnished them with single-burner gas plates for cooking. By the 1920s they had also divided flats and tenement buildings into furnished rooms.[32] The "light housekeeping" rooms, those furnished with gas plates, allowed women to avoid both boarding and eating in restaurants and instead cook their meals in their rooms.[33]

Beginning in the 1890s, entrepreneurs also invested in apartment buildings in Chicago, and, by the second decade of the twentieth century, they began to build apartment buildings with smaller dwelling units. In 1916 a magazine article presented the one-room apartment as a novelty in Chicago's rental market.[34] On the Near North Side, stables and old dwellings were converted into studio apartments during the

1910s, and new buildings of small-unit apartments were constructed during the 1920s.[35] The studio and small kitchenette apartments allowed even greater privacy and freedom of action than the "light housekeeping" rooms, but the higher rent charged for them made them accessible only to higher-paid women.

Women adrift showed their preference for the new institutions. In 1917, Lucile Eaves, an investigator of wage-earning women in Boston, found that, although it cost more to eat in a restaurant than to board, many women chose the former. "It seems probable," she wrote, "that the drift from the old-fashioned boarding house to the restaurant indicates that the latter gives more satisfactory service."[36]

Especially after World War I, reports in Chicago mentioned an increase in the number of women looking for and living in light housekeeping rooms where they might cook their own meals.[37] In 1928 the report of the Chicago YWCA room registry also stated that more women sought the new kitchenette apartments, and in 1929 a committee on women's housing in Chicago reported that "small apartment residences" were "very successful."[38] In a 1922 survey of women adrift in New York, 63 percent of the working women interviewed stated that, if they could afford it, they would prefer to live in housekeeping apartments rather than in furnished rooms or boarding homes. Although fewer black women could afford housekeeping apartments, an especially high proportion of black women, 73 percent, expressed a preference for living in them. "The great drive on the part of the majority of employed women is a home of their own," the report stated, "This was shown in every group studied."[39]

A chronology of the process of change in patterns of boarding and lodging in Chicago might point to two periods of especially rapid change: the World's Columbian Exposition of 1893 and the First World War. During these periods of accelerated migration to Chicago, entrepreneurs responded to acute shortages in housing, board, and entertainment by creating new rooming houses, apartments, restaurants, dance halls, and theaters. After the fair ended and after World War I, the influx of migrants slowed, and some newcomers left the city. In this market, only the most appealing forms of housing, board, and entertainment survived.[40] The decline of boarding homes and of boarding and lodging in private families reflected, at least in part, the preferences of the working women and men who lived apart from family.

The new options provided by entrepreneurs, however, do not explain all of the changes in housing among women adrift in Chicago. Between 1880 and 1930, women turned to more independent forms of housing not only by taking advantage of new institutions but also by creating new options within existing housing forms. An increasing proportion of women adrift chose to head their own households. Rather than rooming or boarding, these women rented entire flats or houses and took in boarders and roomers themselves. From 1880 to 1910, the percentage of women adrift heading households increased from 5 percent to 13 percent (see table 4.1). The change occurred almost wholly among older women, many of whom had lived adrift for several years.[41] After 1910, increasing numbers of women adrift also entered cooperative housing arrangements. These women joined together with others to rent full-sized flats or apartments.[42] It would seem, then, that not only did options change but working women themselves changed as well. Increasingly, they rejected the supervision of surrogate families.

Not surprisingly, women showed similar distaste for employer-owned housing. Many domestic servants did not want to live in their employers' homes for the same reasons that women disliked boarding and lodging in private families—restrictions on freedom of action, lack of privacy, and mistreatment by heads of household and their families.[43] Here, too, black women showed an especially strong preference for living on their own. "The fact remains that they will accept a lower wage and live under far less advantageous conditions for the sake of being free at night," a study of a Chicago employment agency for black women stated, "That is why the 'day work' is so popular. Rather than live in some other person's home and get good wages for continued service, the colored woman prefers to live in this way."[44]

Women also avoided large-scale company-owned housing. According to an article in a Chicago newspaper in 1894, American working women would not imitate the French and English saleswomen who lived in company-owned dormitories. They were "too fond of independence to consent to any restraint upon their perfect liberty of action, manner, and thought." The article concluded: "If she prefers to fight her own battles in life instead of being protected by the people she serves, she deserves credit for her boundless pluck, even though her independence may be exaggerated and aggressive."[45]

In any case, by the late nineteenth century, few employers continued to provide the kind of supervised boarding homes that had characterized many of the earliest American factories.[46] Except for domestic service, the only workplaces likely to provide lodging were institutions, such as hospitals and hotels, with rooms and beds readily available. Like commercial lodging houses, these institutions did not necessarily provide pleasant or familial housing. A 1912 study of fifty hotels in Chicago, for example, found cramped and poorly ventilated sleeping rooms. It is also found that employers supplied no supervision or protection to the chambermaids they hired and lodged.[47]

At least one employer in Chicago, though, did attempt to replicate the middle-class ideal of family life. In 1920 the Illinois Bell Telephone Company opened a home in Chicago for one hundred telephone operators. The company publicized the home, Fairfax Hall, as an example of its concern for its workers' welfare. The home had parlors and music rooms, home-style meals, women supervisors, and carefully selected furnishings in the bedrooms. According to the Bell Company, the residents of the home were "well because they [were] happy."[48] Yet five years later, a new home for working women opened in the same building, with no mention of the Bell Company or telephone operators.[49] Either the company, the operators, or, likely, both had found that a company-owned boarding home did not meet their needs.

Records from the organized boarding homes corroborate the somewhat sketchy evidence from commercial rooming houses, private families, and company-owned housing. More than the other forms of housing that imitated families, managers of these homes aimed avowedly to create a familial atmosphere with parental supervision. They also provided unmistakable benefits to the residents. Despite the benefits, though, the residents complained frequently and publicly about the features of the homes that restricted their independence, curbed their initiative, and invaded their privacy.

In the organized boarding home movement in Chicago, the attempts to create "homes away from home" had several identifiable features. First, the homes had women superintendents who were expected to mother residents as well as manage business. According to one article, the maternal duties of the "housemother" included "to be sympathetic without being partial or sentimental; to be able to care for the tired and sick; to be patient and firm with the hysterical; to understand and direct youth, gayety and extravagance; and to help the girls who are in danger of losing their 'woman's heritage.' "[50] In practice, of course, some superintendents were motherly in this sense, and some were not.

With the same intentions of mothering, several of the homes encouraged their middle- and upper-class women supporters to visit the residents. At the Ruth Club, a home for young Jewish working women, one former resident recalled fondly that a Mrs. Schramm, a wealthy woman in Chicago, occasionally took her on outings.[51] Likewise, the YWCA asked its members to have "a more personal acquaintance" with the residents. "It may help to make the day at the desk or behind the counter pass much more swiftly," one annual report stated, "to know that there are mothers here who sympathize with them in their loneliness and their struggle for life."[52]

The women who managed the homes also took on the parental role of supervision and training in morality. This might include religious services with sermons on moral conduct, outside lecturers invited to speak on deportment, or heart-to-heart talks with the residents. The matrons of the homes also monitored behavior. The common parlor was a recognized feature of any good boarding home. There a working woman might entertain male friends while chaperoned by her house-mates and housemother. Sometimes a matron would intercede as a surrogate parent when a resident's behavior seemed of questionable morality. In one case, in 1891, the matron of the Home for Self-Supporting Women called in the Illinois Humane Society to prevent a resident from going out with a young man from her hometown of Aberdeen, South Dakota. Only after the Humane Society telegraphed the woman's step-mother and received her permission was the case resolved. Although this supervision sounds extreme today, it did not appear unusual in 1891. In fact, the stepmother wrote appreciatively of the attempts to protect her daughter "from the many traps and snares of the city."[53]

Many of the homes hoped to restrain female sexual behavior by offering women a homelike alternative to the unsupervised world of the restaurant and dance hall. In 1887, for example, the admitting committee of the YWCA home asked YWCA members to help entertain the residents. "One of the things to be encouraged," the committee wrote, "is spending their evenings at home. We wish to impress upon the ladies of this association the necessity of doing all in their power to make this home as attractive as possible."[54] And, in 1909, the West Side YWCA home claimed to provide entertainment "so enjoyable that outside attractions will not be a necessity."[55] To the organizers of the YWCA, much of the value of a surrogate home lay in the protection it offered women from predatory men in the public sphere.

In addition to personal training, supervision, and protection, the managers of the organized homes supplied parental discipline by enforcing rules intended to protect and restrain the wage-earning woman. Many of the homes required letters of reference before admission to insure the applicant's respectability. Once admitted, a woman had to return to the home by a specified hour in the evening. In 1899, for example, the St. Francis House of Providence, a Catholic home, set its closing hour at nine, and, in 1921, the Phyllis Wheatley Home for black women closed at ten (see fig. 4.2).[56] In addition, the homes forbade men to enter any rooms except the common parlors. Women who broke the rules risked expulsion.[57] Such institutional substitutes for parenting were widespread and long-lived, existing earlier in the company-owned boarding homes of New England textile factories and continuing into the 1960s in the women's dormitories of colleges and universities.

Finally, most of the managers encouraged sisterly social bonds among the residents. They frequently sponsored events that brought all of the residents together, such as parties, teas, or "family" religious services. In many of the homes, residents celebrated holidays such as

Fig. 4.2. Residents of the Phyllis Wheatley Home, c. 1920. This fund-raising leaflet states: "These girls need a larger building where they may have cafeteria, reading rooms, lounge, gymnasium, swimming pool, club and classrooms." (Source: Chicago Historical Society, neg. qF38JD P4z)

Thanksgiving and Christmas. Most of the homes also served family-style, or communal, meals to the residents.[58]

The economic benefits that the organized homes offered women matched the kinds of subsidies and resource pooling that low-income wage-earning women in families had at home. In the organized homes, "parental" subsidies came from charitable contributions. With one or two exceptions, the homes received substantial financial support from donors, if not continually then at least for initial payments for salaries, furnishings, and building purchase or rent.[59] In addition, the number of working women pooling money weekly for food and fuel allowed the managers of the homes to buy in bulk. And because the homes, by definition, earned no profits, all of the resources pooled went toward home expenses rather than toward the private gain of owners or investors.

The benefits to residents were obvious and direct. All of the homes charged lower rates for room and board than did commercial houses of the same quality accommodations. Some of the homes charged especially low fees or had sliding scales. The Guardian Angel Day Nursery and Home for Girls, a home established by the Catholic church in 1912 for Polish women in the meat-packing industry, had a sliding scale according to income and accepted unemployed women as residents.[60] Similarly, in 1915 the Norwegian-Danish Young Women's Christian Home Society charged from one to four dollars a week for room and board and housed a few women for free.[61]

Other benefits came in the form of house privileges. Almost all of the homes had laundry rooms and parlors for the use of residents. Many had sewing rooms, libraries, and pianos, and offered classes in a variety of subjects. As some of the homes became successful, they expanded to include newer and fancier features. By far the most opulent was the Harriet Hammond McCormick Residence, a YWCA home opened in 1928. Funded by magnate Cyrus McCormick, the home could accommodate 487 women with 455 of them in single rooms. The home included two lobbies, living rooms, writing rooms, a sun room, a small shop, a library, a recreation room, an infirmary, laundry facilities on every floor, a swimming pool, and a beauty parlor.[62]

Additional subsidies resulted from further imitations of family life. The matrons of the homes often allowed unemployed residents to live rent-free for a month or two just as a family might support a daughter through her job search. An investigator noted that Melissia Ann Elam, the ex-slave who owned and managed a home for black women in Chicago, "carrie[d] some of them for two or three months to keep them from wandering into [an] immoral atmosphere."[63] Also, the women who lived in the homes provided each other with the same aid that kinship networks often provided elsewhere. In the homes, women shared information on job openings and collected money for sick housemates.[64]

Given the possibilities for personal relationships, protection, and economic benefit, life in an organized home could provide a pleasant alternative to a bleak and isolated existence in a furnished room. In the organized home, a wage-earning woman might enjoy the daily company of other women. A newcomer, warned of the dangerous city, might feel safe as she learned from the more experienced women around her. Parties, holiday celebrations, informal gatherings, and classes in the evenings might punctuate an otherwise endless daily routine of work, chores, and sleep. And the savings in room and board might allow a low-income woman to indulge in occasional luxuries, such as giving to charity, sending money home, buying a fancy hat, spending an evening at the theater, or even taking a short vacation.

In the late nineteenth and early twentieth centuries, thousands of women took advantage of the homes. In fact, in many years the homes turned women away for lack of sufficient accommodation. As commercial boarding homes declined, the number and size of the organized boarding homes expanded. At the turn of the century, the homes in Chicago housed about six hundred women; by 1914, almost two thousand; and by 1928, over four thousand.[65] These figures give the number of residents at one point in time. Using the YWCA homes as an indicator, it appears that two to three times as many boarders lived in the homes in a year as could be accommodated at any given time. Also, each year thousands of additional women lived in the homes as transients for two weeks or less.[66]

Although the homes were usually full and steadily expanding, the constant volley of criticisms leveled by wage-earning women illustrates the limitations of these surrogate families. Residents disliked the condescension of the managers, the restrictions on their behavior, and their lack of control over fees, food, and decor. And, as in other institutions that crossed class lines, class differences exacerbated the tensions between the women who ran the homes and the women who lived in them.

From the beginning of the organized boarding home movement, self-supporting women resented their image as objects of charity. "For one, I can say we don't want charity. We possess some spirit, though poor and industrious," one working woman wrote in the 1873 Chicago newspaper debate on the merits of organized homes. Working women, she continued, "would rather live in the alley than in a marble mansion" where wealthy donors "in that patronizing tone that to poverty is so unbearable, exclaim, 'my friend, *that* is the home for working girls we were telling you about, to which *we* contributed *ten dollars.*' " This woman favored the building of organized homes if "no charity was asked or received."[67] Through the end of the nineteenth and into the twentieth century, wage-earning women in several cities continued to protest the indignity of charity. "I don't know which is worse," said one New York woman in 1915, "the cramped and the awful loneliness of a hall bedroom, or the humiliating and soul-depressing charity and rules of a Home."[68]

Other women believed that some of the homes charged too much for room and board. If the homes billed themselves as charitable institutions, these women said, they should help the neediest women. Instead, the middle- and upper-class organizers of some of the homes, like the YWCA, erected posh buildings, furnished them in plush middle-class style, and then charged fees prohibitive to the most poorly paid wage-earning women. "I applied at the 'Woman's Christian Association' boarding house . . . for board for a young girl who was clerking at the Boston store," a wage-earning woman wrote to a Chicago newspaper in 1888, "and the matron said four dollars a week was the lowest and washing done outside." In this case, the "young girl" earned only four dollars a week and could not afford to pay the board. "The boarding house . . . cost, if I remember correctly, 44,000 dollars and accommodates 36 boarders," the writer concluded, "It looks like a vast outlay for the amount of accommodation afforded."[69] Twenty-five years later, in 1913, another wage-earning woman wrote that the same boarding home had refused to admit her when she was unemployed and penniless. "They do not take in girls who are stranded," she wrote angrily, "notwithstanding they have numerous little mottoes on their walls reading, 'I was a stranger and ye took me in.' "[70]

Other criticisms came from those who lived in the homes. Soon after the first YWCA home opened in Chicago, residents resisted the managers' efforts to provide the "comforts and blessings of a Christian home." In 1877, less than one month after the home had opened, the superintendent reported that some of the "inmates" did not attend "family worship."[71] In 1878 she reported that boarders complained about the food.[72] And in 1880 the social and educational committee found that the "entertainments" they offered were "not desired by those in the home."[73] Despite the good intentions of the YWCA, wage-earning women neither needed nor appreciated some of the efforts of their wealthier "mothers." And, at the same time, the efforts of the wealthier "mothers" did not prevent the warm home atmosphere from dropping to a chilly institutional air.

The anger of the residents came to a head in 1890 when a group of women from the YWCA home wrote a letter of protest to a Chicago newspaper. In a blistering attack, the women refuted their image as helpless waifs and disdained the implication that they were objects of charity. "The 'good ladies of the board' call it a charitable institution," they wrote, "It is just a little bit galling to a self-respecting and self-supporting young woman to live on charity and pay four hard dollars a week for it." They clearly resented the condescending supervision of the wealthier women. They continued:

> The idea seems to be in circulation that we who are unfortunate enough to be independent, are a collection of ignorant, weak-minded young persons, who have never had any advantages, educational or otherwise, and that we are brought here where we will be philanthropically cared for, and the cold winds tempered for us. A matron is provided, and a committee of women who happen to be blessed with a few thousand dollars worth of aristocracy, has charge of the matron.
>
> The same committee of good ladies furnishes us with preaching services on Sunday evenings so that our untutored minds may learn something of the ways of civilization.

The women also complained of the poor furniture and food, and referred to themselves as "the victims of the home."[74]

The managers of the YWCA were stung. The board considered the letter writers ungrateful, and the executive committee asked them to move out.[75] Later in the 1890s, the YWCA annual reports included references to "ungrateful girls," "chronic grumblers," and those "whose deportment may cast a shadow upon [the home]."[76] The reports, of course, defended the management of the home. In 1899 the report stated proudly, "Most [residents] have shown themselves very willing to conform to the rules of the home—glad to do so in return for its protecting shelter and its privileges."[77]

Nevertheless, investigators in Chicago and other cities uncovered several persistent complaints from the residents of various homes. Women continued to object to the patronizing atmosphere in the homes. They also complained of the rules and regulations, the lack of privacy, and the institutional drabness of the food and decor. More specifically, some women disliked the early closing hours, the watchful eye of the matron, the lack of opportunity to meet men, the Christian atmosphere in many of the homes, and the rooms and meals variously described by investigators as "inadequate," "unattractive," and "funereal."[78] In 1913, in a letter to the National Women's Trade Union League, one wage-earning woman complained of the "little cubby rooms with two or three in them, each girl with a different idea about fresh air and the time to retire."[79] A New York department store clerk explained in 1915 why she would not live in an organized home "if you paid me for it." She said, "There are too many restrictions. I don't know anyone hardly in the city and all I do evenings is to sit in my room by myself. But I'm free and those girls aren't."[80]

By the early twentieth century, a negative stereotype of organized homes appeared in popular literature. For example, in *The Long Day* (1905), Dorothy Richardson described a bleakly furnished home with a thieving and tyrannical superintendent.[81] Even authors who supported the organized homes recognized the negative image. "There will be a thousand things about the home you won't like," an advice book, published in 1908, stated. The book then mentioned the restrictive rules and regulations, the visiting preachers who talk "as though you were an object of charity when you are paying out your hard-earned money for board," the "condescending tone" of the managers, and the "monotony of the bill of fare."[82] Still, the book concluded, the organized home provided a cleaner, purer, and more protective environment than an inexpensive room in a commercial boarding house.

By the late nineteenth and early twentieth centuries, a variety of investigators recommended changes "if we would keep the boarding home popular."[83] In order to avoid the patronizing atmosphere in the homes, investigators suggested that the organized homes become self-supporting and adopt some features of self-government. They also advocated the greater privacy of single rooms and private parlors. A number of studies recommended that residents of the homes be given night keys so that they might come and go at will.[84]

The women who organized and managed the boarding homes wanted to attract wage-earning women to their residences. They responded to criticism and to negative publicity, and they willingly made some changes in the management of the homes. For financial reasons, as well as to escape the taint of charity, an increasing number of homes moved toward self-support. In 1914, nine out of thirty-one homes and, in 1921, almost one-half of the forty-five organized homes investigated in Chicago claimed to be self-supporting.[85] A few homes also instituted self-governing councils composed of residents. The YWCA reported a plan for a house council in 1919, and, in 1921 the West Side Christian Women's Home reported "a self-governing club for home regulation."[86] Several homes responded to the residents' desire for privacy in rooms with two or more occupants. The McKinley Working Girls' Home built small individual dressing rooms for its residents.[87] The Salvation Army

Young Women's Boarding Home, opened in 1912, put folding screens around the beds and, in its annex erected two years later, built only single rooms.[88] In 1925 a citywide committee with representatives from a large number of the organized homes stated, "Wherever economic conditions will permit, single rooms should be provided."[89] Some of the homes also changed their rules on closing hours. When the Salvation Army's home opened in 1912 it closed at ten, but by 1921 it had changed the hour to eleven four nights a week and midnight on the other three. In addition, residents who planned to stay out later could "borrow night keys from the office."[90]

Still, none of the organized homes in Chicago dispensed with supervision. It appears that all of the homes continued to have closing hours, none of the new house councils had the final word in house management, and none of the homes provided keys to all of the residents. "The ideal is, and ever has been," the YWCA stated in 1915, "to maintain a home that would meet the needs and, *so far as possible,* the desires of the young women."[91] The women who managed the homes worked to remedy problems without dropping the original goal of maternal protection.

In their annual reports, the women of the YWCA gave a fuller account of the changes they made. The changes in the YWCA were less a decline of supervision than a softening and a camouflaging of motherly discipline and institutional management. By the 1910s, the leaders of the national YWCA (with which the Chicago branch was not yet affiliated) recognized its negative reputation as an oppressive institution. They admitted past mistakes, especially in the "lack of proper leadership and supervision in the house," and they attempted to change.[92] The stricter discipline of the early YWCA homes gave way to a twentieth-century psychology of lulling the consumer. As the Chicago YWCA Emergency Bureau stated in 1924, "Little can be done in the way of compulsion, and success lies only in the fields of influence and persuasion."[93] The imitation of family remained, but the nature of family relationships had changed. A supervising "mother" now cajoled where earlier she had ruled.

The women who ran the YWCA Central Home in Chicago recorded the details of several specific reforms they adopted to make the home more attractive. First, they stopped insisting upon religiosity among the residents. In the early years of the home, the YWCA managers expected residents to attend "daily family worship" in the home and also to attend church every Sunday.[94] In 1897, however, the managers recognized that many residents "had not come here to be converted or to develop a Christian life." While some residents had "responded" to the YWCA's "invitations," others, they found, "were indifferent to any religious claims." In fact, "some openly defied them." They now stated that residents were under "no obligation . . . to attend a single religious service," but in the years that followed they continued to offer voluntary prayer meetings, circles, and services and to encourage church attendance.[95]

Second, the managers of the YWCA introduced young men into their female sphere. They saw that some women preferred the bright lights of the city to entertainments at home with older and wealthier women. They decided to invite young men to the home to keep the home attractive. In 1906 the matron of the YWCA invited men to the annual reception for the first time and reported the event a big success: "This new feature of inviting the gentlemen friends of the young women was greatly appreciated, and some declared it was the happiest evening spent in Chicago."[96] Throughout the 1910s the annual reports mentioned parties with men invited, often men from the YMCA. By the 1920s the YWCA expressed explicit concern with introducing the residents to suitable men. The 1927 report stated, "Another development this year has been in the effort to find more ways for girls to meet and to know men—not an easy task in a city the size of Chicago. Formerly it has been only the party or dance where this was possible—but now there are added Sunday afternoon Discussion Clubs, with interest groups such as Dramatic Clubs meeting during the week."[97] As the separation of sexual spheres declined in the twentieth century, the women of the YWCA home acquiesced to the sexually integrated urban popular culture in order to enhance their homes' appeal.

Third, the YWCA appealed to women by using the language of cooperation. In its 1915 statement of ideals the YWCA decided "to make [the residents] feel they are an important factor in forming this great co-operative home."[98] Note that the YWCA did not necessarily aim to make the women an important factor, but to make them "feel" they were. In 1919, as the annual report mentioned plans for a new house council, it praised the Central Home for its "spirit of cooperation" as well as its more traditional "home atmosphere."[99] And by 1927 the YWCA no longer wrote of its homes as enclaves protecting women from the city but as training grounds in peer cooperation. "Just to give a girl a place in which to feel she is safe and can live economically is not sufficient excuse for our housing, essential as these things are," the annual report stated. Increasingly, the "test of the effectiveness of housing" was "whether or not girls are learning to live harmoniously," an experience that would make them "better fitted to live and work more happily in the community."[100]

The federal government entered the debate in the organized boarding home movement during World War I, providing a snapshot view of the organized boarding home movement as it changed. When the Bureau of Labor decided to house women clerical workers hired by the wartime government, the U.S. Housing Corporation reported that three schools of thought competed. The first school wanted to build "hotels," run in a businesslike way by experienced hotel managers. The second school advocated "homes" supervised by women "trained in social service" and offering "very special provision to protect these young girls from imprudence and harm." The third school promoted a compromise position, "residences" where the "protection feature could be carried on unostentatiously if women of judgment were in charge."[101] As in Chicago, a popular commercial approach collided head-on with maternal concerns for wage-earning women, and, as in the Chicago YWCA, the compromise position won.

Nevertheless, the compromise position did not curtail the attraction of commercial rentals. By the mid-1920s, the organized boarding homes in Chicago reported an increasing number of vacancies.[102] Women adrift came to see the homes as way stations for newcomers only. One newcomer called the homes "hatching grounds for apartment groups."[103] And a YWCA secretary acknowledged, "Many girls come in here for a short time and then go out into an apartment." Apartments, she conceded, offered "privacy, a place to entertain friends, a chance to satisfy a girl's taste for domesticity, and an escape from the monotony of an institution."[104]

The criticisms of the homes and the changes in management parallel the criticisms and changes in the other forms of housing that imitated families. Yet the organized homes differed substantially from the commercial rooming houses and the lodgings in private families. Unlike the commercial houses and private families, many of the organized homes suffered from the problems of large institutions. In addition, the class differences between the managers and the residents as well as the charitable subsidies created special tensions in the organized homes. Furthermore, the residents of the organized homes did not quite represent the larger group of women adrift. Because many homes excluded women over thirty, the residents were on average younger than other women adrift. Also, because a disproportionate number of the homes catered to native-born white women, the residents, in general, worked disproportionately in clerical and sales jobs.[105]

Despite these differences, the parallels between the organized homes and the commercial lodgings should not be dismissed. Wage-earning women had the same two complaints about all of the forms of housing that imitated family life. First, the surrogate families rarely met the family ideal. If families often did not meet the expectations of their members, then surrogate families had even less success. Stingy landladies, impersonal relationships among lodgers, or cold institutional management might ruin the home atmosphere that reformers hoped for. Second, many women adrift disliked certain features of the family ideal, particularly the parental supervision which restricted their freedom and invaded their privacy. Whether the surrogate families did not meet the family ideal or whether they mirrored the ideal too closely, women adrift desired independence.[106]

By the early twentieth century, wage-earning daughters who remained at home also expressed reservations about the restrictions of family life. A social investigator in Chicago, Louise Montgomery, found that daughters who worked for wages "manifested a little more self-assertion."[107] Chicago settlement worker Mary McDowell noted that young women "became discontented with their home and estranged from their mothers, especially the daughter of the old-country mother who does not know the exciting world into which the daughter goes every day."[108] And community activist Jane Addams observed "that sense of independence which the first taste of self-support always brings."[109] In fact, in many cases, wage-earning women who lived at home directed their greatest acts of rebellion against parental authority.[110]

 Historians and sociologists often attribute events in history to the rebellion of sons who would not or could not live up to the ideals of their fathers. It is worth noting that daughters sometimes rebelled against their mothers. In the late nineteenth and early twentieth centuries, women's roles were expanding rapidly beyond the traditional female domestic sphere. Many working-class women left home to go to work, to high school, to dance halls, and to movies. As they departed from traditional home roles, the advice and rules of old-fashioned mothers sounded increasingly obsolete. While some daughters at home expressed discontent, the women who actually moved away rejected imitations of family life, and sometimes defied the mother figures who tried to protect and support them in surrogate families.

 The city had changed and so had women adrift. New options in housing, board, and entertainment had shown women new possibilities for greater independence. And the experience of living on their own and of supporting themselves had perhaps given women adrift a sense of themselves as capable individuals who were not simply daughters, wives, and mothers. The women adrift who went out daily to work led less cloistered lives than many of the women who lived with their families, many of the domestic servants who lived with their employers, and even many of the mid-nineteenth century seamstresses who had worked and slept in their rented rooms. Yet, because of low wages, most of these women could not afford a comfortable independence. Many of them turned instead to their peers and set up alternatives to families in which they might live without maternal supervision.

Chapter Five
"Friends to Help Them"

In the early 1890s, May Churchill, a fifteen-year-old Irish widow alone in Chicago, learned to earn her own living. "The World's Fair," she wrote later, "was a gold mine to me and my friends." On her "first big" job, May worked with a partner, Dora Donegan. May invited a man to the Sherman House hotel. "I went through with the job," she wrote, "and Dora lifted nearly a thousand dollars out of the gent's clothes, while I was putting up a barrage of laughs, shrieks, and expostulations." Dora helped May out further "by steering the gink away from the place and allowing me to escape." On lesser jobs, May cooperated with hotel managers. She would register at a hotel with a man who would pay two dollars for a room; she would then excuse herself for a glass of water and leave. She "often . . . had as many as ten Johns this way, in one night." In another situation, May came up with a "brilliant idea in handling suckers." She would "throw a John's pants out of the window and beat it." By her own characterization, May "ran wild" in Chicago until "business went on the blink." When she left for New York in 1894, her "gang" of friends and partners was "sorry to lose" her.[1]

"Chicago May" belonged to an underworld of criminals that flourished in the red-light districts of turn-of-the-century Chicago.[2] By the early twentieth century, this underworld was only one among several visible peer subcultures that attracted "women adrift."[3] In rooming houses, at workplaces, and in commercialized recreation institutions, women adrift lived, worked, and socialized in settings where men and women mingled freely. In these settings, many women entered unsupervised social networks, and some entered extramarital sexual relationships as well. Chicago May's behavior, then, is an early and colorful example of a more common pattern in which women adrift replaced familial support and supervision with relationships with their peers.

Two types of informal relationships formed the bedrock of the urban peer subcultures. On the one hand, women cooperated as equals with friends and acquaintances, pooling and sharing resources. On the other hand, women, especially young women, depended on their higher-paid male peers, exchanging companionship and sometimes sexual services for various "treats" and "gifts." In some cases, these cooperative and dependent relationships provided women adrift with both emotional and economic support. In other cases, they were primarily economic, governed by the need to stretch and supplement inadequate wages. In the following interchange, a Chicago working woman stated the case simply to an investigator who asked about low wages: "Q. 'How did they manage to exist?' A. 'Well, they used to get friends to help them.' "[4]

Historians of wage-earning women in the United States find cooperative relationships primarily in two institutions: the family and the trade union.[5] With this institutional bias, they sometimes neglect informal cooperation. In certain American subcultures, informal cooperative relationships supplemented family and kin networks and sometimes preceded formal organization in clubs or trade unions.[6] In the 1830s and 1840s, for example, women factory workers in Lowell, Massachusetts, created communities within their company-owned boarding homes.[7] Similarly, in the late nineteenth and early twentieth centuries, many wage-earning women who did not live with family or kin developed informal bonds of mutual dependence.

The most obvious and probably the most prevalent form of this informal cooperation among women adrift was the sharing of rooms. Women reduced their rent by doubling up in furnished rooms and pooling funds for food and fuel. In some cases, writers suggested that low-income women could choose between poor housing and shared rooms. One investigator in Boston wrote, "Roommates are another form of economy in rent. And hall bedrooms, unheated rooms, rooms without light, all come cheap."[8] Or, as a wage-earning woman in Chicago wrote in 1913, "The cheapest board a girl can get—without living in so-called philanthropic homes that always smack of charity—is five dollars a week. This sometimes gives her a little closet-like room alone, or she may have a larger room by sharing it with another girl."[9] The available figures on the extent of shared rooms are few and imprecise. Our best estimates come from two surveys of wage-earning women in Boston published in 1911 and 1917. These surveys indicate that anywhere from 30 percent to 60 percent of women adrift had roommates.[10]

When a woman had more than one roommate, her rent dropped lower still. Among the poorest immigrant workers in Chicago, several lodgers, men and women together, often shared a room. A 1910 federal investigation in Chicago's meat-packing industries found one woman who slept in a ten-by-fifteen-foot room with seven other lodgers. This woman and several others in similar situations spent on average less than one-and-a-half dollars per week for all living expenses.[11] In the same year, the Immigrants' Protective League reported a number of cases in Chicago in which women shared rooms with several other lodgers. In one case, a nineteen-year-old Polish woman lived in a three-room flat with a married couple and six other boarders. While many women paid two dollars per week for rent, this woman paid only two dollars per month.[12]

In addition to sharing rooms, increasing numbers of women adrift rented entire flats or houses together. In the late nineteenth century, this "cooperative housekeeping" attracted attention because it seemed novel. "Some self-supporting girls have inaugurated a great reform which it would be possible to operate for the benefit of thousands," wrote one investigator in 1890. "Five newly-landed Irish flax mill operatives club together, hire a tenement, furnish it plainly in common, and, while one keeps house, four work in the factory."[13] As in this account, several early descriptions of cooperative rentals stated that one of the housemates did or should serve as housekeeper while the others worked.

By the early twentieth century, reports of shared homes appeared with frequency. Writers no longer expressed surprise at cooperative housekeeping arrangements, nor did they expect to find a housekeeper in every household. In Chicago, in 1910, the Immigrants' Protective League reported without further comment, "Occasionally a group of women rent rooms and live together. Five Polish girls, all under twenty, were found living in two rooms. They all work in factories and each does some part of their simple housekeeping."[14] Native-born white women also shared apartments with increasing frequency. A 1909 advice book, apparently aimed at native-born white women, stated that "many girls who desire to avoid both 'homes' and boarding houses" wrote to ask whether they could live feasibly in cooperative housekeeping arrangements. By the late 1910s, reformers and popular literature acknowledged that cooperative housekeeping was not only feasible but respectable and widespread.[15] The survey of wage-earning women in Boston published in 1917 found that the two groups of women most likely to enter cooperative housekeeping were at opposite ends of the wage scale. The most poorly paid women crowded several tenants into two or three rooms, and the better-paid women rented flats where each roommate had her own bedroom.[16]

Often women who shared rooms and flats together also shared meals. Women cooked together in the common kitchen or on gas burners in their rooms, or they took turns fixing dinners. In some house-holds, roommates bought the food together, and one woman chosen as cook prepared the meals. Wilma M., who lived with three friends in Chicago, explained, "Josephine rented a three-room apartment . . . and she cooks our meals for us. We pay her. It's a nice arrangement."[17]

Many women moved into shared rooms or apartments solely for economic reasons. They pooled resources temporarily in order to rent housing that they could not afford alone. They did not necessarily enjoy this arrangement.[18] As in the organized boarding homes, some women disliked the lack of privacy in shared bedrooms. They also distrusted roommates whom they hardly knew. In 1921, for example, a black woman in Chicago found herself arrested when her suspicious roommate accused her of stealing.[19] To avoid such situations, many women chose to live alone as soon as they could afford to pay higher rent. A 1911 study found that when a woman earned over nine dollars a week, she paid higher rent in order to have "a room to herself, heat of some sort and sunshine."[20]

Other women enjoyed the companionship of shared homes. As Wilma M. stated simply, "We like each other. . . . and we get along very well."[21] Some of these women formed long-term friendships and partnerships with their roommates. In the 1890s, Mary Anderson, later a labor activist, shared a room for several years with a sister buttonhole maker she met at work. She and her roommate lived together first in Chicago. They then traveled to Dixon, Illinois, for work, later to Milwaukee, and eventually back to Chicago when unemployed.[22] Similar partnerships occurred in the twentieth century. In the late 1920s, for example, two friends went to Chicago together from their small hometown in Michigan. During the next three years, they lived together "in apartments, rooming houses, and finally at a girl's club."[23] These long-term partnerships suggest that close personal bonds may have existed among some wage-earning women similar to the strong bonds of friendship described by historians of nineteenth-century American middle-class women.[24]

In a few of these long-term partnerships, one of the women posed as a man and thereby earned higher wages. Newspapers at the turn of the century carried sensational stories about women adrift discovered passing as men. Such was the case with Cora Anderson, a Native American woman, and Marie White. The *Chicago Day Book,* a mildly sensational newspaper, carried their story. In 1901 the women, student nurses in Chicago, "found out how hard it was for a woman (especially a woman with a dark skin) to make an honest living, and decided to double up and form a home." Rather than pooling their funds as working women, however, Cora Anderson assumed the identity of a man, Ralph Kerwineio, and Marie White lived as her wife. They left Chicago and lived together for thirteen years, first in Cleveland and then in Milwaukee. Cora Anderson undoubtedly had complex motives for assuming a male identity. Her relationship with Marie White was most likely lesbian. In addition, she expressed an unusual recognition of male privilege. "The world," she wrote, "is made by man—for man alone. . . . Is it any wonder that I determined to become a member of this privileged sex?" Still, in 1914, after her arrest for cross-dressing (officially disorderly conduct), she allegedly justified her defiance of sexual convention specifically with a protest of women's wages: "A girl or woman needs more money to live decently than a man. . . . there are thousands of young women who are living in a state of semi-starvation."[25]

Anderson's self-justification points to an underlying feature of wage-earning women's cooperative relationships in the late nineteenth and early twentieth centuries: in purely monetary terms, one woman had little to offer another. Women with inherited wealth or professional jobs could easily form the comfortable long-term partnerships known as "Boston marriages," but most wage-earning women adrift who formed long-term cooperative partnerships could expect lives of continuing poverty. When many women contributed small amounts to a common fund, however, they might have sufficient resources to achieve certain limited ends. Such enterprises required greater planning and more organization. Accordingly, a smaller number of women joined together in larger groups to gain additional benefits. These organizations represent the more visible and structured aspect of the cooperative impulse that led to shared housing and food.

The most successful such organization of women adrift in Chicago was the Jane Club, a well-publicized model of cooperative housing. Named after settlement worker and community activist Jane Addams, the club opened with her aid in 1892. In her memoirs, Addams recounted how the idea for the club arose at a meeting of women shoe workers during a strike. "The discussions made it clear," she wrote, "that the strikers who had been most easily frightened, and therefore first to capitulate were naturally those girls who were paying board and were afraid of being put out if they fell too far behind." After a discussion of the problem, one shoe worker asked, "Wouldn't it be fine if we had a boarding club of our own, and then we could stand by each other in a time like this?"[26] Addams enlisted the help of Mary Kenney, a young bookbinder active in the Chicago labor movement. Addams supplied the first month's rent and furnishings, and Kenney supplied the initial members.[27] The club opened with two bookbinders, two shoemakers, and one shirtmaker. Five years later, the club size had stabilized at thirty members. It continued at about that size at least into the 1920s, although by the twentieth century, it housed more teachers and clerical workers than factory workers.[28]

From the beginning, members managed the Jane Club democratically. They paid a weekly sum for room and board, and gave an hour each week for general housework. Housekeepers hired by the club were also eligible for membership. Members assessed themselves for small amounts when additional funds were needed, elected officers, and voted on applicants.[29] Like the organized subsidized homes, the Jane Club had problems with drab food and cramped quarters, but, unlike the organized homes, the residents of the Jane Club took an active role in finding remedies. They discussed problems in general meetings. In 1894, for example, the members resolved not to air grievances about the cooking privately but to report them to the house committee only.[30] And in 1897, while discussing the prospect of a new building, the members claimed to be "willing to lay bricks themselves if single rooms and other conveniences might be thus secured."[31] The democratic management of the Jane Club inspired discussion of cooperative housing among other groups of women.[32] In Chicago, the founders of the Gertrude Club for kindergarten teachers and the Eleanor Clubs for wage-earning women and students emulated some features of self-government.[33]

The Jane Club fostered a cooperative social atmosphere among its members. "The social spirit was just as cooperative as the financial relationship," remembered Mary Kenney O'Sullivan, "We enjoyed doing things together."[34] The members partied together frequently and entertained each other with musicales, hops, a glee club, and a reading club. They celebrated the anniversaries of the club, and several members held their weddings in the home.[35] Other members spent much of their adult lives in the Jane Club. A report in 1921 stated that one member had lived in the home since its establishment thirty years earlier, and several members had lived there for over ten years.[36]

While the members of the Jane Club encouraged sisterly cooperation, they did without institutional maternalism. First, the Jane Club had no matron or controlling board of managers. Although Mary Kenney's invalid mother lived in the home in the 1890s and "mothered the cooperators as though they had been her own," she did not have supervisory or disciplinary privileges.[37] Second, no rules regulated closing hours or supervised sexual behavior. According to Jane Addams, "Those things are left for the girls to take care of in their own way. Any girl who can come into the city and earn an honest living knows enough to run her own evenings." Each member had her own key to the home.[38]

Third, members refused several offers of charitable contributions which they considered patronizing.[39] As one investigator noted, boarding clubs like the Jane Club were "unquestionably a revolt against authority."[40]

In addition to the Jane Club, women adrift joined other wage-earning women in a variety of clubs for insurance, education, and recreation. While some wealthier women and employers financed and ran working women's clubs, wage-earning women themselves appear to have managed other clubs as genuine cooperatives. The Alpha Sorosis Club was a self-governing club in Chicago founded "for the purpose of giving to busy women through cooperation advantages which as individuals they could not enjoy." In 1897 the club had 350 members, most of whom worked in offices and stores. For three dollars a year, the members had access to classes, a restaurant, clubrooms, and a library. The club also offered a limited number of furnished sleeping rooms which members could rent for twenty-five cents per night or one to one-and-a-half dollars per week.[41]

Foreign-born women formed numerous local mutual aid societies. In 1890 a German-language newspaper reported a working women's club with a mutual aid system that paid unemployed members three to five dollars per week.[42] In the early twentieth century, Polish and Lithuanian women in Chicago formed similar small self-assessment groups. One account of Lithuanian women in Chicago stated, "all belong to at least one friendly insurance society. The poorer women and the more recent immigrants are associated in little parish self-assessment societies, in which each pays a small monthly fee, usually twenty-five cents."[43] Most of the larger immigrant fraternal orders and lodges, however, catered to men and charged fees prohibitive to poorly paid wage-earning women.[44]

Lodges among blacks in Chicago, though, seem to have included women adrift. Black migrants to Chicago organized "states clubs" for migrants from their home states. Clubs like the Alabama Club and the Georgia Club and some clubs for migrants from cities like the Natchez Club gave aid and a social life to newcomers. The clubs met migrants at train stations, provided information on homes and work, and sponsored parties and dances.[45]

Similar kinds of cooperation occurred in some of the black churches in Chicago. Some of the black migrants to Chicago shunned the established churches managed by middle-class blacks and instead organized new storefront churches that replicated the "old-time shouting religion" of the rural South. The preachers themselves were often uneducated migrants, sometimes women. The churches held prayer meetings several times per week, providing a social and spiritual center for new-comers to the city.[46]

Investigators in the early twentieth century reported clubs formed exclusively for social purposes among white working women and men in several cities. In the rooming house districts of Philadelphia the clubs, with names like the Red Rose Social, put on parties, and in New York they gave dances.[47] In Chicago at least one early version of today's singles' clubs existed for women and men apart from family. The Lonesome Club, founded in 1915, gave weekly chaperoned dances "to facilitate the social contacts of those who are alone and without friends in the city." The club's motto was "A Bright Spot in a Blue World."[48]

Some women adrift preferred to arrange their social lives informally and to organize instead to increase wages and better working conditions. "I had been a member of a working girls' club and I was much disgusted with the talk of the group. It was always about outings," wrote Mary Kenney. "I thought that helping to get better wages was much more important. If you had good wages you could have your own outings. I left the club to give my time to work for trade organization."[49]

As Kenney's statement indicates, most women adrift did not have the same degree of political commitment. And because most employers opposed organization and many trade unions treated women with indifference, if not hostility, women without strong political convictions often did not join unions. While freedom from family responsibilities may have enabled women adrift to attend union meetings held in the evening, lack of family support may have made them less likely than other working women to go out on strike or chance unemployment. On balance, it seems that women adrift probably joined unions as frequently (or infrequently) as wage-earning women who lived at home. Despite the injustice of low wages and the merits of worker solidarity, the difficult and risky trade union efforts had less immediate and certain results for women adrift than did the pooling of resources to lower expenses in housing, food, and entertainment.

One union in Chicago, though, spoke particularly for women adrift.[50] Waitresses, many of whom lived away from home, organized Local 484 of the Hotel and Restaurant Employees International in Chicago in 1902.[51] In well-publicized actions, union members, both black and white, won wage increases and other benefits. Unorganized waitresses also benefited from the union's victories which set new standards for restaurant owners throughout Chicago.[52] In addition, the Waitresses' Union had an insurance fund, an important cushion for wage-earning women without family support. As one observer noted, "Many waitresses are lonely roomers. . . . To save the girls from the dangers of the nobody-to-know and nobody-to-care feeling, the waitresses early inaugurated a sick benefit fund." The fund supplied money for "room rent or other necessaries" to self-supporting waitresses who could not work due to illness.[53] The early successes of the Waitresses' Union made it an example of what organization could do for self-supporting women (see fig. 5.1). Unlike many of the unions formed by

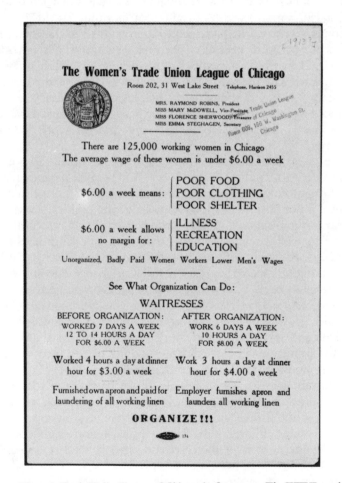

The Women's Trade Union League of Chicago

Room 202, 31 West Lake Street   Telephone, Harrison 2455

MRS. RAYMOND ROBINS, President
MISS MARY McDOWELL, Vice-President
MISS FLORENCE SHERWOOD, Treasurer
MISS EMMA STEGHAGEN, Secretary

There are 125,000 working women in Chicago
The average wage of these women is under $6.00 a week

$6.00 a week means: { POOR FOOD
POOR CLOTHING
POOR SHELTER

$6.00 a week allows
no margin for: { ILLNESS
RECREATION
EDUCATION

Unorganized, Badly Paid Women Workers Lower Men's Wages

See What Organization Can Do:

WAITRESSES

BEFORE ORGANIZATION:	AFTER ORGANIZATION:
WORKED 7 DAYS A WEEK 12 TO 14 HOURS A DAY FOR $6.00 A WEEK	WORK 6 DAYS A WEEK 10 HOURS A DAY FOR $8.00 A WEEK
Worked 4 hours a day at dinner hour for $3.00 a week	Work 3 hours a day at dinner hour for $4.00 a week
Furnished own apron and paid for laundering of all working linen	Employer furnishes apron and launders all working linen

ORGANIZE !!!

Fig. 5.1. Women's Trade Union League of Chicago leaflet, c. 1913. The WTUL used the success of the Waitresses' Union to show what organizing could accomplish for the self-supporting woman. (Source: Schlesinger Library, Radcliffe College)

women in the first years of the twentieth century, the Waitresses' Union remained vital for several decades.[54] Despite a disastrous strike in 1914, the union recovered its strength. In the mid-1920s, it had five-hundred members.[55]

Just as the Jane Club received occasional support from Hull House, so the Waitresses' Union received funds for organizing, strikes, and publicity from the Women's Trade Union League of Chicago. Without outside financial support, other organizations of wage-earning women suffered from the same problem as did the informal partnerships in housing. As early as 1892, Eliza Chester, author of *The Unmarried Woman*, recognized the problem. "They have not much money in advance," she wrote, "and it is hard for 20 or 30 women to combine satisfactorily in any new scheme where it is necessary for each to risk almost all her savings."[56] When a wage-earning woman sought a higher standard of living, she could turn to the charity of wealthier women or the conventional dependence on higher-paid men. Many women disliked charity and the supervision it often entailed; they turned instead to their male peers.

In the late nineteenth and early twentieth centuries, wives depended customarily on husbands for economic support. Among women adrift, a partial and less permanent dependence on men appeared outside of marriage. The higher wages of men, plus the social sanction given to a courtship in which a man plied a woman with gifts, encouraged forms of dependence that fell somewhere between professional prostitution and marriage. This dependence covered a range of behavior from respectable "dating" to cynical "gold digging" to "occasional prostitution." Men provided limited support, paying for entertainment, luxuries, gifts, and sometimes necessities. Women, in return, gave limited sexual favors, such as charming companionship, a good-night kiss, heavy petting, and sometimes sexual intercourse. Like the cooperative relationships among women adrift, this "sex game," as one writer named it, offered peer-oriented, unsupervised substitutes for family companionship and support.

At its simplest, a woman adrift who could not afford to pay for her own amusements could accept a date with a man who, by convention, paid for the evening's entertainment. The 1910 federal report on wage-earning women adrift stressed the importance of gentlemen friends: "Even if most of the girls do not spend money for amusements, it is no proof that they go without them. Many of the girls have 'gentlemen friends' who take them out. 'Sure I go out all the time, but it doesn't cost me anything; my gentleman friend takes me,' was the type of remark heard again and again."⁵⁷ A woman adrift with a "steady" could expect to supplement her income regularly with free meals in restaurants and free evenings on the town. As the 1910 report stated, "Girls who have 'steadies' are regarded as fortunate indeed."⁵⁸

A woman need not have a "steady," however, to engage in dating. Women adrift, especially young and conventionally pretty women, could go out with acquaintances or even strangers known as "pickups." The 1910 federal report suggested that a woman who wore "presentable" clothing could meet men in public places who would pay for her entertainment: "They can 'take a walk' on the street, go into the free dance halls, where they meet men who will treat them to the entertainment the place affords. . . . Or they will take a car to some amusement park where they often make acquaintances who take them the rounds of the resort."⁵⁹

As this quotation indicates, the new commercialized recreation institutions promoted these patterns of urban dating. Women frequented dance halls and amusement parks with the hope of meeting men who would "treat" them. In 1911, an investigator in Chicago met several women adrift in dance halls who asked him "to take them to shows or dances."⁶⁰ In addition, when a woman "picked up" a man on the street, they often began their evening in the restaurants, dance halls, amusement parks, movies, and cabarets where men paid for the food, drink, and entertainment. In 1921, for example, Gladys B., an eighteen-year-old black woman "went cabareting" with James P. after she met him at the corner of Thirty-fifth and State streets on Chicago's South Side.⁶¹

Working-class women who lived in their parents' homes also participated avidly in the new urban dating patterns.⁶² For women adrift, however, economic need added a special imperative. They were highly aware of the economics of dating. A waitress said, "If I did not have a man, I could not get along on my wages."⁶³ And a chambermaid in a hotel said, "If the girls are good and refuse invitations to go out, they simply have no pleasure."⁶⁴ Some women adrift calculated their appearance to attract men who took them out and bought them gifts. In 1911 a saleswoman in a department store explained why she powdered her face: "I might get invited out to supper and save twenty cents."⁶⁵ And in the mid-1920s, a taxi dancer told an interviewer, "The Filipinos [whom she dated] will spend a lot more money on you if you wear nice light dresses."⁶⁶

Dating, of course, affected men as well as women. A man needed extra cash to date a woman who expected gifts and entertainment. In 1919 a *Chicago Tribune* article carried the headline "Man Getting $18 a

Week Dares Not Fall In Love." The story itemized the budget of a returning soldier who refused to work for the eighteen dollars offered him by a retail store. With no funds for entertainment, the young man "could not even buy a young lady an ice cream cone," not to mention dinner and treats.[67]

The custom of paying for companionship led some men to aggressive or devious behavior. Some men offered women adrift what amounted to bribes or hounded them with false promises of material comfort. Women complained bitterly of men who had bribed them or lied to them. "I know how it is," a woman who worked in a Chicago store explained in 1913. "A fellow you think is all right asks you to go for a walk or to the nickel show and you pass gay windows with pretty dresses displayed. You stop to look. 'Like that dress?' the fellow says. 'Oh, it's lovely,' you say. 'Well, I can buy you prettier ones,' he says 'if you will come and be my sweetheart,' and sometimes the girl is fool enough to do it."[68] In another case, a Chicago woman who had earned eight dollars a week became a prostitute when, in her own words, she was "tempted by lies and overpowered by the evil in men." Men, she wrote, "seemed to consider me their prey. . . . They wanted to be nice to me, they said, and take me to the theaters and treat me fair—and give me a chance to enjoy life. I didn't know men were bad, all bad—where a girl is concerned."[69]

While some men took advantage of women, some women in turn took advantage of men. Most women adrift probably dated only men whom they liked and accepted dinners, entertainment, and gifts as conventional and useful expressions of male affection. But some women became self-avowed and cynical opportunists who feigned interest in order to sucker men into spending money. Two women hospital workers told a Chicago investigator in 1911 that "they had two 'Interns' on their staff, and were 'bleeding' them for all that was in it."[70] In 1915, Virginia Brooks reported several such stories of gold digging in a sensational book that recounted her antiprostitution work in Chicago. In search of vice, Brooks, disguised as a working woman, discovered the dance halls and cabarets where women induced men to give them gifts or money. A co-worker in a department store told her, "Don't let nothing get away from you that you can grab. . . . I'll take you to Dreamland [Dance Hall]. It won't cost us a cent if we make a killing. There's always a bunch of guys around there and it's dead easy to date up."[71] In 1930 a woman summed up the gold digger's ethos: "what I get is mine. And what they have is mine, too, if I am smart enough to get it. . . . I'll show you how to take their socks away."[72]

In the mid-1920s, Alma Z., a sixteen-year-old migrant from Wisconsin, gave an especially detailed description of one of her gold digging scams. "The first impression a girl has to make," she said, "is that she is a good girl under hard circumstances." When a man asked her for a date, she would first have him pay the wages she would earn if she stayed at the dance hall where she worked. "When he ask[s] how much that is, I make it seven or eight dollars rather than the four dollars which it usually is." Then she would let him treat her to a meal in a nice café or restaurant. After dinner, she would find some way to escape. She might excuse herself for a moment and leave through a back door. Or she might telephone an older woman friend "to come right down to where I am, to walk in and claim me as her niece and to threaten to make a scene." She and her friend would leave together; the friend would get half of the "rake-off."[73] For Alma Z., gold digging was a thrilling game: she accepted gifts and money, then plotted to escape without payment of sexual favors.

What other women gave in return for the gifts they received is not usually known. In many cases, they were probably friends and companions to men who found them attractive. For some women who cared for or loved the men they dated, the economic support expected after marriage simply began earlier. In other cases, women adrift most likely gave sexual favors in return for gifts regardless of whether or not they liked the man involved. As one man in Chicago explained, they "draw on their sex as I would on my bank account to pay for the kind of clothes they want to wear, the kind of shows they want to see."[74] These women looked for short-term and immediate gain and did not necessarily seek the long-term economic benefits of marriage. "She doesn't want to marry anybody," said one ex-steady of his former girlfriend, "only wants a good time with lots of money."[75] Not surprisingly, these women rarely admitted the details of their sexual lives to interviewers.

One group of sexually active women adrift, though, did attract the attention of investigators in the early twentieth century. These women, known as "occasional prostitutes," worked in stores, offices, factories, and restaurants during the day and sold their sexual services on occasional nights for gifts or extra money. The massive report on vice in Chicago, published in 1911, included numerous accounts of women adrift who worked as occasional prostitutes. One woman, about twenty years old, worked in the basement of a department store for six dollars a week. She paid three dollars for her meals, two dollars for her room, and sixty cents for carfare. The investigator wrote, "She 'hustles' three nights a week for extra money to pay for washing, clothes and other things."[76] A twenty-one-year-old woman solicited an investigator at an amusement park. She told him she worked in a butter factory for one dollar a day. She paid two dollars per week for her room and ate two meals a day at a restaurant. She offered to "go out" with the investigator for two dollars.[77] Another woman, nineteen years old, had arrived in Chicago from Indiana three months earlier. She worked in a restaurant and lived in a rooming house on Michigan Avenue. The report stated, "Is not a regular prostitute, goes out with men for presents or money. Is poorly paid at restaurant."[78]

Other women supplemented or replaced their wages in relationships that more closely resembled marriage. These "kept" women supported themselves by providing sexual services to one man in return for economic support. The 1911 report of the Chicago Vice Commission included several examples. One twenty-year-old cashier in a restaurant left her job when she met a streetcar conductor who became her "steady fellow." This man had bought her a new hat and had promised her a winter coat. She occasionally went out with other men "to get a little more spending money."[79] Sometimes these women lived with the men who supported them. One such woman, twenty-one years old, could not live on the money she earned as a waitress. Then she met a man "who took her out, bought her some clothes, gave her money and not long afterward they took a room together."[80] Like the occasional prostitutes, these women did not belong to a pariah caste of "fallen women." They belonged instead to an urban subculture that sanctioned what investigator Albert Benedict Wolfe labeled "temporary alliance."

In 1906, Wolfe, an investigator of lodging houses in Boston, described how a women adrift might enter such a relationship. In Wolfe's scenario, a woman meets a man, "perhaps at a cafe table." They see each other again, "by chance perhaps, and then by tacit consent or appointment." At first, she "pays her own way," but then she allows him "to pay for dinner or to take her to the theatre." Eventually the man "comes unconsciously to think he has some claims upon her, and she, bowing to traditional ways of thinking, also comes to something of the same feeling." They then "strike up a temporary alliance," motivated in some cases by "genuine and lasting regard." In other cases, however, "the motive of the girl is simply to find support, and that of the man gratification."[81]

Wolfe's scenario resembles the courtship of Louise D., a young migrant to Chicago from Wisconsin. In 1925, Louise D. worked as a waitress during the day and danced at night in a dance hall. There she met a man who "went with her regularly" for six months before they had "sexual contact." Soon after, he began to pay the rent on her apartment and also some of her board bill. In return, Louise gave him a "pass key" to her apartment. A few months later, the couple broke up, and Louise returned to the dance halls.[82]

For women adrift, the "sex game" held the obvious danger of unwanted pregnancy. The more sophisticated women had access to contraceptive devices and abortions.[83] Some women, though, found themselves alone with children born out of wedlock. These women probably had fewer means of securing marriage or support from the child's father than did wage-earning women who lived at home.[84] Without family to help them, some women turned to the courts. A study of bastardy cases in the Chicago Court of Domestic Relations in 1913 found that women who boarded or lived alone pursued a fairly high number of cases.[85]

Even when they avoided unwanted pregnancies, women adrift found that dates, steadies, pickups, suckers, and alliances provided them with only temporary means to supplement income. Older women adrift often withdrew from the "sex game" as they lost the youthful appearance that readily attracted men. Furthermore, for some women, the cost of attractive clothing exceeded the benefits of free nights on the town. In addition, some women tired of the nightlife. One black woman adrift explained, "I used to go to cabarets a lot, used to dress and spend plenty of money. . . . I used to go to these all night parties about two or three years ago. I had a beau, I didn't miss it. . . . I was good looking then, you know. . . . I am just sorry I let so much of my time waste up."[86] Other women avoided relationships as they learned to mistrust men. Ann J., a forty-nine-year-old widow, "had several offers to live with men in free unions." She refused them, she said, "because all men are weak." While she rejected free unions, she would have remarried had she met an "elderly, kind, clean, unburdensome man."[87] Like Ann J., most women adrift eventually hoped for marriage, which offered more stable companionship and support.

Cooperation with friends and dependence on men had, of course, existed earlier.[88] But by the early twentieth century, these relationships seemed more visible and widespread than in the past. The growth of sexually integrated workplaces and new entertainment industries provided settings in which the steadily increasing number of wage-earning women could make friends and meet men. In factories and department stores, in cabarets and dance halls, at amusement parks and cheap theaters, observers noted that working women and men participated not only in informal relationships, but also in elaborate peer-oriented sub-cultures.[89] Women adrift were especially active in such networks. Separation from family supervision plus the need for companionship and support encouraged them to engage in social and sexual experimentation.[90] In Chicago, studies of waitresses and taxi dancers described these peer subcultures.[91]

In a book published in 1920, Frances Donovan examined the lifestyle of Chicago waitresses. "It is the group life in the waitress world," she wrote, "that makes the appeal." Or, as a waitress told her, "If it wasn't for the fun I have [at the restaurant] cutting up with the girls, I'd go mad." The waitress, Donovan noted, approached the issue of sex with "the incredible candor of men," was "looser in her sex relations," and accepted gifts from men she dated in "a life of semi-prostitution." The peer networks she described extended beyond the workday. "For the unmarried waitress," she wrote, "home is usually a furnished room and she spends only the time there that is necessary for washing, ironing, and mending her clothes. Practically all her leisure is spent at the movies, cabarets, and restaurants, where she goes with her 'friend' or with some other girl." She concluded that waitresses had different standards than their parents and that they made "a new group life in which these standards are approved."[92]

In a detailed study of taxi-dance halls conducted in Chicago in the 1920s, sociologist Paul Cressey discovered a similar occupational subculture. Like waitresses, taxi dancers, women who danced with male customers for a small fee, created a cooperative atmosphere with each other both in the closed dance halls where they worked and outside of the workplace.[93] The dancers developed common mannerisms and patterns of speech at work. Many of them also lived together, with groups of three or four sharing apartments or furnished rooms. Like the waitresses described by Donovan, the dancers dated patrons in return for entertainment, clothes, or even rent money. One taxi dancer described her subculture, "I lived with other dance-hall girls, met my fellows at the dance hall, got my living from the dance hall. In fact, there was nothing I wanted that I couldn't get through it."[94]

A few of the taxi dancers joined together more formally by organizing themselves into all-female gangs. "The gangs are formed . . . ," wrote Cressey, "among a group of congenial girls who frequent the same dance hall." In some gangs, the members rented apartments together. These women formed tight bonds of friendship with one another and shared a cynical, get-all-you-can attitude toward men. The gang members "in their association with patrons seem to be motivated wholly by utilitarian or exploitative interests. . . . They are reputed to be some of the most active in 'fishing' gullible patrons."⁹⁵ Gangs, such as Roses's Gang and Minnie's Gang, were named for their female leaders.

Timid women adrift, women who had no desire to enter peer networks, and women who spoke no English might choose to board or lodge in private families in residential neighborhoods of the city. But women adrift who felt comfortable in the city and who sought new experiences could choose to live in the furnished room districts where peer subcultures appeared most obviously. In these districts where lodgers concentrated, both observers and inhabitants recognized communities in which working women and men lived unsupervised by family and sometimes unfettered by convention.

By the end of the nineteenth century, most major American cities had districts where rooming houses abounded. These districts often first appeared in the city center and, later, as business displaced downtown housing, moved outside the center along major transportation lines.⁹⁶ The large proportion of adults and the small proportion of children distinguished these districts demographically from other neighborhoods of the city.⁹⁷ A residential street in a furnished room district usually resembled other residential streets in the city: a typical block would consist of single-family homes, buildings of flats, large tenements, or older mansions. The owners of the buildings, however, converted the interiors into one- or two-room dwellings. They might divide a flat into two or three smaller units or divide a large tenement into an "apartment hotel" with as many as one hundred furnished rooms. In a mansion, an owner might convert a large sitting room or parlor into two or three sleeping rooms. The owner might live in and care for the rooming house, or a widow or older single woman might rent it and keep it for her living. Caretakers or janitors usually managed the larger buildings while the owners lived elsewhere.⁹⁸

In Chicago, three such districts emerged in the late nineteenth century (see fig. 5.2). On the South Side, the furnished room district covered an especially large area that included major portions of the Chicago black community and also what was, before the 1912 raids, the segregated vice district of the city. Few immigrants lived in this district. On the West Side, the district housed a population of predominantly white service and factory workers. Several organized homes for working women and the offices of many labor organizations were nearby. A transient male hobo population congregated on the inner boundaries. On the North Side, where rents were slightly higher, sales and clerical workers lived in rooming houses alongside white service and manufacturing workers, artists, bohemians, and radicals of all stripes. In the

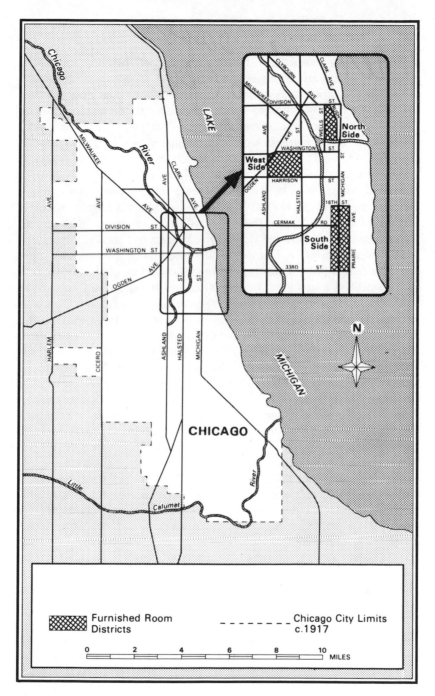

Fig. 5.2. Map of the furnished room districts of Chicago, c. 1917. (Source: Abbott, Tenements of Chicago, 1908–1935*)*

early twentieth century, the North Side district included substantial numbers of Irish and Swedish roomers.[99]

These districts burgeoned in the early 1890s when migrants and visitors streamed to Chicago for the World's Columbian Exposition. They continued to expand into the 1930s. After 1915 the South Side, where most black migrants settled, grew especially rapidly. By 1923 the Illinois Lodging House Register reported over eighty-five thousand lodgers in about five thousand rooming houses in the three major furnished room districts. By 1930, several smaller districts for white roomers had emerged on the North and South sides farther from the city center. And residents of the new small-unit apartments (with private bathrooms and kitchenettes) joined the lodgers in furnished rooms.[100]

Several distinctive features of furnished room districts promoted the development of relationships among peers. Most obviously, women and men lived together in houses where most people did not live in families. In these neighborhoods, lodgers found numerous opportunities to create social and sexual ties with their neighbors. Further, the high geographic mobility in the furnished room districts made informal, transient relationships the norm. One observer went so far as to claim that the entire population of Chicago's North Side furnished room district changed every four months.[101] This high turnover rate created an atmosphere of anonymity in which lodgers rarely knew their neighbors well. Community pressures to conform to conventional familial roles were weaker than in more stable neighborhoods. And parental authorities were absent. Many rooming house keepers, eager to keep their tenants, refrained from criticizing or interfering with roomers' sexual behavior.[102] In addition, the sex ratios in the North and West Side districts may have encouraged women to participate in extramarital heterosexual relationships. The predominance of men in these districts must have made it easy for women to meet men and difficult to avoid them.[103]

In any case, the prevalence of prostitution in these districts fostered a climate where open expressions of sexuality were common. In the first decade of the twentieth century, the most prominent vice district of Chicago lay in the South Side furnished room district. Brothels were tolerated in sections of the West and North Side districts as well.[104] In addition, on the South, West, and North sides, some keepers of rooming houses and hotels rented rooms by the hour or night to prostitutes and their customers.[105] Around 1910 a missionary worker described the North Side of Chicago: "On all the cross streets, from the river to Chicago avenue, one can see soliciting going on almost any time of night."[106]

After the municipal government closed many of the brothels in the 1910s, investigators in the furnished room districts repeatedly found rooming houses and hotels used for prostitution. In 1917, in the West Side district, for example, an investigator entered a hotel that advertised for "steady roomers." The maid there told him that "they had no girls on hand but that I could bring a girl up to the hotel and she would rent a room for $1.50 and I would pay the girl what she charged."[107] A 1922 study concluded, "The furnished room situation in Chicago is particularly bad, especially on the South Side. Many of the women who operate upon the streets and in the cabarets utilize the rooming houses."[108]

The "bright light" centers of the furnished room districts provided settings in which men and women could socialize. Investors who hoped to profit from the market of lodgers built cafeterias, cheap restaurants, tea rooms, soft-drink parlors, saloons, dance halls, cabarets, and movie theaters in the furnished room districts. These institutions served as social centers. One observer of cabarets in the North Side district discovered, "Considerable companionship grows up around these resorts. One is struck by the fact that the same people visit and re-visit the same cabaret time and again."[109]

On the North Side, Clark Street and, on the West Side, Halsted Street were well known for their night life. In 1918 the section of Clark Street that ran through the North Side district housed fifty-seven saloons, thirty-eight restaurants, and twenty cabarets.[110] "Halsted Street . . . mak[es] a constant appeal to those living either east or west of it," wrote Edith Abbott in a classic study of Chicago's housing, "Here are the great West Side theaters, the old saloons. . . . Here also are the dance halls, the movies, hotels, peddler's carts, the rush of 'through cars,' and the ever present possibility of excitement."[111]

In the South Side furnished room district, the State Street "Stroll" and, by the 1920s, Thirty-fifth Street emerged as the "bright light" centers of the black community.[112] Dance halls, restaurants, movies, and saloons for black customers coexisted with "black and tan" cabarets which offered racially integrated recreation.[113] When young men and women who lived at home went out for a night on the town and when wealthier people went "slumming," they often went to the furnished room districts of the city.

By the early twentieth century, the furnished room districts of Chicago and other large cities were known as havens for working women and men who chose to defy conventions.[114] For these lodgers, the furnished room districts not only provided settings for economic cooperation with and dependence on peers but also a chance to have adventures, break taboos, and express ideas in a community without parental authorities. Women and men could live together outside of marriage or with members of their own sex in homosexual relationships. In many rooming houses, occasional or professional prostitutes could come and go at all hours without arousing concern of family or neighbors. Teenage runaways could live apart from family with little fear that their parents would find them. As one dismayed observer noted, the furnished room districts attracted "people who want to get away from their neighbors."[115]

The tolerance of unconventional behavior, the commercialized recreation, the proximity of prostitution, the high mobility, and the predominance of unmarried lodgers encouraged the growth of a variety of peer subcultures in the furnished room districts. While some women adrift who lived in these districts led lonely lives alienated from their peers, others formed complex networks of cooperative and dependent relationships. Although these networks provided some women with the economic support and the social and sexual companionship they may have desired, they were not necessarily ideal, deeply binding, or conflict free. The following account, from a study of Chicago's North Side written in 1918, shows the complexity and the casual nature of relationships in the furnished room districts:

> [J. and V.] went to the North Clark Street section where they posed as man and wife. They took a couple of furnished rooms . . . , and remained there for two years. Both of them worked often bringing in as much as $30.00 a week together. They took their meals out and got along very well.
>
> Then two of the girl's sisters came to Chicago to find work and rented rooms next to them. These girls had good intentions but not securing very lucrative positions, they soon learned how to supplement their wages by allowing young men to stay with them.
>
> These girls struck up an acquaintanceship with another girl who used to remain overnight with them now and again when they had been out to a dance or cabaret. J. liked this new girl and as he put it could not "help monkeying with her" and when V. found it out she became extremely jealous and shortly afterwards left him. Her sisters and the other girl followed her.[116]

Other accounts provide additional glimpses of how women formed casual social networks in the furnished room districts. In 1911, two women, seventeen and twenty years old, met at a South Side dance hall. The older woman persuaded the younger woman to leave her parents' home and room with her on Chicago's North Side. After they moved in together, they made "pickup acquaintances" with men at dance halls and on the street.[117] Around 1913, Myrtle S., who roomed in the North Side furnished room district, made friends with another woman at the restaurant where she ate her meals. This woman introduced her to a man, Lew W., with whom she spent several evenings drinking beer in a North Side inn. Myrtle testified that she lost her virginity when Lew took advantage of her: "one night she lost consciousness after her drink of beer and awoke next morning in the Superior Hotel." Despite this betrayal, she returned to the hotel with Lew on two other occasions. Later, Myrtle met another man in a "chop suey" restaurant.[118]

Some newcomers to the furnished room districts remained aloof from social encounters until they became accustomed to the freer sexual expression. "The men and women living in the [rooming] house were mostly a tough lot," one woman recounted. "There were goings on that shocked me then—though I would pay scant attention to them now." This woman had trouble making friends in her rooming house and at her job. "A girl brought up on the Commandments," she said, "doesn't make friends in rooming houses or as a waitress very readily." Eventually, though, she made friends with another woman and shared a room with her. Then, she met a man at a restaurant and lived with him briefly. "He said that he loved me, and I was willing not to question too closely." Loneliness, she felt, had led her into the social networks she had at first avoided.[119]

Several of the social circles that developed in the furnished room districts were distinguished by unconventional life-styles, sexual preferences, or political leanings. In the North Side district of Chicago, for example, a subculture of hoboes congregated in and around Washington, or Bughouse, Square. In her autobiography, hobo "Box Car Bertha" wrote, "Girls and women of every variety seemed to keep Chicago as their hobo center. . . . They all centered about the Near North Side, in Bughouse Square, in the cheap roominghouses and light housekeeping establishments, or begged or accepted sleeping space from men or other women there before them." Bertha remembered one house in particular, the Martha Biegler Boarding House, where "Red Martha" herself sheltered and fed women hoboes who had no money. The women hoboes engaged casually in sexual relationships. One woman, Bertha wrote, had "a group of sweethearts," others lived and traveled with men "to whom by chance or feeling they had attached themselves," and still others engaged in "careless sex relations."[120]

By the 1920s, lesbian communities were also apparent in the furnished room districts of Chicago.[121] Among black women, blues singer Ma Rainey, a bisexual, suggested that lesbians frequented State Street,

a central street of the South Side rooming house area. In a song recorded
in 1924, she included these references to State Street among other more
sexually suggestive verses: "Goin' down to spread the news/State Street
women wearing brogan shoes/ . . . There's one thing I don't understand/
Some women walkin' State Street like a man."[122] According to "Box
Car Bertha," "several tea shops and bootleg joints on the near-north
side . . . catered to lesbians." Bertha found a large number of lesbians
among the Chicago hobo population.[123] Another observer found lesbians in the somewhat less transient population of the Near North Side
furnished room district's bohemia. He, too, noted that lesbians and
homosexual men frequented the tea rooms of the area and held parties
in their apartments and rented rooms.[124]

From the limited evidence available, the lesbian community seems
similar to the other subcultures of the furnished room districts in that
it was based on unsupervised, informal cooperative and dependent relationships. Lesbians shared rooms and flats, and socialized and partied
together. Like other women adrift, some lesbians depended on men,
earning money as prostitutes, although they had "women sweethearts."
Others depended on higher-paid or wealthier women to support them.
For example, in the North Side district in the late 1920s, Beatrice lived
in a basement flat with several other lesbians and a few men. She was
supported by her lover, Peggy, who earned money as a prostitute. Peggy,
wrote Box-Car Bertha, "has had a dozen sweethearts, all lesbian, and
has always supported them." Bertha also reported a form of gold digging
or, more precisely, veiled blackmail among lesbians. After a North Side
party, some lesbians persuaded the wealthier women attending to pay
for their companionship: "The lesbians would get their names and
addresses and borrow money by saying, 'I met you at . . . [the] party.' "
Some lesbians also prostituted themselves to other women.[125] As with
heterosexual women adrift, not only desire and romance but also economic need shaped the relationships in a social and sexual community.

The best-known subcultures of the furnished room districts were
undoubtedly the bohemian subcultures of artists, political radicals, and
sexually permissive intellectuals. Black bohemians congregated in the
South Side furnished room district, and some white socialists and an-
archists lived in the West Side district.[126] But the heart of Chicago's
Bohemia was on the North Side where one well-known study found
that "most of the experimenters are young women."[127]

The stereotypic image of these female bohemians pictures a young
native-born white woman from a middle- or upper-class background.
While some middle- and upper-class women moved to the furnished
room districts in search of independence, working-class women adrift

also chose to enter this subculture. For example, in the 1910s, Eulalia B., from an impoverished home in Indiana, moved to a flat in the West Side district where she lived with political radicals of both sexes. Influenced by the ideas of her roommates, she eventually joined the Industrial Workers of the World.[128]

In the bohemian subculture and in other subcultures of the furnished room districts, women tried to shed their social backgrounds in an attempt to conform to new group norms. Natalie Feinberg, the daughter of poor Jewish immigrants from Russia, gradually withdrew from her family as she attempted to enter Chicago's North Side bohemian community. After she left school, Natalie took a job as a clerk in a radical bookstore. There she met "various people of the 'Bohemian' type" whom she found attractive. As she made friends, she spent less time at home, withheld her paycheck from the family fund, and finally moved away. She waited tables in a restaurant where bohemians congregated, modeled for artists, and acted in an amateur theater. According to the sociologist who described her, "she frequented the various gathering places of the group and by attempting to outdo the older members in unconventionality, sought approval and admittance as one of them. She won the reputation of wishing to become a great courtesan." As part of her rejection of her background and her entrance into a new community, she changed her name to Jean Farway.[129]

The furnished room districts, it seems, were physical settings where behavior considered unacceptable elsewhere was accepted matter-of-factly and even encouraged. In working-class residential communities of Chicago, neighbors often stigmatized sexually active unmarried women. The case of Mamie, a young woman who lived with her parents in a working-class neighborhood, is illustrative. Mamie first encountered problems in 1918 when a policewoman reported her for "unbecoming conduct with sailors." The unbecoming conduct continued, and, two years later, rumor had it that her neighbors talked of signing a petition to expel her from the neighborhood.[130] Contrast Mamie's brief case history with the comment of a student of Chicago's South Side furnished room district: "It is said that an attractive woman who does not 'cash in' is likely to be considered a fool by her neighbors, instead of any stigma being attached to a woman who 'hustles' in this neighborhood."[131]

By the 1910s, a woman adrift in Chicago found a number of peer-oriented subcultures open to her. These subcultures offered economic support, companionship, physical pleasure, adventure, and romance. But they also promoted female dependence, fostered peer group pressures to conform to new sexual standards, and encouraged women to see themselves as sexual objects. In some ways, the relationships in these subcultures imitated the family, especially relationships between siblings and between spouses. They differed from family, though, in the absence of parental supervision, the acceptance of extramarital sex, the transiency of relationships, and the immodesty of public behavior. Because these differences reflect patterns of behavior still prevalent today, the sub-cultures of women adrift seem decidedly more modern than early twentieth-century family life.

Until a few years ago, historians identified the early twentieth-century "sexual revolution" as a middle-class phenomenon that only gradually trickled down to the working class.[132] In this literature, historians remember the peer subcultures of the furnished room districts primarily for the articulate middle- and upper-class members of the bohemian communities. These bohemians appear as vanguards of modern sexuality—women and men who experimented freely with new sexual possibilities learned from Sigmund Freud, Havelock Ellis, and other sexologists.[133] They replaced the nineteenth-century middle-class image of sex as danger with a twentieth-century image of sex as pleasure.[134]

Recent historical works, though, suggest that working-class women and men also engaged in rebellions against the conventions of their parents and of middle-class reformers. Like the middle-class flapper, these women danced, drank, flirted, and adopted bawdy language and sexually suggestive clothing styles. Not infrequently they engaged in premarital sexual intercourse.[135]

Among women adrift, the "revolution" does not seem to have trickled down from a bohemian and middle-class vanguard to the working class. The various peer subcultures of women adrift appeared at least as early as the bohemian communities and predated the more widespread mixed-sex subcultures of middle-class youth of the 1920s.[136] In fact, it seems more likely that the bohemians learned of new sexual possibilities not only from the "highbrow" writings of the sexologists but also from the "lowbrow" behavior of their less intellectual working-class neighbors. The working-class women adrift did not simply follow middle-class patterns; they helped chart the modern sexual terrain. For these women, sexual expression not only promised pleasure; in a variety of forms, it also promised financial reward.

Chapter Six
Urban Pioneers

In 1900, Doubleday, Page, and Company tried to break its contract with Theodore Dreiser for the publication of *Sister Carrie*. Mr. and Mrs. Doubleday themselves, it seems, deemed the book immoral. What troubled the Doubledays, and later many reviewers, was not that Sister Carrie went "astray" in the novel, but that she went willingly and without disastrous consequence. Unlike the heroines of romance novels, she represented neither endangered virtue nor innocence ruined. For Carrie, the opportunities of the city outweighed its perils. She pursued fame and wealth successfully and flouted the Victorian moral code. When Dreiser refused to relinquish his contract, Doubleday, Page, and Company withheld the book from wide distribution. The novel did not attract a large readership until 1907 when Dreiser arranged republication with another company.[1]

With *Sister Carrie,* Theodore Dreiser joined a small minority of writers who challenged the dominant public image of orphaned and innocent "women adrift." In the late nineteenth century, a few conservatives condemned women adrift as frivolous self-seekers who ignored their domestic duties.[2] In addition, writers of semipornographic literature sometimes portrayed self-supporting women as uncontrollably exuberant and eager for new experiences. An advertisement for one such book described its heroine as "one of those WILD, RECKLESS DARE-DEVILS, that every now and then dashes upon the world like a Blazing Meteor. . . . Her own words, in one striking passage, tell what she is: 'Mother,' she said, 'I will *not* go home! I will *not* be good! I will *not* reform!' "[3]

Variations on these undercurrents became more prevalent in the first decades of the twentieth century. Here the self-supporting woman, headstrong and openly sexual, lived boldly in a fast-paced urban environment. In the earlier dominant discourse, unfortunate circumstance—poverty or death in the family—forced timid young women, soon to be victims, from happy parental homes. Or foolish young women left their homes and soon regretted it. In the newer discourse, women like Sister Carrie chafed at the restrictions of domesticity. They left their homes willingly and never regretted their decision. "Why do they come to the city?" asked Frances Donovan in 1920, "Because life is dull in the small town or on the farm and because there is excitement and adventure in the city. The lure of the stage, of the movie, of the shop, and of the office make of it the definite El Dorado of the woman. It is her frontier and in it she is the pioneer."[4] By the 1920s, the woman adrift had stepped ashore as a trailblazer.

The entrepreneurs who developed new mass culture industries publicized this image. Movies, cabaret reviews, and pulp magazines used the woman adrift, and especially her sexuality, as a symbol of urban energy, allure, and adventure. She represented both the attractive pleasures of urban life and their dissipating influence on men who could not resist them. Just as the entrepreneurs who built cheap restaurants and small-unit apartments appealed to the desire of boarders for independence, so the entrepreneurs who sold entertainment appealed to the desire of city dwellers for adventure, pleasure, and thrills. By the 1920s, reformers' earlier image of women adrift, evoking pity rather than excitement, could not compete.

In any case, by the 1920s, many reformers had modified their earlier picture of pure and innocent women helpless in an evil environment. They now credited the wage-earning woman with a more active role in her own fate. Not until the mid-1920s, though, did large numbers of intellectuals adopt the newer images publicized by the mass culture industries. Then, academic sociologists, centered at the University of Chicago, portrayed the city as a less constraining environment than the small town and chose the popular image of the self-supporting woman as a symbol of both the positive and negative features of urban liberation.

When social investigators first discovered the peer subcultures of women adrift, they expressed reservations. As one author wrote, "It may be set down as a general rule that there is danger wherever young people congregate without restraining influences."[5] Although investigators sometimes applauded the efforts of sisterly cooperation among women adrift, often they qualified their support. For example, in 1898 one author wondered whether most low-income women workers could "safely undertake cooperative housekeeping . . . without the moral support of a head to the home."[6] And, eleven years later, an advice book to wage-earning women concluded that newcomers to the city should avoid cooperative housekeeping: "Danger lurks in her ignorance of neighborhoods and in the too sudden intimacy with girls of whom she knows nothing."[7]

In the case of women who turned to men for support, the early response of investigators was, predictably, more negative. In 1887, Grace Dodge, founder of the first Working Girls' Society in New York, advised working women, "It is dangerous as well as wrong to allow a man to give you money or presents of value, to accept invitations from one you do not know all about, to put yourselves in any way in a man's power."[8] Books, articles, and leaflets warned of the dangers that men posed to women without family protection, not only men who abducted women and sold them to brothels, but also the Tom, Dick, and Harrys who simply wanted "gratification."[9]

Even as reformers sought to protect women, however, some of them began to acknowledge that wage-earning women had wills and desires of their own. By the end of the first decade of the twentieth century, reformers often conceded that women adrift relied on their peers not simply from economic necessity but also by active choice. In 1909 the Immigrants' Protective League acknowledged its unsuccessful attempts to persuade Polish working women to leave lodgings where unrelated men and women lived together. "We have usually tried to induce a girl so situated to change from scrubbing in a restaurant on State Street to scrubbing in the Presbyterian hospital where she would also live," the annual report stated. "This is, however, a very lonesome performance for the girl. She hates to leave the Polish district, where she has many friends, to do work where she sees and hears strange things and eats stranger food. As a result we have not been able to persuade many to move."[10] Rather than women who drifted wherever the forces of the city pushed and pulled them, some investigators now described women who actively pursued companionship, adventure, and entertainment.[11] By giving the wage-earning woman a will, they rejected the extreme environmental determinism inherent in the image of the passive woman adrift.

Increasing numbers of writers stated as well that women adrift had sexual urges. In 1910, one campaigner against prostitution, who described women adrift as innocent, naïve, and unprotected, wrote in a distinctly modern passage, "it must not be forgotten that every normal girl or woman has primal instincts just as strong as her brother's."[12] Jane Addams, Louise DeKoven Bowen, and others rejected the earlier image of female passionlessness. Instead, they blamed overwork, commercialized recreation, and alcohol for bringing out natural yearnings and instincts that they preferred to see repressed.

The reformers' concern for the woman adrift continued, but they dropped their earlier emphasis on her helplessness. In a book of morality stories for wage-earning women published in 1913, reformer Clara Laughlin pointed to the change. In one story, the protagonist, Eugenia, "did not suddenly find herself obliged to seek a livelihood like the story-heroines of two and three decades ago. Her father did not die; their investments did not 'prove worthless.' " Instead Eugenia chose to leave home because "she had a sturdy desire to do for herself—to be adequate to her own support." She also wished, Laughlin wrote with approval, "to gratify some of her long-repressed desires." And, full of verve, Eugenia "loved the adventure of it."[13] In another story, Laughlin's protagonist, Mary, moved away from the urban home of her tyrannical father. In contrast to her father, Mary "felt that women had a right to be something besides daughters, wives, and mothers."[14] And Laughlin agreed: Mary supported herself capably and, with a friend, rented a three-room kitchenette apartment.

As the concept of women's special helplessness began to lose its appeal, organizations that had catered originally to women adrift extended their protective services to include some men as well. On a national level, the National League for the Protection of Colored Women, founded in New York in 1905, merged in 1911 with two other organizations to form the National League on Urban Conditions among Negroes, known today as the National Urban League. The new organization continued to aid black women migrants to cities but only as part of a more varied agenda to help both men and women.[15] In Chicago, the Immigration Committee of the Women's Trade Union League, established in 1907, reorganized in 1908 to become an independent group, the League for the Protection of Immigrants, later called the Immigrants' Protective League. The independent organization still worked primarily with women, but it also opened its work to young male newcomers "suspected of being under the control of padrones."[16] Similarly, in 1914 the Travelers' Aid Department of the Chicago YWCA joined with representatives from Jewish, Catholic, and Protestant organizations to form an independent Travelers' Aid Society working for all travelers in need regardless of sex, race, religion, or nationality. The articles of incorporation defined the travelers in need as "innocent, unwary, ignorant and inexperienced travelers, especially boys, girls, women, invalids and the aged."[17] In this organization and in the others, the protection of women remained a priority but no longer the sole activity.

Meanwhile, the reformers in the organized boarding home movement publicized their work with decreasing frequency. As many of the homes moved toward self-support, they no longer made public appeals to donors. In addition, some of the older homes now entered a period of internal consolidation. During the First World War, the Chicago YWCA, the largest organization managing homes in Chicago, centralized its operations and created a coordinate branch system much like those found in major corporations. The YWCA, involved in war work, asked for and received substantial grants and loans from the National War Work Council, obviating the need for fund-raising and publicity campaigns.[18]

The public discussion of organized homes also disappeared from national social reform periodicals. Coordination on a local level lessened the need for public discussion in a national literature. In 1915, New Yorkers formed the Association to Promote Proper Housing for Girls.[19] In the early 1920s, representatives from at least twenty-five organized boarding homes for women in Chicago began to meet as the Subcommittee on Housing of the Chicago Council of Social Agencies. The group discussed problems in managing homes and set standards for housing. It continued to meet into the 1950s.[20]

Other social reform literature on women adrift also dwindled. In the 1910s, much of the new literature on the poverty of women adrift came from the efforts for a living wage for women workers. But in 1922 a Supreme Court decision nullified the minimum wage law in the District of Columbia and set back further efforts for legislation with the likelihood that the court would also declare new laws unconstitutional. Although reformers continued to support protective legislation, minimum wage literature declined until the 1930s.

Into the 1920s, sporadic voices echoed the earlier message. In 1920 the Chicago YWCA Room Registry Bureau stated, "It is a dangerous thing to let these girls go into rooms where they can come and go as they like, pay prices they cannot afford, and be released from all home ties."[21] And the Travelers' Aid Society of Chicago distributed a leaflet that graphically portrayed an innocent woman adrift as a predatory man approaches her. In four smaller pictures, the leaflet then spelled out "what might have happened." Lonely in a barren room, jobless, and cold on the snowy streets of Chicago, the once innocent young woman ends up dancing in the arms of a man in a seedy cabaret (see fig. 6.1). In 1924 the *Literary Digest* published a "warning for country girls" that stated that the "peril" of urban life warranted "a nationwide movement to keep girls away from the great cities."[22] These occasional warnings and descriptions of women adrift from the 1920s, however, seem bland when compared to similar fare from the 1890s and 1900s.[23]

Fig. 6.1. Travelers' Aid Society of Chicago leaflet, c. 1920. The Travelers' Aid matron saves the innocent migrant from the city slicker. (Source: University of Illinois at Chicago, University Library, Travelers' Aid Society Records)

By the end of the 1920s, even these watered-down descriptions had virtually vanished. When reformers and social investigators observed women migrants to cities, they generally concluded, as did Orie Latham Hatcher, that "none had changed her condition for the worse by coming."[24] By 1928, even the most avid promoters of the earlier image reassessed their work. The Chicago YWCA *Annual Report* stated, "One may discover a room through a daily newspaper ad; there are innumerable employment bureaus where jobs are to be found; . . . and friends are to be found at work, or at play in the many commercial recreation features of this great city."[25] Fifty years earlier the women of the YWCA had introduced protective services precisely because they considered newspaper ads, employment bureaus, workplaces, and commercial recreation facilities dangerous to women. When wage-earning women seemed more capable and the city seemed less threatening, the woman adrift lost her place as a symbol that evoked reformers' sympathies. In 1929 the Subcommittee on Housing, comprised of representatives from organized homes throughout the city, asked its members, "What type of person is next in need of housing care—the older woman, the industrial girl, the student or who?" At its next meeting, the committee members answered that older women and students had the more urgent needs.[26]

The earlier image of the orphaned and innocent woman adrift faded for several reasons. First and foremost, women adrift themselves forced reformers to recognize them as competent adults. The managers of the organized homes toned down their sentimental descriptions of orphans in order to attract residents who resented the image of helpless victims.[27] At the same time, reformers and journalists, adopting the new social science method, undertook detailed social investigations that brought them into daily contact with women who contradicted the image of the weak and innocent woman adrift. They learned that most wage-earning women, though poor, did not starve. They saw women who supported themselves ably on low wages. And they acknowledged that many sexually active women adrift were neither forced by poverty nor deceived by men.

As reformers observed women adrift, their fears about women's sexual vulnerability diminished. They saw that many women adrift lived in a world that attached less stigma to female sexual activity. Reformers interviewed women who had given up their virginity without an inkling that they had chosen a "fate worse than death," and they saw that a wage-earning woman might choose to sell her sexual services without ruining her life. "The fact that she has earned money in this way does not stamp her as 'lost,' " a 1911 federal report stated. "And the ease with which, in a large city, a woman may conceal a fall of this kind, if she desires to do so, also helps to make a return to virtuous ways easy . . . occasional prostitution holds its place in their minds as a possible resource, extreme, to be sure, but not in the least unthinkable."[28] The reformers may not have approved of such behavior, but they saw that it did not spell disaster.

Observant reformers discovered a spectrum of behavior between the chastity that they preferred and the sexual slavery they decried, a spectrum that further blurred the line between pure and fallen. They noticed that chaste working women sometimes adopted the clothing, makeup, and speech that had earlier distinguished prostitutes and relegated them to a visible pariah caste. "To those accustomed to reserve and decorum on a woman's part, the freedom of manner sometimes met with is suggestive of much evil," the 1911 federal report explained, ". . . any one who has had experience with working women in clubs or classes or homes knows that this freedom is entirely compatible with perfect rectitude of conduct."[29] In 1910, one writer stated in a condemnatory tone that many women "would not accept money from any man, but would let the man give them a present of anything from a pair of stockings to an automobile, and think they were lucky."[30] Other authors came to accept such arrangements more complacently. The 1911 federal report, for example, noted the lack of compunction with which women adrift accepted presents from male friends. "They simply take this means," the report stated, "of securing more amusements, excitements, luxuries, and indulgencies than their wages would afford them. They are not promiscuously immoral."[31]

By the mid-1910s, the observations of reformers coincided with broader changes in middle-class thought and behavior. In the years before World War I, increasing numbers of middle-class urban women imitated the more open sexual behavior that reformers described among wage-earning women. Observers reported that middle-class daughters danced, drank, smoked, and petted. Young, white, middle-class women, by the mid-1910s labeled "flappers," wore shorter dresses and shorter hair, once the styles of prostitutes. More recent studies of sexual practices reveal that, by the 1920s, rates of extramarital intercourse had indeed increased among middle-class women.[32] This change in middle-class morals further undermined the older image of female innocence and passionlessness, and challenged the Victorian fear that female sexual behavior denoted female victimization.

The First World War accelerated the process of change. As young, urban middle-class women entered the paid labor force to work at wartime jobs, some of them rejected their parents' moral standards and

attacked the stereotypes that portrayed self-supporting women as vulnerable innocents. One woman stated that, during the war, middle-
class women had discovered a new morality through self-support and
self-expression. "For the first time in the memory of man," she wrote,
"girls from well-bred, respectable middle-class families broke through
these invisible chains of custom and asserted their right to a non-chalant,
self-sustaining life of their own with a cigarette after every meal and a
lover in the evening." In contrast to these modern women, she denounced the chaste "Victorian spinster prototypes" as "meek and pet-
ulant and useless . . . parasites to the social body."[33]

By the mid-1920s, self-consciously modern middle-class women
began to adopt the role of women adrift. They moved temporarily into
the new kitchenette apartments of the furnished room districts to live
with their friends. With better education and often with better wages,
these women imitated the freedom of life without parental supervision
while avoiding the threat of permanent poverty. "It has been compar-
atively easy for [middle-class girls] to leave home, to sever their economic ties with their families, and to go 'on their own,' " noted one observer
in 1926. "It has become a great adventure, this going on one's own, the
thing to do!"[34]

While some middle-class women asserted their independence, the
federal government led an attack against female sexuality that further
subverted the older image of the helpless and passionless woman adrift.
During World War I, in a massive crusade against prostitution, the
government detained thirty thousand women suspected as prostitutes.
Unlike the earlier antivice crusaders, the government officials did not
intend to protect women from exploitation but rather to protect soldiers
from venereal disease. They rejected the image of women as pure and
helpless, and replaced it with an image of women as corrupting. They
acted as if "any woman who was mobile, unchaperoned, and outside
traditional contexts of moral control was a potential prostitute."[35] After
the war, several state governments also treated women with more hostility, enacting statutes that allowed the conviction of women as prostitutes without proof of solicitation. The city no longer threatened
women; now women threatened the city.

In the 1920s, other factors further diminished reformers' interest
in women adrift. First, women's real wages rose.[36] While many wage-
earning women still earned inadequate incomes, the increase in the
average wage probably made the poverty of self-supporting women
seem less dire. Second, the interest in the most poorly paid working
women declined with the end of most immigration from Europe during
and after World War I. The predominantly white social investigators

never paid as much attention to the black women who filled the unskilled manufacturing and service jobs that European-born women had held earlier. Finally, reformers who did not lose their interest in women adrift lost their audience and their clout. After World War I, in a conservative political climate, many Progressive era reform movements suffered from declining public interest and from government repression and indifference.[37] Middle-class women reformers, once recognized as moral guardians, had lost the power to shape popular cultural images.

As the older image of women adrift faded, the manufacturers of mass entertainment publicized a newer image. Rather than a victim of poverty and vice, the self-supporting woman now symbolized the vitality and appeal of the modern age. In the earlier image, her suffering signified the high cost of urban living; in the newer image, her pleasure pointed to its rewards. The fun-loving woman adrift of the furnished room districts, the "jazz baby," replaced the Victorian angel. She represented a working-class variant of the modern New Woman of the early twentieth century. This new discourse was ambiguous, though. In the guise of the gold digger, the self-supporting woman also personified the dangers to men who indulged naïvely in urban pleasures. The new discourse celebrated the city and female energy while it warned against excessive pleasure seeking and expressed underlying hostility toward an increasingly public female sexuality.

The new image appeared in the first decade of the twentieth century in the stories of chorus girls who achieved stardom and married wealth. In 1900 the Floradora Girls, who dated and married wealthy men, showed the chorus line as "a potential stepping-stone to personal happiness and self-advancement."[38] Unlike the timid heroines of romance novels, these women strutted boldly across the stage, displaying their bodies and commanding attention. The glamour of the chorus line received wide publicity in 1908 when the trial of Henry Thaw made sensational headlines and reached larger audiences still in a movie, *The Great Trial*. Thaw had murdered architect Stanford White in a jealous rage over White's affair with Thaw's wife, Evelyn Nesbit. During the trial, Nesbit, a former chorus girl, told how wealthy men entertained, courted, and, in her case, married the sexually attractive dancers who worked in cabarets and theaters. She recounted her rise from the life of a poor and hardworking chorus girl to a life of luxury and extravagance. For wealthy men, the trial revealed the disastrous consequences that resulted from succumbing to the chorus girl's sexuality. For wage-earning women, however, the trial publicized the romantic and material opportunities that seemed to open when a woman lived without family supervision.[39]

In the following years, as the number of movie theaters expanded rapidly and the size of audiences grew, the woman adrift emerged as a central character in feature films. At first, in the early "white slavery" films, the heroines, like the romance novel heroines, faced threats to their virtue and sometimes eventual tragedy. At the same time, though, in the early serials—*The Perils of Pauline, The Hazards of Helen,* and *Dolly of the Dailies*—the heroines, often adrift, were "healthy, robust, and self-reliant." Apart from family, they met available and often moneyed men whom they attracted with their native allure. Like the earlier romance heroines, they encountered dangers and difficulties, but they also enjoyed the daring nightlife in cabarets and dance halls as well as the high life in opulent villas.[40]

Soon the movies portrayed increasingly competent and more overtly sexual heroines. By 1915, Mary Pickford had made her career as the first major movie queen by playing "women striving to be economically free and morally emancipated."[41] In her films, Pickford, though always chaste, portrayed characters who flirted, danced, wore revealing clothing, and enjoyed energetic activities. She combined the purity of the Victorian angel with the sexuality of the chorus girl. Her exuberance and spunk attracted male suitors, leading to upwardly mobile marriages. For example, in *Behind the Scenes,* released in 1914, Pickford played a small-town woman who migrates to the city. After a stint at office work, the heroine dances in the chorus line at a cabaret. There she attracts a man who shows her the entertainments of the city and then marries her. The story continues as Pickford refuses to exchange her fun-loving life-style for a traditional marriage.[42] Pickford played a rural daughter in search of urban freedom in *The Eternal Grind,* released in 1916. She takes a low-paying and dull job sewing in a factory, but her attractive energy and her battle against injustice lead eventually to her marriage to the wealthy son of her boss.[43]

While the earlier romance novel heroines endured agony until rescued, the movie heroines often managed to stand up for themselves and sometimes for others. In *The Outcast,* a 1915 film, the heroine, Netta, a cabaret dancer, neither faints nor waits for her hero when a masher pins her against a wall. Taking matters into her own hands, she finds a gun and shoots him.[44] Similarly, in *June Friday,* the heroine, June, stabs the man who seduced and abandoned her.[45] Neither woman pays for her crime: both Netta and June end up happily married.

By the 1920s, the movies drew clear connections between separation from family, on the one side, and female sexuality and material gain, on the other. In some movies, the woman adrift was the stock heroine of rags-to-riches stories. The following description of *At the*

Stage Door typifies the formula: "Mary leaves home to become a chorus girl in New York, and soon she achieves stardom. Philip Pierce, a young millionaire, is attracted to her."⁴⁶ In other movies, the heroine, a wife or daughter, rejected her Victorian heritage by leaving her family temporarily for a short period of freedom in the city's cabarets and dance halls. She appeared eager to escape the restrictions and routine of family. In still other films, self-supporting and openly sexual women, often chorus dancers, won men away from the homebodies who insisted upon clinging to outmoded Victorian standards. In most movies, the heroines and heroes returned home in the end, but often they brought with them, in a tempered form, the sexuality they discovered when separated from family.⁴⁷

As the sexual activities and the assertive behavior of the woman adrift became more explicit in the movies, so did the dangers she posed to men. The woman adrift as gold digger appeared at least as early as 1915. In *The Model; Or, Women and Wine,* wealthy young Dick Seymour pursues a woman adrift, Marcelle Rigadont, an artist's model. Marcelle, as one character advises her, wants to "play him for a sucker. . . . and bleed him for every cent he's got." She convinces Dick to take her to Paris and buy her jewels. Then, when he has no money left, she confesses, "I never loved you—It was only your money I was after."⁴⁸

In the 1920s, at least thirty-four films included the gold digger with her "aggressive use of sexual attraction."⁴⁹ This character followed in a long and popular tradition of seductive vampires whose sexual powers drained male energy. Earlier "vamp" characters, however, including those played in the movies by the famous Theda Bara, were usually independently wealthy women, or else they were women wronged by men.⁵⁰ For example, in the popular play *The Easiest Way,* written in 1908, playwright Eugene Walter described his character Elfie St. Clair as "more sinned against than sinning," a woman who men had "imposed upon, deceived, illtreated and bulldozed" until she "had turned the tables and with her charm and beauty gone out to make the same slaughter."⁵¹ By the 1920s, gold diggers, young and separated from family, needed no justification for their behavior. In a well-known movie, *Gentlemen Prefer Blondes,* written as a novel in 1925 by Anita Loos and first released as a movie in 1928, Lorelei Lee, the gold digger from Little Rock, Arkansas, has neither an evil nature nor an unhappy past. She stalks her male prey with a comical and bald-faced directness and wins audience approval with a curious mixture of clever connivance, naïveté, and sincerity. In one typical line, Lorelei states openly that love interferes with a woman's material interests: "I mean I always seem to think that when a girl really enjoys being with a gentleman, it puts her to quite a disadvantage and no real good can come of it."⁵²

The new image of women adrift was not limited to the movies. Although unrecorded forms of entertainment are harder to document, it seems that the same image appeared in the chorus revues of cabarets and theaters. In "The Girl from My Hometown," the opening number of the Midnight Frolic's "Just Girls," staged in 1915, "girls from 24 cities and one small town came to New York for adventure, men, and a new life."⁵³ "Sally," a Ziegfield revue staged in 1920, told the story of a working-class orphan who climbed from "the chorus to theatrical fame, wealthy admirers and riches."⁵⁴

More accessible to the historian are the pulp romance magazines that grew to popularity in the 1920s. These magazines, usually issued monthly, contained short stories of romance, purported true and illustrated with photographs.⁵⁵ An early and successful publication entitled *True Story Magazine* appeared first in 1919. Geared to working-class readers, it included numerous stories, usually anonymous, about hardworking women adrift. In the 1920s, *True Story Magazine* provided the pattern for imitators, such as *True Romances, Dream World,* and *Real Love Magazine* (see fig. 6.2). Publisher Bernarr MacFadden owned several of these magazines.⁵⁶

In the stories about women adrift, the plots usually resembled the formula found in earlier romance novels. A young, white, native-born woman, often an orphan, had troubles in the city and eventually married the man she loved. The stories depicted love, marriage, and family life as the most desirable and permanent solution to hardship, loneliness, and ambition. In this sense, they reinforced traditional values for women: domesticity triumphed in the end.

Despite the similarity in plot, however, the pulp magazines differed markedly from the earlier novels. For one, they were more realistic. Ordinary working women replaced beautiful heiresses; rooming houses, shops, factories, and offices replaced "the seething whirlpool of vice and crime"; everyday seductions and harassments replaced dramatic abductions and suicide attempts. As one heroine says of her arrival in New York, "What made me feel so utterly insignificant was the fact that nobody noticed me at all. I wasn't accosted; nobody tried to lure me anywhere; I just didn't seem to make any impression on the city at all."⁵⁷

In contrast to the helpless heroines of romance novels, the women adrift of magazine stories were competent, bold, and courageous. When Juliette "Jimmie" Jones, a newcomer to the city, encounters an unscru-

My Adventures in a Rooming House

By a

Lonely Girl in

Harlem

*She was a nice girl
and she came from way
down East. She was
not a dumb-bell, either,
but she did not know
Harlem—and she
found more than one
surprise behind the
curtains of the win-
dows where dangled
the cardboard sign
"Rooms to Let."*

THOSE folks who think every
Follies girl lives on Riverside Drive,
takes a milk rub before retiring, and
goes to sleep with the fizz of champagne
jazzing her off to dreamland, haven't
got our number. If I should say that a
Follies girl, far from being a working girl
de luxe, is a homeless wanderer in comparison with her type-hitting sisters,
you'd probably label me a candidate for
Bloomingdale.
But here it is: a beautiful young girl—
plus clothes, plus the theatrical pro-
fession—has hardly a pillow to lay her
Dutch clip on. Nobody wants her.
Every landlady from the Bronx to South
Ferry looks on a chorus girl with disgust,
contempt—and suspicion. Let me say
right now that getting yourself landed in
the Ziegfeld Follies isn't half the job of
getting yourself landed in a respectable
rooming house in New York if you appear to be able to recognize a Bronx cocktail from a fruit lemonade.

A Follies girl, far from being a working girl de luxe, is a homeless wanderer in comparison with her type-hitting sisters.

Fig. 6.2. True Romances, *October* 1923. *The woman adrift is the protagonist of this confession magazine story. (Source: Library of Congress)*

pulous cab driver, the author announces explicitly, "She was neither cowardly nor resourceless."[58] In another story, when "strong, independent" Grace Harper learns that a man tried to "trick her into a mock marriage," the author states, "But if her trust was gone, her courage was not."[59] In yet another story, Minnie Brown, a divorcée, shows "strength of character" in crisis. In this story and others, a woman scorned carries "herself with dignity," goes "through it dry-eyed," and then gets revenge.[60] As another character takes her revenge, she proclaims her sense of control: "In the past you found that I had a will of my own. You will do just as I say."[61]

A highly unusual story highlights the boldness of women magazine characters. In "The Face with the Three Crosses," Pepita Ortiz, a southwestern woman adrift in New York, learns that the man she trusted, Bob Guthrie, is a cad. She does not faint, cry, or run away. She knocks him out, ties him to a chair, brands three crosses on his forehead, and pours carbolic acid in the wounds! With racist overtones, the story attributes her behavior to her "boiling Spanish blood," but it leaves no doubt that Pepita is the heroine and Bob the villain who deserves his punishment.[62]

The magazine stories differed most clearly from the earlier romance novels in the sexual behavior of women adrift. With surprising frequency, the magazine heroines, like the movie heroines, held sexually expressive jobs such as chorus dancing and nude modeling. (In contrast, when told to go on the stage, one nineteenth-century romance novel heroine says, "I would *die* first," and she does.)[63] Other magazine heroines attended cabarets, dance halls, and wild parties. Their sexual behavior ranged from chastity to premarital sexual intercourse with a lover to prostitution. And, regardless of their sexual behavior, the stories ended happily with the heroine married to the man she loved.

A common theme was the bad girl redeemed. In one such story, the heroine, a prostitute, returns to respectability when a man's "love so noble, so true, so pure, so all-sustaining . . . drew me back up the road that for most girls who take it, is the Road of No Returning."[64] In another story, a respectable widow helps a reformed prostitute, her soon-to-be daughter-in-law, by admitting that, in her youth, she too had sinned and made money from men. The message is straightforward: "I hope my story may reach a woman somehow, somewhere who is trying to 'come back' and 'encourage her.' "[65] In the pulp magazines, as opposed to the earlier romance novels, extramarital sex, while still illicit, did not lead to death or even necessarily to a ruined life.

In the magazines, love could cleanse a woman of past mistakes and, in some cases, it could justify them. In "Love Is Not a Plaything," an orphaned wage-earning woman, "in the madness of . . . passion," makes love to her wealthy fiancé.[66] She has a baby out of wedlock and then marries a kind financier. The baby's father, returned from abroad, searches for her and finds her. She gets a divorce and marries him, her one true love. The stories glorified heterosexual love and elevated it above conventions of propriety.

In the magazine stories, as in the movies, the gold digger made her appearance. As often as not, she was the story's heroine, an energetic woman who hoped and plotted to marry or date a wealthy man. In one story, Joy Waring, an orphaned chorus girl, chooses "the career of marrying money."[67] Her amusing chicanery, her ability to outwit the wealthy, shows her daring and intelligence. She meets George Crawley, a wealthy college boy, cajoles him into proposing, and forces his disapproving mother to acquiesce to the marriage. But then, despite her victory, she has a change of heart: "Suddenly I saw myself as I had been . . . , scheming, planning, working to get ahead, being catty and malicious and contemptible. I was so ashamed I could have wept."[68] She leaves George's mansion with his streetwise chauffeur and marries him instead.

In the nineteenth-century romance novels, the greedy woman, devious to the core, eventually blundered and suffered. In the magazine stories, the greedy heroine, like Joy Waring, proved herself clever, triumphant, and ultimately good-hearted. In a new version of the sexual double standard, she did not necessarily pay for her behavior, but men literally paid for theirs. When she made fools of wealthy men, she demonstrated the sexual power of women. But, equally important, she redeemed herself only by relinquishing that power voluntarily.

The competent, bold, and sexual women adrift of the magazine stories rarely feared the city's perils. More often, the stories played down danger and exaggerated urban opportunities for adventure, romance, and upward mobility. In several stories, the city fared favorably when compared to the small town. In "Be My Husband," the heroine, orphan Ruby Carlton, leaves "dull" Little Falls for "the world where life would really be worth the living." The city fulfills its promise: Ruby rises to stardom, earns a comfortable living, and eventually marries her wealthy employer.[69]

While some magazine heroines returned happily to their hometowns, others denounced the small town as narrow-minded and restrictive. One heroine states directly, "I was glad to get away from Mapleton, and I have never wanted to go back. I have found more of the better part of human nature, more real kindness, more tolerance, more friendship, and more love in the big cities of the world than I have ever found in any small town."[70] In another story, "Small Town Morals," the heroine, a store clerk from a poor West Virginia family, loses her "reputation" through no fault of her own. The town rejects her, and she leaves for Akron, Ohio. When rumors of her past reach Akron, she finds, "it wasn't as bad in the big city as it had been back home. There everyone was against me. Here I had many friends left."[71] Urban opportunity and urban tolerance outweighed the dangers of the metropolis.

The young woman adrift as the modern New Woman provided the popular culture industries with an especially choice symbol for conveying urban energy and female sexuality. The romance novels of late-nineteenth-century popular culture probably used the orphaned and innocent woman adrift because, without family protection, she could enter dangerous and suspenseful situations menacing to her virtue. In contrast, the popular culture of the 1910s and 1920s probably used the new woman adrift because, without family interference and at large in the city, she could explore urban nightlife freely and experience titillating and romantic adventures.

The newer image of women adrift may well have changed some women's self-perceptions. It probably helped timid women to see themselves as individuals outside of family roles and to participate in urban life with less fear. In fact, by the 1920s, increasing numbers of female migrants stated that they came to the city not simply for work but also for "new experiences" or "adventure."[72] It may also have encouraged women to see themselves as bait for men, for in the newer image a woman's success in life depended on her ability to attract men sexually. In addition, like the romance novels, the stories may have created false expectations of undying love and upward mobility.

Whatever their influence, the magazines and movies fit the needs of their creators: they attracted readers and viewers. In 1924, five years after first publication, *True Story Magazine* circulated to over 848,000 readers, and, five years later, the circulation surpassed two million.[73] The movies were more popular still. In the 1920s they attracted between twenty and thirty million viewers weekly.[74] By using wholesome women as sexual objects, the directors and writers attracted both the kind of male patrons who had long frequented bawdy theaters and the patrons who preferred their sexual objects packaged in respectability. By creating fantasies of adventure, romance, and success, they attracted women and men dissatisfied with home life or with low-paying, dead-end jobs. By investigating shocking topics, such as premarital sex, they appealed to women and men with prurient curiosity. And, by emphasizing the chastity, or at least the redemption, of their heroines and the dangers of dissipation, they managed to appease the reformers who, in the early years, balked at the sexual implications of the new entertainments.[75]

As the new image of women adrift gained in popularity, it appeared occasionally in literary works written for more elite audiences. For example, in Anzia Yezierska's autobiographical novel *Bread Givers*, life apart from family offers freedom, upward mobility, and romance. The heroine, Sara Smolinsky, runs away from the home of her immigrant Jewish parents despite her father's patriarchal stranglehold on all of the other women of the family. On her first day on her own, she bristles with joy: "I felt I could turn the earth upside down with my littlest finger. I wanted to dance, to fly in the air and kiss the sun and stars with my singing heart." And when she goes to the door of the room she will rent, it symbolizes her freedom. "This door was life," writes Yezierska, "It was air. The bottom starting-point of becoming a person."[76] Unlike the movie heroines, Sara does not leap up the ladder to wealth through marriage. She works in a laundry, attends night school, puts herself through college, teaches school, and then in the end marries the man she loves.

From the turn of the century to 1925, when Yezierska published *Bread Givers,* attitudes toward female sexuality had changed dramatically. Theodore Dreiser's *An American Tragedy* illustrates some of the changes. The book won immediate and widespread acclaim, although it had many of the features that had made *Sister Carrie* offensive in 1900. Hortense Briggs, the vain, heartless, and successful gold digger in *An American Tragedy,* makes Carrie look virtuous. In contrast to Carrie, Hortense aggressively exploits men; yet, she escapes without punishment. By 1925, few readers expected a sexually active character to pay for her "sins." The tragic central character of the novel, Clyde Griffiths, however, succumbs to female sexuality and pays with his life for his inability to resist the attractions of women and wealth. With Roberta Alden, an innocent country woman who comes to the city for work, Dreiser gives an unusual twist to the classic woman adrift. Roberta suffers not because poverty and predatory men push her inevitably toward dishonor and, in her case, death, but because she insists upon an old-fashioned morality. Roberta clings to Clyde while other female characters assert their independence. She dies in the end because she lets love and outdated morals guide her behavior.[77]

By the 1920s, few writers took the older image of the woman adrift seriously. In Carl Van Vechten's *Firecrackers: A Realistic Novel,* for example, a hard-boiled, cocaine-snorting, promiscuous actress named Lottie becomes the voice of authority, while the green woman adrift from Michigan, Wintergreen Waterbury, plays the part of a fool. In the following conversation, Lottie suggests that Wintergreen blackmail her married suitor:

> "I mean you gotta get wise. This ain't a boilermaker. These Wall Street johns can be trimmed."
> "Why, what do you mean?" Wintergreen repeated.
> "Make him say something or do something."
> "I'm as pure as you are, Lottie Coulter! How dare you!"
> "Snap it off, kid, snap it off."

Lottie then explains her less-than-pure life-style, but Wintergreen does not understand the slang. The conversation ends as Lottie admonishes Wintergreen, " 'Open your eyes, kid, open your eyes.' Wintergreen obeyed her literally."[78]

Aside from a few exceptional literary examples, academic sociologists rather than novelists spread the newer image of women adrift to elite audiences. Inaugurated in the 1890s, the academic discipline of sociology thrived at the University of Chicago where faculty members and students, mostly male, undertook intensive investigations of urban life. At first, many of the sociologists, with backgrounds of religious training, approached the city with an antiurban moralism reminiscent of the Young Men's and Young Women's Christian Associations. By the 1920s, however, the sociologists, influenced by German social theorists, developed an outlook that differed from earlier reformers.[79] They began to stress the "objectivity" of their "scientific" observations. One founding sociologist, Robert Park, "directly attacked the humanitarian attitude" of some of his students.[80] Others chose quietly to take a more detached stance that approached cultural relativism. They stopped identifying victims and vices, and turned instead to more rarefied theoretical questions.

As part of their new outlook, the sociologists shared a vocabulary of social change. Cities, they wrote, were composed of "natural areas" which developed without human planning or intention. Some of these areas or zones were distinctly urban, part of an inevitable evolution of social "reorganization" as cities grew. In these zones, the traditional family and village life of the small town disintegrated. This disintegration led to a "disorganization" in the city characterized by "individuation" or "atomization" in which individuals stood alone without the cohesive group life of the village community. Individuals in the city, free from traditional "social control," now experimented with new ways of fulfilling their desires. The "disorganization" in the city, a transitional stage in an evolutionary process, gave way eventually to a new "social organization."

The sociologists turned to the furnished room districts and their residents as a vanguard of "individuation." Robert Park placed the furnished room districts at the forefront of urban evolution: "Everywhere the old order is passing, but the new has not arrived. . . . This is particularly true of the so-called rooming-house area."[81] And Harvey Warren Zorbaugh found that individualism replaced conventional family in the furnished room districts. "Old standards disintegrate," he wrote, "and life is reduced to a more nearly individual basis. . . . It is a world of atomized individuals, of spiritual nomads."[82] Other sociologists found that the furnished room districts and other "disorganized" areas, such as skid row, had high rates of divorce, prostitution, suicide, and certain mental disorders.[83]

As the term "disorganization" suggests, some sociologists saw the furnished room districts as an unfortunate feature of urban evolution. Some of them equated individualism with loneliness. According to Ruth Shonle Cavan, "In lodging-houses the people are detached, uncontrolled by the opinions of their neighbors, and often very lonely."[84] Others lamented the lack of tradition and restraints, disliked the pursuit of cheap thrills, and feared the "hazards involved in promiscuous acquaintanceships."[85] These sociologists often found life in the furnished room districts soulless and hollow.

For the most part, however, the sociologists had a stronger faith in progress. As the vanguard of urban evolution, the furnished room districts were, in a sense, the most advanced development of city life. With a marked ambivalence, these sociologists described the furnished room districts as "emancipated" as frequently as they called them "disorganized." In the furnished room districts, women and men escaped social pressures to conform to community standards. Ernest Mowrer found that wives and husbands who lived in the districts were "emancipated" from traditional family roles.[86] And E. Franklin Frazier, in his book on black families in Chicago, saw the migration of blacks from small towns and farms to "disorganized" furnished room districts as a "second emancipation."[87] Of the founding generation of sociologists at the University of Chicago, W. I. Thomas and Robert Park showed special interest in the urban "freedom from the conventional social control of the village."[88]

The woman adrift symbolized the emancipation and freedom of urban life. Park and Zorbaugh agreed that women were the chief adventurers and experimenters of the furnished room districts.[89] In the small town, women usually adhered to conventional expectations of domesticity and premarital chastity; in the furnished room districts, however, they found opportunities for upward job mobility and for open sexual expression. Frazier used a female example to explain the opportunities open to blacks in Chicago. In the bright light area of Chicago's South Side, he wrote, "the mulatto girl from the South who, ever since she heard that she was 'pretty enough to be an actress,' had visions of the stage, realized her dream in one of the cheap theaters."[90] In a study of "business girls," Cavan stated, "leaving the restriction of home and living in large cities are two of the simplest and most easily attained ways of securing excitement, new experiences, wider contacts."[91] From this point of view, home life restrained women more than it protected them. It contrasted with "the freer life which the great cities offer them."[92] Walter Reckless stated the case more bluntly: "The homeless woman of modern cities is the emancipated woman. She has broken away from her home community, frequently the small town. And approximating the activities of man, she . . . is acquiring more self-reliance and greater individuality."[93]

Popular culture may well have influenced the sociologists. After all, the image of women adrift presented by sociologists seems curiously similar to the image appearing in movies and pulp magazines. Like the movies and magazines, the sociologists found that the city released women from the "monotony of settled family life" in the small town.[94] From a barren and restricted life, the woman moved to "a section of the old frontier transplanted to the heart of the modern city" where, competent and self-seeking, she could pursue her individual desires and ambitions.[95]

In all of the areas where earlier reformers and investigators had discovered exploitation of unprotected women, sociologists now found willing participation. Of dating for money, Frances Donovan wrote, "She is not . . . exploited nor driven into it, but goes with her eyes wide open."[96] Walter Reckless attempted to prove that "white slavery," the abduction of women to prostitution, had scarcely existed.[97] And W. I. Thomas stated that prostitutes were no longer exploited by procurers or pimps. They had "become 'wise,' " he wrote, and were "going more 'on their own,' " a change he attributed in part to the "general individualization."[98] In a 1929 book on saleswomen, Frances Donovan summed up the new image: "The working girl no longer depends upon heaven to protect her; she protects herself."[99]

The sociologists also mirrored the movies and magazines in their focus on female sexuality. A key component of the "emancipation" they described was greater freedom to engage in sexual activities outside of marriage. Several sociologists discussed the sexual behavior of various types of women adrift, including taxi dancers, "unadjusted girls," and bohemians. As in the movies, some of the sociologists depicted the sexually "emancipated" woman as a threat to men. In the early writings of the Chicago school, the stimulations of the city attracted residents but injured them in the end. In a 1916 essay, for example, Ernest Groves described the restlessness of rural youth and their attraction to the city. He concluded pessimistically that "city dwellers," as they searched for stimulation, would "face either the breakdown of physical vitality or the blunting of their sensibilities."[100] By the 1920s, the woman adrift personified these urban stimulations: she attracted men and threatened them with dissipation and poverty. Thomas wrote that women use their "charm" as a "lure" for "procuring entertainment, affection, and perhaps gifts."[101] Paul Cressey, in his study of taxi dancers, used the word "exploitation" to describe the ways in which women made money from gullible men. "In the quest after the material equipment of life which seems of such importance," he wrote, "the girl becomes not only an individualist but also—frankly—an opportunist."[102] In the earlier image of the woman adrift, men exploited naïve women; in the sociologists' image of the "urban pioneer," women, like the gold diggers in the movies and magazines, exploited naïve men.

No less than the earlier discourse on the innocent woman adrift, the new discourse on the "urban pioneer" reduced wage-earning women to stereotypes. It exaggerated certain features of life adrift and neglected others. Like the earlier discourse, the new discourse focused almost wholly on young, white, native-born women adrift. The sociologists used these self-supporting women as examples of uniquely urban personalities, and, accordingly, they emphasized those aspects of women's lives that supported their theories of urban evolution: individualism, unconventional sexual behavior, transient personal relationships, and freedom from social control. Their commitment to the idea of evolutionary progress encouraged them to accept these urban features as at least somewhat positive and liberating. At the same time, they played down the negative constraints of low wages, sexual harassment, and economic dependence that many women adrift continued to face. They also expressed an underlying fear of uncontrolled female sexuality. With the new stereotype, the sociologists undermined reform efforts and gave intellectual legitimacy to the neglect of female poverty.

The earlier discourse on women adrift drew on a stereotype of women as passive, passionless, and innocent, while the sociologists, moviemakers, and pulp magazine writers tapped an older stereotype of women as wild, sexual, and potentially dangerous. The changing discourse highlights a larger change in the portrayal of women in America, from the Victorian angel to the sexy starlet. In the late nineteenth century, women adrift epitomized the purity of women; in the early twentieth century, the same women were among the first "respectable" women broadcast as sexual objects.

For the fifty years between 1880 and 1930, the special position of living apart from family attracted public attention to the woman adrift. When large numbers of women left their homes, Victorian Americans, especially women reformers, predicted the worst. As they would have it, women depended on the protection of a harmonious home life, and the home depended upon women's moral guardianship. In contrast, the rapidly growing cities were cruel and ruthless, the domain of the stronger and coarser male sex. Without female care the home might collapse, and without the family's protection a woman at large in the city might fall prey to poverty and evil men. By the early twentieth century, however, the city had its celebrants, the home its detractors. Entrepreneurs profited when they promoted and sold the vitality of urban life. City dwellers responded to the lure of the bright lights and the appeal of energetic entertainment. In contrast to the vibrant city, the peaceful haven of the home appeared dull and restrictive. Moreover, the worst predictions had not come true. From all observations, women adrift, though poorly paid, lived ably, often cooperating with and depending on their peers. And as middle-class moral standards changed, political conservatism increased, the average woman's wages rose, and immigration ended, both the sexual vulnerability of women and the problems of poverty claimed less notice. In this context, the woman who left her home seemed much like Sister Carrie, an unbounded individualist who might use her sexual appeal to increase her personal wealth.

Conclusion

In the late nineteenth and early twentieth centuries, thousands of women moved apart from family to support themselves in the city. Black and white, native born and immigrant, young and old, rural and urban, these women often came from backgrounds of poverty and sometimes from families disrupted by death, desertion, abuse, or conflict. They came to the city in search of jobs, and some hoped also for adventure, romance, or careers. In a sense, the city failed them. Despite their expectations, many women encountered poverty, sexual exploitation, loneliness, and stigma. In another sense, though, the city offered possibilities. In new neighborhoods and at new jobs, women created social networks that provided them with companionship and support. Here they also found the opportunity for a limited measure of self-assertion.

What the "women adrift" asserted most adamantly was their desire for independence from supervision. Gradually they rejected the surrogate families that cast them, regardless of age, in the role of daughter. To the dismay of middle-class reformers, many wage-earning women clearly preferred the company of their peers. Alert to a new market, urban entrepreneurs responded readily. In the 1890s they invested in restaurants, apartments, furnished rooming houses, and dance halls where lodgers, male and female, could eat, sleep, and socialize without the presence of parental authorities. By the 1910s, women adrift flocked to and shaped these institutions, creating new peer-oriented subcultures.

Several historians of American wage-earning women have focused recently on the challenges that women in trade unions and informal work cultures posed at the turn of the century to the power of employers.[1] While women adrift participated in such efforts, as a group they posed their greatest challenge to sexual conventions. Observers recognized this early on. Late-nineteenth-century reformers feared that women without kin to protect them would succumb to sexual temptation, and early-twentieth-century sociologists saw women without kin to restrain them as avid sexual experimenters. In fact, women adrift ran the gamut from sexually inactive to sexually adventuresome. Those who chose to defy the conventions of their parents and of the middle class entered urban subcultures that sanctioned extramarital heterosexual and sometimes homosexual activity. The relationships they formed often combined sexual expression with economic strategy. Through dating, pickups, gold digging, temporary alliances, and occasional prostitution, they sometimes found excitement, companionship, and, not least, some relief from poverty.

These women adrift were not "emancipated" women in the sense that people often use the word today. The subcultures they formed failed to remedy low wages, promoted female economic dependence, and encouraged women to value themselves as sexual objects. Still, as they knew, their challenge had genuine, though limited, meaning. They defied the sexual double standard, explored sexual desire, and established independence from supervision, at least in their leisure hours. In so doing, they helped forge the modern sexual expression that replaced Victorian reticence.

From the 1880s to the 1920s, the woman adrift, and especially her sexual behavior, captured public notice. With the onset of the Great Depression, though, the public interest all but died. During the 1930s, the poverty of self-supporting women seemed little different from the more widespread poverty of women, men, and children who lived in families. In fact, the situation of self-supporting women often seemed less dire than that of unemployed women and men who had dependent children. Furthermore, by the end of the 1920s, many middle-class women had adopted a more sexually expressive style; in this context, the sexual behavior of women adrift no longer provoked alarm or even comment. In addition, during the 1930s the number of women adrift declined temporarily. Fewer migrants arrived in the city looking for work, and many unemployed migrants returned to rural small-town homes where food for subsistence might be grown more easily.[2] When migration increased again during and after World War II, few Americans noticed the woman adrift. She had become an accepted figure in the urban landscape.

The history of women adrift is not an isolated episode in American women's history. Other historians note that wage work promoted autonomous female migration to cities. They also describe sexual experimentation among the female migrants. From at least the 1830s to at least the 1960s, women who left their families and came to the cities for work sometimes explored the boundaries of sexual convention.[3]

Sociologists and anthropologists today draw a similar picture of change in some third world nations. In parts of Latin America, Asia, and Africa, women leave their homes in increasing numbers for work in the cities and in the export zones where multinational corporations operate factories.[4] The obvious and major differences of time and place, economy and culture distinguish third world nations today from the United States at the turn of the century. In kinship configurations, filial piety, marriage customs, occupational distribution, and employment conditions, the women adrift of turn-of-the-century Chicago differ vastly from, say, the contemporary women migrants to the export zones of Malaysia. Nevertheless, the similarities are in some ways striking.

In the broadest of outlines, the story of third world women migrants resembles the story of women adrift. As in the United States, third world women today leave their homes for both economic and non-economic reasons. Poverty pushes them from their homes, and jobs lure them to the cities. At the same time, abusive patriarchal authority, stigmatized premarital pregnancies, oppressive arranged marriages, and other "female" motives impel autonomous migration.[5] Working primarily in service and manufacturing jobs, these women find, as did women adrift, that employers often pay them the low wages of dependent daughters or wives.[6] Further, in some cities, these migrants also find themselves vulnerable to sexual exploitation and stigmatized as sexually suspect because of their lone status.[7] With little social, political, or economic power, most autonomous women migrants today face limited options in some ways similar to those faced by women adrift in American cities earlier. They can work for low wages, or they can accept higher-paying sexual service jobs.[8] They can maintain tradition, or they can assert their independence from the customs of their parents.[9] They can lead isolated lives, or they can cooperate with and depend on others. As in the United States, observers notice and often lament changes in sexual mores, in some cases the "Westernization" of life-styles.[10] Here too sexual expression is often tied to financial reward. Temporary heterosexual alliances and occasional prostitution offer poorly paid women a means to supplement income.[11]

To point to these similarities is not to suggest that the complex and diverse experiences of self-supporting women in various third world nations today replicate the experiences of women adrift of turn-of-the-century Chicago. Stated simply, they do not. The similarities are important, though, for they place the women adrift in their broader historical context—the ongoing world history of industrial capitalism, urban growth, and autonomous female migration.

Appendix
Women Adrift Samples

Much of the quantitative data in this book is derived from two samples of "women adrift" drawn from the federal manuscript censuses of Chicago of 1880 and 1910. The samples were drawn systematically from the entire city of Chicago; they are equivalent to random samples. For 1880, I selected all women adrift on every fourth page of the manuscript census of Chicago. For 1910, when the city was much larger, I selected all women adrift on every thirty-fifth page.* The 1880 sample had 957 women; the 1910 sample had 905.

I defined women adrift as gainfully employed women who did not live with kin or with employers. To select these women, I used the following census categories: surname, relationship to household head, sex, and occupation. I selected gainfully employed women who had no familial relationship to the household head, who were not employees of the household head, and who had a different surname from all other members of the household. Almost all of these women were listed (under relationship to household head) as boarders, lodgers, roomers, or tenants. I also selected gainfully employed women who lived alone, and I included gainfully employed women household heads when all other members of the household had different surnames from her and no listed familial relationship to her. In the few multiperson households without listed heads, I coded data on gainfully employed women who had different surnames from all other members of the household. I included women who lived in hotels and organized boarding homes but excluded women who lived in institutions such as prisons and convents.

For each woman selected, I recorded all of the census information available. I also coded data on the household head and the household size and composition. Much of this data appears in the tables and in

*Thanks to Ian Reiff of the Newberry Library for help in constructing these samples.

the text. Finally, for households with more than one roomer, I recorded how many of the fellow boarders and lodgers were born in the same state or foreign nation as the women adrift, how many of her fellow female boarders and lodgers worked in the same occupation, and what occupational categories they worked in. After analyzing this last-mentioned data with the computer, I found virtually nothing of major interest: in both 1880 and 1910, few women lived with other roomers who worked in the same specific occupation, and, not surprisingly, service and factory workers (often blacks and immigrants) did not usually live with clericals, sales workers, or semiprofessionals (often native-born whites); native-born women migrants (black or white) did not cluster with other roomers from the same state of birth, but immigrants (especially recent immigrants) tended to live with other roomers from the same nation of birth. Because most women married and changed their names after marriage and because many women were not listed in city directories, I did not attempt to trace individuals over time.

A traditional occupational classification (unskilled labor, semis-killed labor, skilled labor, low white collar, professional) did not capture the female labor market; therefore, I used my own categories in this study. These categories are service (day-working servant, waitress, dish-washer, etc.), needle trades (seamstress, dressmaker, etc.), other manufacturing (meat-packer, bookbinder, etc.), clerical (file clerk, stenographer, etc.), sales (saleswoman, cashier, etc.), entrepreneurial/ managerial (store keeper, rooming house keeper, supervisor, etc.), sem-iprofessional (nurse, teacher, etc.), professional (doctor, lawyer, etc.), and other (fortune-tellers, ragpickers, etc.).

The results of the quantitative study are only as accurate as the raw data. In this respect, as social historians know, the manuscript census falls short. Census data are notoriously rife with error. Among other inaccuracies, census takers may well have undercounted the number of women adrift. Heads of crowded homes, fearing the housing inspector, may have failed to list all of their lodgers. And women adrift themselves, fearing stigmatization, may have claimed to live with family or kin. While the census provides the best (and sometimes the only) available source for quantitative assessment, the inadequacies of the data should be kept in mind.

Notes

Introduction

1. On middle- and upper-class New Women, see June Sochen, *The New Woman: Feminism in Greenwich Village, 1910–1920* (New York: Quadrangle Books, 1972); Elaine Showalter, ed., *These Modern Women: Autobiographical Essays from the Twenties* (Old Westbury, N.Y.: Feminist Press, 1978); Rosalind Rosenberg, *Beyond Separate Spheres: Intellectual Roots of Modern Feminism* (New Haven: Yale University Press, 1982); Carroll Smith-Rosenberg, "The New Woman as Androgyne: Social Disorder and Gender Crisis, 1870–1936," in *Disorderly Conduct: Visions of Gender in Victorian America* (New York: Alfred A. Knopf, 1985); Esther Newton, "The Mythic Mannish Lesbian: Radclyffe Hall and the New Woman," *Signs: Journal of Women in Culture and Society* (Summer 1984): 557–75.

2. U.S. Bureau of the Census, *Tenth Census, 1880, Population*, vol. 1, p. 712; idem, *Fifteenth Census, 1930, Population*, vol. 3, pt. 1, p. 12.

3. I use the phrase "women adrift" as it was used in the early twentieth century, to refer to wage-earning women who did not live with kin or with employers. In the nineteenth century, writers often used the adjective *adrift* to describe women who had no family nearby and who were not live-in domestic servants, but the label "woman adrift" was not popularized until a federal report of 1910.

4. U.S. Bureau of the Census, *Statistics of Women at Work* (Washington, D.C.: Government Printing Office, 1907), p. 27. This figure does not include the large group of women working as "servants and waitresses," most of whom lived in the homes of their employers.

5. See appendix.

6. One possible solution was to purchase from the Census Bureau "public use samples" or summaries of raw census data from targeted neighborhoods in 1920 and 1930. Unfortunately such samples were not feasible for this study. While the Census Bureau will summarize one or more variables for targeted tracts, it will not select out women adrift, whom I defined fairly complexly by looking at several census variables simultaneously. (To select a woman adrift, I looked at relationship to household head [no relation and not

employee], occupation [gainfully employed], sex [female], and surname [different from all other members of household]).

7. Edward Shorter, *The Making of the Modern Family* (New York: Basic Books, 1975), p. 260. This once-standard interpretation was adopted by both orthodox Marxists and liberal historians. Shorter's study of eighteenth-century European women is probably the most strongly stated recent account.

8. Leslie Woodcock Tentler, *Wage-Earning Women: Industrial Work and Family Life in the United States, 1900–1930* (New York: Oxford University Press, 1979), p. 86. This interpretation emerged as a refutation of Edward Shorter's work; see Louise Tilly, Joan W. Scott, and Miriam Cohen, "Women's Work and European Fertility Patterns," *Journal of Interdisciplinary History* (Winter 1976); and Louise A. Tilly and Joan W. Scott, *Women, Work, and Family* (New York: Holt, Rinehart and Winston, 1978). See also Virginia Yans-McLaughlin, *Family and Community: Italian Immigrants in Buffalo, 1880–1930* (Ithaca: Cornell University Press, 1977); Miriam Cohen, "Italian-American Women in New York City, 1900–1950: Work and School," in Milton Cantor and Bruce Laurie, ed., *Class, Sex, and the Woman Worker* (Westport, Conn.: Greenwood Press, 1977); Tamara K. Hareven, *Family Time and Industrial Time: The Relationship between the Family and Work in a New England Industrial Community* (Cambridge: Cambridge University Press, 1982); Sarah Eisenstein, *Give Us Bread but Give Us Roses: Working Women's Consciousness in the United States, 1890 to the First World War* (London: Routledge and Kegan Paul, 1983); Judith E. Smith, *Family Connections: A History of Italian and Jewish Immigrant Lives in Providence, Rhode Island, 1900–1940* (Albany: State University of New York, 1985).

9. Tentler, *Wage-Earning Women*, p. 116.

10. See, for examples, Barbara Melosh, *"The Physician's Hand": Work Culture and Conflict in American Nursing* (Philadelphia: Temple University Press, 1982); Susan Porter Benson, *Counter Cultures: Saleswomen, Managers, and Customers in American Department Stores, 1890–1940* (Urbana: University of Illinois Press, 1986); Dolores Janiewski, *Sisterhood Denied: Race, Gender, and Class in a New South Community* (Philadelphia: Temple University Press, 1985); Kathy Peiss, *Cheap Amusements: Working Women and Leisure in Turn-of-the-Century New York* (Philadelphia: Temple University Press, 1986); Christine Stansell, *City of Women: Sex and Class in New York, 1789–1860* (New York: Alfred A. Knopf, 1986).

11. For the pioneering essay on women's culture, see Carroll Smith-Rosenberg, "The Female World of Love and Ritual: Relations between Women in Nineteenth-Century America," *Signs* (Autumn 1975); for sociological theories on networks and subcultures, see David J. O'Brien and Mary Joan Roach, "Recent Developments in Urban Sociology," *Journal of Urban History* (February 1984); Claude S. Fischer, "Toward a Subcultural Theory of Urbanism," *American Journal of Sociology* (May 1975).

12. The Fall 1985 issue of *Feminist Studies* explores the potential for change in women's work cultures. In that issue see Micaela di Leonardo, "Women's Work, Work Culture, and Consciousness (an Introduction)"; Cynthia B. Costello, "WEA're Worth It! Work Culture and Conflict at the Wisconsin Education

Association Insurance Trust"; Louise Lamphere, "Bringing the Family to Work: Women's Culture on the Shop Floor"; and Patricia Zavella, " 'Abnormal Intimacy': The Varying Work Networks of Chicana Cannery Workers."

13. See John D'Emilio, "Capitalism and Gay Identity," in Ann Snitow, Christine Stansell, and Sharon Thompson, eds., *Powers of Desire: The Politics of Sexuality* (New York: Monthly Review Press, 1983).

14. Frederick Lewis Allen, *Only Yesterday* (New York: Harper and Brothers, 1931); William Leuchtenburg, *The Perils of Prosperity, 1914–1932* (Chicago: University of Chicago Press, 1958); Henry May, *The End of American Innocence: A Study of the First Years of Our Own Time, 1912–1917* (New York: Alfred A. Knopf, 1959); James McGovern, "The American Woman's Pre–World War I Freedom in Manners and Morals," *Journal of American History* (September 1968); Gerald Critoph, "The Flapper and Her Critics," in Carol V. R. George, ed., *"Remember the Ladies": New Perspectives on Women in American History* (Syracuse: Syracuse University Press, 1975).

15. Daniel Scott Smith, "The Dating of the American Sexual Revolution: Evidence and Interpretation," in Michael Gordon, ed., *The American Family in Social-Historical Perspective* (New York: St. Martin's Press, 1973); Lewis A. Erenberg, *Steppin' Out: New York Nightlife and the Transformation of American Culture, 1890–1930* (Westport, Conn.: Greenwood Press, 1981); Peiss, *Cheap Amusements*.

Chapter 1. Apart from Family

1. Theodore Dreiser, *Sister Carrie* (New York: Random House, 1932).

2. On women's work in the family economy in the late-nineteenth- and early-twentieth-century United States, see Virginia Yans-McLaughlin, "Italian Women and Work: Experience and Perception," and Miriam Cohen, "Italian-American Women in New York City, 1900–1950: Work and School," in Milton Cantor and Bruce Laurie, eds., *Class, Sex, and the Women Worker* (Westport, Conn.: Greenwood Press, 1977); Elizabeth Pleck, "A Mother's Wages: Income Earning among Married Italian and Black Women, 1896–1911," in Michael Gordon, ed., *The American Family in Social-Historical Perspective*, 2d ed. (New York: St. Martin's Press, 1978); Leslie Woodcock Tentler, *Wage-Earning Women: Industrial Work and Family Life in the United States, 1900–1930* (New York: Oxford University Press, 1979); Tamara K. Hareven, *Family Time and Industrial Time: The Relationship between the Family and Work in a New England Industrial Community* (Cambridge: Cambridge University Press, 1982); Judith E. Smith, *Family Connections: A History of Italian and Jewish Immigrant Lives in Providence, Rhode Island, 1900–1940* (Albany: State University of New York Press, 1985); Sarah Eisenstein, *Give Us Bread but Give Us Roses: Working Women's Consciousness in the United States, 1890 to the First World War* (London: Routledge and Kegan Paul, 1983).

3. Julie A. Matthaei, *An Economic History of Women in America: Women's Work, the Sexual Division of Labor, and the Development of Capitalism* (New York: Schocken Books, 1982), chap. 3; Mary P. Ryan, *Womanhood in America: From*

Colonial Times to the Present, 2d ed. (New York: New Viewpoints, 1979), pp. 11, 14, 15, 31; Mary Beth Norton, *Liberty's Daughters: The Revolutionary Experience of American Women, 1750–1800* (Boston: Little, Brown, 1980), chap. 5; on colonial slaves, see Winthrop D. Jordan, *White over Black: American Attitudes toward the Negro, 1550–1812* (Chapel Hill: University of North Carolina Press, 1968); Edmund S. Morgan, *American Slavery American Freedom: The Ordeal of Colonial Virginia* (New York: W. W. Norton, 1975); on indentured servants, see Abbot Emerson Smith, *Colonists in Bondage: White Servitude and Convict Labor in America, 1607–1776* (Chapel Hill: University of North Carolina Press, 1947); James Axtell, *The School upon a Hill: Education and Society in Colonial New England* (New York: W. W. Norton, 1974); for a nineteenth-century example of indentured servitude, see Harriet E. Wilson, *Our Nig; Or, Sketches from the Life of a Free Black* (New York: Vintage Books, 1983); on early-nineteenth-century household help, see Faye Dudden, *Serving Women: Household Service in Nineteenth-Century America* (Middletown, Conn.: Wesleyan University Press, 1983), chap. 1; on early-nineteenth-century apprenticeship as servants, see Michael Katz, *The People of Hamilton, Canada West: Family and Class in a Mid-Nineteenth-Century City* (Cambridge: Harvard University Press, 1975), p. 270.

4. Jane Riblett Wilkie, "The Black Urban Population of the Pre–Civil War South," *Phylon* (September 1976): 257, 260; Suzanne Lebsock, *The Free Women of Petersburg: Status and Culture in a Southern Town, 1784–1860* (New York: W. W. Norton, 1984), p. 99.

5. Joseph F. Kett, *Rites of Passage: Adolescence in America, 1790 to the Present* (New York: Basic Books, 1977), p. 96.

6. Katz, *People of Hamilton, Canada West,* p. 266.

7. Joseph A. Hill, *Women in Gainful Occupations, 1870–1920* (Washington, D.C.: Government Printing Office, 1921), p. 36.

8. The best recent account of early-nineteenth-century self-supporting women is found in Christine Stansell, *City of Women: Sex and Class in New York, 1789–1860* (New York: Alfred A. Knopf, 1986), pp. 83–85.

9. Matthew Carey, "Address to the Ladies in New York Who Have Undertaken to Establish a House of Industry," in Matthew Carey, *Miscellaneous Essays* (New York: Burt Franklin, 1966; orig. 1830), p. 280. In her sample from the New York State Census of 1855, Stansell counted 151 boarders among the 400 single working women selected from New York City's Fourth Ward. Whether this high proportion of lodgers is representative of other wards or other cities is not yet known. Stansell, *City of Women,* p. 253.

10. Helen L. Sumner, *History of Women in Industry in the United States,* vol. 9 in the *Report on Condition of Woman and Child Wage-Earners in the U.S.* (Washington, D.C.: Government Printing Office, 1910), p. 22.

11. Alice Kessler-Harris, *Out to Work: A History of Wage-Earning Women in the United States* (New York: Oxford University Press, 1982), p. 76.

12. Sumner, *History of Women in Industry,* p. 22.

13. Barbara Mayer Wertheimer, *We Were There: The Story of Working Women in America* (New York: Pantheon Books, 1977), p. 153; on earlier protests

by seamstresses, see Kessler-Harris, *Out to Work,* p. 40; on protests in New York, see Stansell, *City of Women,* chap. 7.

14. On the hardships of seamstresses, see Mary Christine Stansell, "Women of the Laboring Poor in New York City, 1820–1860," Ph.D. dissertation, Yale University, 1979, pp. 68–75; Kessler-Harris, *Out to Work,* pp. 77–81.

15. Virginia Penny, *The Employment of Women: A Cyclopedia of Women's Work* (Boston: Walker, Wise, 1863), pp. 309, 310, her emphasis.

16. *Chicago Daily Tribune,* September 4, 1873, p. 2.

17. U.S. Bureau of the Census, *Statistics of Women at Work* (Washington, D.C.: Government Printing Office, 1907), derived from table 26, pp. 198, 199.

18. Ibid., table 28, pp. 228, 230.

19. U.S. Bureau of the Census, *Tenth Census, 1880, Population,* vol. 1, p. 712; idem, *Fifteenth Census, 1930, Population,* vol. 3, pt. 1, p. 12.

20. *Fifteenth Census, 1930, Population,* vol. 4, p. 42.

21. *Tenth Census, 1880, Population,* vol. 1, p. 720; *Fifteenth Census, 1930, Population,* vol. 3, pt. 1, p. 12.

22. Hill, *Women in Gainful Occupations,* p. 36; *Fifteenth Census, 1930, Population,* vol. 4, pp. 60–62.

23. Hill, *Women in Gainful Occupations,* p. 138; see also David Katzman, *Seven Days a Week: Women and Domestic Service in Industrializing America* (New York: Oxford University Press, 1978).

24. *Tenth Census, 1880, Population,* vol. 1, p. 870; *Fifteenth Census, 1930, Population,* vol. 4, p. 440.

25. *Fifteenth Census, 1930, Population,* vol. 4, p. 80.

26. Ibid., vol. 3, pt. 1, p. 22. The census defines cities as places with over twenty-five hundred inhabitants.

27. These estimates are derived from systematic samples of women adrift drawn from the federal manuscript censuses of Chicago; see appendix.

28. Other studies include: Commissioner of Labor, *Fourth Annual Report, 1888: Working Women in Large Cities* (Washington, D.C.: Government Printing Office, 1889); Illinois Bureau of Labor Statistics, *Seventh Biennial Report, 1892,* pt. 1: *Working Women in Chicago* (Springfield, Ill.: H. W. Rokker, 1893); Illinois Bureau of Labor Statistics, *Fifteenth Biennial Report, 1908,* pt. 3: *Women Employed in Department Stores* (Springfield, Ill.: Illinois State Journal Co., 1910); Charles P. Neill, *Wage-Earning Women in Stores and Factories,* vol. 5 in the *Report on Condition of Woman and Child Wage-Earners in the United States* (Washington, D.C.: Government Printing Office, 1910); Hill, *Women in Gainful Occupations;* U.S. Women's Bureau, *Women Workers in Flint, Michigan,* Bulletin 67 (Washington, D.C.: Government Printing Office, 1929).

29. This estimate is the more conservative of two estimates calculated. It is 14 percent of the nonservant adult female labor force in 1930. Earlier surveys of Chicago and other cities of comparable size showed that women adrift consistently comprised over 14 percent of the nonservant adult female labor force. In the second method of estimation, I multiplied the proportions of women adrift in Chicago in each race and nativity category in 1910 by the

numbers of adult women in each race and nativity category in Chicago in 1930. The sum here was approximately 57,200.

30. I use the term *single* to refer to women never married. Unless otherwise noted, the statistical evidence here and in the following pages is drawn from my census samples of women adrift in Chicago in 1880 and 1910; see appendix.

31. Anderson, "Life History of a Rooming House Keeper," c. 1925, Burgess Papers 127:2, University of Chicago Manuscript Collections; interview conducted by author at the Amalgamated Clothing and Textile Workers Union Retirement Center, August 27, 1980.

32. Interview conducted by author with Pauline R., September 12, 1980.

33. Case records of Sarah K. and Caroline O., U.S. Women's Bureau Papers, Record Group 86, Bulletin 158, Survey Materials, Box 347: 584–M27– Woodlawn and 578–M21–Woodlawn, National Archives, Washington, D.C. I am grateful to Lois Rita Helmbold for sharing these records with me.

34. U.S. Bureau of the Census, *Thirteenth Census, 1910, Population,* vol. I, p. 619.

35. *Statistics of Women at Work,* p. 29.

36. Ibid., p. 29. For similar findings among white male and female boarders and lodgers in late-nineteenth-century Boston, see Mark Peel, "On the Margins: Lodgers and Boarders in Boston, 1860–1900," *Journal of American History* (March 1986): 817. On the high proportion of black women "adrift" in New York in 1905 and 1925, see Herbert G. Gutman, *The Black Family in Slavery and Freedom, 1750–1925* (New York: Pantheon Books, 1976), pp. 450, 453.

37. For examples, see E. G. Ravenstein, "The Laws of Migration," *Journal of the Statistical Society* (June 1885): 199; Adna Ferrin Weber, *The Growth of Cities in the Nineteenth Century: A Study in Statistics* (New York: Macmillan, 1899), pp. 276–80; Donald J. Bogue, *Principles of Demography* (New York: John Wiley, 1969), p. 169. For more recent findings, see Ester Boserup, *Women's Role in Economic Development* (New York: St. Martin's Press, 1970), pp. 186–87; Elizabeth Jelin, "Migration and Labor Force Participation of Latin American Women: The Domestic Servants in the Cities," *Signs: Journal of Women in Culture and Society* (Fall 1977): 129–41; Orlando Patterson, "Migration in Caribbean Societies: Socioeconomic and Symbolic Resource," in William H. McNeill and Ruth S. Adams, eds., *Human Migration: Patterns and Policies* (Bloomington: Indiana University Press, 1978), p. 115; James T. Fawcett, Siew-ean Khoo, and Peter C. Smith, eds., *Women in the Cities of Asia: Migration and Urban Adaptation* (Boulder, Colo.: Westview Press, 1984).

38. Bengt Ankarloo, "Agriculture and Women's Work: Directions of Change in the West, 1700–1900," *Journal of Family History* (Summer 1979): 118.

39. U.S. Bureau of the Census, *Farm Population of the United States, 1920* (Washington, D.C.: Government Printing Office, 1926), p. 62.

40. Carle C. Zimmerman, "The Migration to Towns and Cities," *American Journal of Sociology* (November 1926): 450–55; C. Warren Thornthwaite,

Internal Migration in the United States (Philadelphia: University of Pennsylvania Press, 1934), p. 32; E. C. Young, *The Movement of Farm Population* (Ithaca: Cornell University Agricultural Experiment Station, 1924), pp. 16, 20.

41. In 1880 and in 1910, most of the women adrift who listed northeastern birthplaces were, in fact, older than most of the migrants from the Midwest. Some had probably lived in Chicago for many years; others had probably moved more than once, perhaps settling in Ohio or Indiana before moving on to Chicago. Census data give the state of birth only. With this limited information, we cannot tell when a woman migrated to Chicago nor can we tell how many women adrift came from rural areas and how many came from towns and cities.

42. Inez Evangeline Bolin, "Religious Adjustments of the Newcomer Girl in Chicago," M.A. thesis, University of Chicago, 1931, p. 4.

43. *Fifteenth Census, 1930, Population,* vol. 2, pp. 216–18; see also, Allan H. Spear, *Black Chicago: The Making of a Negro Ghetto, 1890–1920* (Chicago: University of Chicago Press, 1967).

44. Because Poland did not exist as an independent nation in 1910, it was not listed as a place of birth in the 1910 census. Polish immigrants are distinguished in the census from Germans, Austrians, and Russians by the language listed in the census category "mother tongue." This may well provide an inaccurate enumeration of Poles in Chicago, but it is the best (and only) enumeration available.

45. On Italian and Jewish women in strong family and kin networks, see Virginia Yans-McLaughlin, *Family and Community: Italian Immigrants in Buffalo, 1880–1930* (Ithaca: Cornell University Press, 1977); Cohen, "Italian-American Women in New York City, 1900–1950"; Elizabeth Ewen, *Immigrant Women in the Land of Dollars: Life and Culture on the Lower East Side, 1890–1925* (New York: Monthly Review Press, 1985); Smith, *Family Connections.* We have no comparable work on German-American women. For a contrasting picture of independent Irish women, see Hasia Diner, *Erin's Daughters in America: Irish Immigrant Women in the Nineteenth Century* (Baltimore: Johns Hopkins University Press, 1983).

46. See, for example, Peter A. Morrison, "The Functions and Dynamics of the Migration Process," in Alan A. Brown and Egon Neuberger, eds., *Internal Migration: A Comparative Perspective* (New York: Academic Press, 1977), p. 63.

47. Young, *Movement of Farm Population,* pp. 20, 23, 24. In 1900, 23 percent of adult women in larger cities (population of one hundred thousand or more) worked in the wage labor force; only 18 percent worked for wages in the rest of the nation. By 1920, the gap had widened. Thirty-three percent of adult women worked for wages in larger cities while only 21 percent worked for wages in smaller cities, towns, and rural areas. In both years, this rural-urban gap in jobs per capita was larger for women (more than twice as large) than it was for men. Derived from *Twelfth Census, 1900, Population,* vol. 2, pp. 550–601; Hill, *Women in Gainful Occupations,* p. 9; *Fourteenth Census, 1920, Population,* vol. 4, pp. 33, 128.

48. For example, in 1900 only 16.6 percent of adult women worked for wages in Youngstown while 23.2 percent worked for wages in Chicago. *Twelfth Census, 1900, Population,* vol. 2, pp. cliii, clv.

49. Travelers' Aid Society of Chicago, *Report of the General Secretary for the Year Ending March 31, 1919.*

50. Paul G. Cressey, *The Taxi-Dance Hall: A Sociological Study in Commercialized Recreation and City Life* (Chicago: University of Chicago Press, 1932), p. 56.

51. See, for example, "Dance School Investigated," copy of news item, c. 1920, Juvenile Protective Association of Chicago Papers 104, University of Illinois at Chicago Manuscript Collections.

52. Travelers' Aid Society of Chicago, *Ninth Annual Report, 1923.*

53. Emmett J. Scott, *Negro Migration during the War* (New York: Arno Press, 1969), p. 17.

54. Emmett J. Scott, "Letters of Negro Migrants of 1916–1918," *Journal of Negro History* (July 1919): 333.

55. Emmett J. Scott, "Additional Letters of Negro Migrants of 1916–1918," *Journal of Negro History* (October 1919): 413.

56. Anderson, "Life History of a Rooming House Keeper."

57. Louise DeKoven Bowen, *The Department Store Girl* (Chicago: Juvenile Protective Association of Chicago, 1911), p. 11.

58. Mary Kenney O'Sullivan, typewritten autobiography, Schlesinger Library, Radcliffe College, p. 27.

59. Scott, "Letters of Negro Migrants," p. 316.

60. E. Franklin Frazier, *The Negro Family in Chicago* (Chicago: University of Chicago Press, 1932), p. 81.

61. Scott, "Additional Letters of Negro Migrants," p. 426.

62. Ruth Shonle Cavan, *Business Girls: A Study of Their Interests and Problems* (n.p.: Religious Education Association, 1929), p. 1.

63. Vice Commission of Chicago, *The Social Evil in Chicago: A Study of Existing Conditions with Recommendations by the Vice Commission of Chicago* (Chicago: Vice Commission of Chicago, 1911), p. 132.

64. Some readers might question the veracity of explanations women migrants gave to charity workers and social investigators. To screen out unreliable accounts, I have not included any "stories" that seemed inconsistent, overtly self-serving, or maudlin. The accounts of pregnancy, seduction, prostitution, incest, and self-seeking included here seem to me at least as honest or sincere as the accounts that focus on economic need. In an era that placed a high value on female chastity and selflessness, most women would probably not fabricate such potentially embarrassing reasons for leaving home.

65. Travelers' Aid Society of Chicago, *Report of the General Secretary for the Year Ending March 31, 1919.*

66. Seth Cook Rees, *Miracles in the Slums, or Thrilling Stories of Those Rescued from the Cesspools of Iniquity, and Touching Incidents in the Lives of the Unfortunate* (Chicago: Seth Cook Rees, 1905), p. 120.

67. Interview with Philiminia P., conducted by author, October 24, 1980.

68. See, for example, interview with Pauline G., Oral History Archives of Chicago Polonia GOL-027, Chicago Historical Society.

69. Louise DeKoven Bowen, *The Straight Girl on the Crooked Path: A True Story* (Chicago: Juvenile Protective Association of Chicago, 1916), p. 2.

70. John Regan, *Crimes of White Slavers and the Results* (Chicago: J. Regan and Co., 1912), p. 94.

71. "Alma N. Z——r," Paul Cressey notes, c. 1926, Ernest Burgess Papers 129:6, University of Chicago Manuscript Collections.

72. See, for example, Illinois General Assembly, *Report of the Senate Vice Committee* (Chicago: n.p., 1916), p. 388.

73. Case record, 1/7/88, Illinois Humane Society Papers 3, University of Illinois at Chicago Manuscript Collections.

74. Rees, *Miracles in the Slums,* p. 120.

75. Case record, Juvenile Protective Association of Chicago Papers, Supplement I:7, University of Illinois at Chicago Manuscript Collections.

76. *Social Evil in Chicago,* p. 95.

77. Travelers' Aid Society of Chicago, *Report of the General Secretary for the Year Ending March 31, 1919.*

78. Walter C. Reckless, *Vice in Chicago* (Chicago: University of Chicago Press, 1933), p. 46.

79. YWCA of Chicago, *36th Annual Report* (1912), p. 29.

80. See Tentler, *Wage-Earning Women,* pp. 73, 89; Louise Montgomery, *The American Girl in the Stockyards District* (Chicago: University of Chicago Press, 1913), pp. 57, 58; Ewen, *Immigrant Women in the Land of Dollars,* pp. 104–8, 208–14.

81. *Social Evil in Chicago,* p. 189; Louise DeKoven Bowen, *Safeguards for City Youth at Work and at Play* (New York: Macmillan, 1914), p. 165.

82. "Lillian S. W——n," Paul Cressey notes, c. 1926, Ernest Burgess Papers 129:6, University of Chicago Manuscript Collections.

83. Case record, 11/15/99, Juvenile Protective Association of Chicago Papers, Supplement I:9, University of Illinois at Chicago Manuscript Collections.

84. YWCA of Chicago, *38th Annual Report* (1914).

85. Quoted in William A. McKeever, *Farm Boys and Girls* (New York: Macmillan, 1912), p. 238. John Mack Faragher has argued that farm daughters also migrated to escape the drudgery that befell farm wives; see John Mack Faragher, "Sister Carrie's Sisters: White Country Girls in the City of Chicago, 1880–1930," typescript, 1983.

86. Ruth Shonle Cavan, "Suicide: A Study of Personal Disorganization," Ph.D. dissertation, University of Chicago, 1926, p. 66.

87. Cressey, *Taxi-Dance Hall,* p. 65.

88. See, for examples, YWCA of Chicago, *45th Annual Report* (1921), p. 17; Cavan, *Business Girls,* p. 1.

89. Frazier, *Negro Family in Chicago,* p. 7.

90. Bolin, "Religious Adjustments of the Newcomer Girl in Chicago," p. 16.

91. See, for example, Elizabeth Rauh Bethel, *Promisedland: A Century of Life in a Negro Community* (Philadelphia: Temple University Press, 1981), p. 36.

92. For a recent example of the "resilient family" model, see Hareven, *Family Time and Industrial Time*.

93. See especially Louise A. Tilly and Joan W. Scott, *Women, Work, and Family* (New York: Holt, Rinehart and Winston, 1978), p. 121.

94. On the family as a "locus of struggle" in a different context, see Heidi I. Hartmann, "The Family as the Locus of Gender, Class, and Political Struggle: The Example of Housework," *Signs: Journal of Women in Culture and Society* (Spring 1981): 368.

95. Dreiser, *Sister Carrie*, pp. 75, 78.

Chapter 2: "A Lone Woman Can't Be Too Careful"

1. U.S. Bureau of the Census, *Tenth Census, 1880, Social Statistics of Cities,* pt. 2, p. 494; idem, *Tenth Census, 1880, Population,* vol. 1, p. 417.

2. U.S. Bureau of the Census, *Fifteenth Census, 1930, Metropolitan Districts,* p. 49; idem, *Fifteenth Census, 1930, Population,* vol. 3, p. 61.

3. *Historic City: The Settlement of Chicago* (Chicago: Department of Development and Planning, 1976); Bessie Louise Pierce, *A History of Chicago,* vol. 3, *The Rise of a Modern City, 1871–1893* (New York: Alfred A. Knopf, 1967).

4. Harvey Warren Zorbaugh, *The Gold Coast and the Slum: A Sociological Study of Chicago's Near North Side* (Chicago: University of Chicago Press, 1929), p. 76.

5. Interview with Pauline G., Oral History Archives of Chicago Polonia GOL-027, Chicago Historical Society.

6. "How Chicago YWCA Solves Girl Problem," *Chicago Whip,* May 20, 1922; YWCA of Chicago, *48th Annual Report* (1924), p. 17.

7. League of the Protection of Immigrants, *Annual Report, 1909–1910,* pp. 16, 17.

8. Immigrants' Protective League, *Seventh Annual Report* (1916), p. 9.

9. Travelers' Aid Society of Chicago, *Report of the General Secretary for the Year Ending March 31, 1919.*

10. Case record, 6/25/91, Illinois Humane Society Papers 5:6/91, University of Illinois at Chicago Manuscript Collections.

11. Jean Turner-Zimmerman, *Chicago's Black Traffic in White Girls* (n.p., 1912), p. 37.

12. See, for examples, YWCA of Chicago, *21st Annual Report* (1897), p. 36; YWCA of Chicago, *34th Annual Report* (1910), p. 31; Travelers' Aid Society of Chicago, *Second Annual Report* (1916), p. 10.

13. "Louise T——n," Paul Cressey notes, 2/24/26, Ernest Burgess Papers 129:6, University of Chicago Manuscript Collections.

14. See, for example, Mary Kenney O'Sullivan autobiography, typewritten manuscript, Schlesinger Library, Radcliffe College, p. 28.

15. Letter from Anna H——k, 3/3/28, Immigrants' Protective League Papers 50, University of Illinois at Chicago Manuscript Collections.

16. Emmett J. Scott, "Letters of Negro Migrants of 1916–1918," *Journal of Negro History* (July 1919): 317. Domestic servants did not always find the safety they sought. Some employment agencies cheated women or charged outrageous fees; some employers abused their servants. See Frances A. Kellor, "Southern Colored Girls in the North: The Problem of Their Protection," *Charities*, March 18, 1905, pp. 584–85.

17. In 1880, 11.3 percent of the women adrift I sampled from the manuscript census lived alone; in 1910, 12.7 percent. For a description of the sample, see appendix.

18. Louise DeKoven Bowen, *The Straight Girl on the Crooked Path: A True Story* (Chicago: Juvenile Protective Association of Chicago, 1916), p. 2.

19. Chicago Commission on Race Relations, *The Negro in Chicago* (Chicago: University of Chicago Press, 1922), p. 165.

20. Mrs. John Van Vorst and Marie Van Vorst, *The Woman Who Toils: Being the Experiences of Two Ladies as Factory Girls* (New York: Doubleday, Page, 1903), p. 101.

21. For a description of room registries in Chicago, see Ann Elizabeth Trotter, *Housing of Non-Family Women in Chicago: A Survey* (Chicago: Chicago Community Trust, c. 1921), pp. 22–26.

22. Chicago Commission on Race Relations, *Negro in Chicago*, p. 16; see also Franklin Kline Fretz, *The Furnished Room Problem in Philadelphia* (n.p., 1912), p. 59; for a fictional account, see Anzia Yezierska, *Bread Givers* (New York: Persea Books, 1975; orig. 1925), p. 157.

23. Group interview at Amalgamated Clothing and Textile Workers' Union Retirement Center in Chicago, conducted by author, August 27, 1980; also see Theresa Wolfson, *The Woman Worker and the Trade Unions* (New York: International Publishers, 1926), p. 43.

24. Frances Donovan, *The Woman Who Waits* (Boston: Richard G. Badger, Gorham Press, 1920), p. 99.

25. Theodore Thomas Cowgill, "The Employment Agencies of Chicago," M.A. thesis, University of Chicago, 1928.

26. See Bowen, *Straight Girl*, p. 6.

27. William T. Stead, *If Christ Came to Chicago! A Plea for the Union of All Who Love in the Service of All Who Suffer* (London: Review of Reviews, 1894), p. 245.

28. Wolfson, *Woman Worker and the Trade Unions*, p. 115; see also YWCA of Chicago, *12th Annual Report* (1888), p. 21; for a fictional account, see Theodore Dreiser, *An American Tragedy* (New York: New American Library, 1964; orig. 1925), p. 240.

29. YWCA of Chicago, *19th Annual Report* (1895), p. 34.

30. Ruth Shonle Cavan, *Suicide* (Chicago: University of Chicago Press, 1928), p. 277.

31. See David M. Katzman, *Seven Days a Week: Women and Domestic Service in Industrializing America* (New York: Oxford University Press, 1978).

32. See Estelle Hill Scott, *Occupational Changes among Negroes in Chicago* (Chicago: Illinois Work Projects Administration, 1939), pp. 33, 68, 118, 184, 232.

By 1930, over one-half of native-born white women adrift also worked in clerical jobs; see Inez Evangeline Bolin, "Religious Adjustments of the Newcomer Girl in Chicago," M.A. thesis, University of Chicago, 1931, p. 11.

33. See Scott, *Occupational Changes among Negroes in Chicago,* pp. 33, 68, 118, 184, 232.

34. Ibid.

35. On Irish women as domestic servants, see Hasia Diner, *Erin's Daughters in America: Irish Immigrant Women in the Nineteenth Century* (Baltimore: Johns Hopkins University Press, 1983), chap. 4; on Jewish women as garment workers and Polish women as factory workers, see Alice Kessler-Harris, *Out to Work: A History of Wage-Earning Women in the United States* (New York: Oxford University Press, 1982), p. 138; and Sarah Eisenstein, *Give Us Bread but Give Us Roses: Working Women's Consciousness in the United States, 1890 to the First World War* (London: Routledge and Kegan Paul, 1983), p. 53. See also Barbara Klaczynska, "Why Women Work: A Comparison of Various Groups— Philadelphia, 1910–1930," *Labor History* (Winter 1976).

36. In 1910, rooming house keepers comprised 4.0 percent of women adrift, but only 2.5 percent of the Chicago female labor force. In the same year, nurses comprised 6.2 percent of women adrift, but only 3.0 percent of the Chicago female labor force. Restaurant workers (dishwashers, waitresses, and what census takers labeled "in restaurant") accounted for 6.1 percent of women adrift; published census data only include waitresses at 1.6 percent of the Chicago female labor force. Laundresses comprised 8.4 percent of women adrift and 5.7 percent of the Chicago female labor force. The figures drawn from published census data are based on calculations that exclude domestic servants. The job titles published in the 1880 census are not specific enough to permit similar comparisons for that year.

In various studies and surveys, other jobs appear to have high proportions of women adrift. The findings vary greatly from study to study. For example, two studies conducted in 1908 surveyed department store saleswomen in Chicago. One study found that 48 percent of saleswomen lived adrift; the other found only 20 percent adrift. The 1900 special census report on women at work showed teachers and stenographers as overrepresented among women adrift; my sample from 1910, however, found both teachers and stenographers underrepresented. The year of the study, the sampling techniques, and the definition of women adrift apparently led to different results.

On the proportion of saleswomen adrift found in surveys of various cities, see Susan Porter Benson, *Counter Cultures: Saleswomen, Managers, and Customers in American Department Stores, 1890–1940* (Urbana: University of Illinois Press, 1986), pp. 310–11.

37. *Chicago Times,* August 3, 1888.

38. Illinois General Assembly, *Report of the Senate Vice Committee* (Chicago, n.p., 1916), p. 33.

39. Louise Montgomery, *The American Girl in Stockyards District* (Chicago: University of Chicago Press, 1913), p. 58.

40. Neill, *Wage-Earning Women in Stores and Factories,* pp. 106, 113, 118. These figures take into account layoffs and fines.

41. Louise Marion Bosworth, *The Living Wage of Women Workers: A Study of Incomes and Expenditures of 450 Women in the City of Boston,* Women's Educational and Industrial Union, Department of Research, Studies in Economic Relations of Women, vol. 3 (New York: Longmans, Green, 1911), p. 16.

42. National Industrial Conference Board, *Wages in the United States, 1914–1930* (New York: National Industrial Conference Board, 1931), p. 52. For an extended discussion of women's wages, see Leslie Woodcock Tentler, *Wage-Earning Women: Industrial Work and Family Life in the United States, 1900–1930* (New York: Oxford University Press, 1979), chap. 1.

43. *Report and Year-Book of the Women's Trade Union League of Illinois, 1907–1908.*

44. Bosworth, *Living Wage of Women Workers,* p. 11.

45. *Report of the Senate Vice Committee,* p. 116.

46. *Chicago Tribune,* June 10, 1911.

47. "What Is a Living Wage for Girls?" newspaper article, c. 1910, in Chicago Women's Trade Union League Papers, University of Illinois at Chicago Manuscript Collections, folder 1.

48. Quoted in Thomas H. Russell, *The Girl's Fight for a Living: How to Protect Working Women From Dangers Due to Low Wages* (Chicago: M. A. Donahue and Co., 1913), p. 189.

49. *Report of the Senate Vice Committee,* pp. 340, 338.

50. Neill, *Wage-Earning Women in Stores and Factories,* p. 116.

51. *Report of the Senate Vice Committee,* p. 388.

52. *Wages in the United States,* pp. 214, 215.

53. Elyce J. Rotella, *From Home to Office: U.S. Women at Work, 1870–1930* (Ann Arbor: University Microfilms International Research Press, 1981), p. 201.

54. *Los Angeles Times,* June 1, 1930; clipping found in National Consumers League Papers C49: IV R-16, Library of Congress.

55. "Employment of Colored Women in Chicago," *The Crisis,* January, 1911, p. 24.

56. Chicago Urban League, *Two Decades of Service, 1916–1936* (n.p., c. 1936). These jobs were lost when Sears closed some of its offices during the depression of 1921 and 1922.

57. Alma Herbst, *The Negro in the Slaughtering and Meatpacking Industry in Chicago* (Boston: Houghton Mifflin, 1932), p. 30. See also Jacqueline Jones, *Labor of Love, Labor of Sorrow: Black Women, Work, and the Family from Slavery to the Present* (New York: Basic Books, 1985), chap. 6.

58. Protective Agency for Women and Children, *Second Annual Report* (1888).

59. Edith Abbott and S. P. Breckinridge, "Women in Industry in the Chicago Stockyards," *Journal of Political Economy* (October 1911): 646.

60. Neill, *Wage-Earning Women in Stores and Factories,* p. 25.

61. Ibid., pp. 47, 42.

62. Mary Anderson, as told to Mary N. Winslow, *Woman at Work: The Autobiography of Mary Anderson* (Minneapolis: University of Minnesota Press, 1951).

63. Frances R. Donovan, *The Saleslady* (Chicago: University of Chicago Press, 1929), p. 183.

64. Donovan, *Woman Who Waits,* p. 96.

65. Anderson, "Life History of a Rooming House Keeper," c. 1925, Ernest Burgess Papers 127:2, University of Chicago Manuscript Collections, p. 9.

66. Neill, *Wage-Earning Women in Stores and Factories,* pp. 47, 42.

67. Case record, Caroline O., U.S. Women's Bureau Papers, Record Group 86, Bulletin 158, Survey Materials, Box 347: 584–M27–Woodlawn, National Archives, Washington, D.C.

68. Case record, Cora J., U.S. Women's Bureau Papers, Record Group 86, Bulletin 158, Survey Materials, Box 346:482–K34–Union Park, National Archives, Washington, D.C.

69. Case record, Sarah K., U.S. Women's Bureau Papers, Record Group 86, Bulletin 158, Survey Materials, Box 347: 578–M21–Woodlawn, National Archives, Washington, D.C.

70. Anderson, "Life History of a Rooming House Keeper," pp. 10, 15, 18, 19.

71. Louise DeKoven Bowen, *The Department Store Girl: Based upon Interviews with 200 Girls* (Chicago: Juvenile Protective Association of Chicago, 1911), p. 11.

72. *Chicago's Dark Places: Investigations by a Corps of Specially Appointed Commissioners* (Chicago: Craig Press and Women's Temperance Publishing Association, 1891), p. 130.

73. "Ill, Penniless Girl Tries to Die but Is Rescued," *Chicago Sunday Tribune,* September 28, 1919.

74. *Chicago Record-Herald,* January 4, 1912, p. 3.

75. Vice Commission of Chicago, *The Social Evil in Chicago: A Study of Existing Conditions with Recommendations* (Chicago: Vice Commission of Chicago, 1911), pp. 228, 272. Many of these women would not be classified as women adrift, since those in brothels with madames, like live-in domestic servants, boarded with their employers.

76. Russell, *Girl's Fight for a Living,* p. 162.

77. *Report of the Senate Vice Committee,* p. 211.

78. On the lives of prostitutes, see Ruth Rosen, *The Lost Sisterhood: Prostitution in America, 1900–1918* (Baltimore: Johns Hopkins University Press, 1982); for a perceptive discussion of prostitutes in the early nineteenth century, see Christine Stansell, *City of Women: Sex and Class in New York, 1789–1860* (New York: Alfred A. Knopf, 1986), chap. 9.

79. Harold R. Vynne, *Chicago by Day and Night: The Pleasure Seeker's Guide to the Paris of America* (Chicago: Thomas and Zimmerman, 1892), p. 49.

80. Junius B. Wood, *The Negro in Chicago,* reprint of series of articles in the *Chicago Daily News,* December 11–27, 1916.

81. Taxi dancers were women who worked in closed (as opposed to public) dance halls. They danced with male customers who paid a small fee, usually a dime per dance.

82. *Chicago's Dark Places,* p. 125.

83. *Report of the Senate Vice Committee,* pp. 477, 506.

84. Louise DeKoven Bowen, *The Road to Destruction Made Easy in Chicago* (Chicago: Juvenile Protective Association of Chicago, 1916), p. 13.

85. Letter from Rose to Hymie, April 5, c. 1926, Paul Cressey notes, Ernest Burgess Papers 129:6, University of Chicago Manuscript Collections.

86. Florence Wenderoth Saunders, *Letters to a Business Girl* (Chicago: Laird and Lee, 1908), p. 73.

Chapter 3. Orphans and Innocents

1. *Chicago Daily Tribune,* September 1, 1873.

2. Ibid., September 14, 1873.

3. Ibid., September 16, 1873; November 2, 1873.

4. Ibid., September 8, 1873.

5. Ibid., September 17, 1873.

6. Ibid., November 17, 1873.

7. Ibid., September 21, 1873.

8. For an early-nineteenth-century version of middle-class sentimental images of working-class women, see Christine Stansell, *City of Women: Sex and Class in New York, 1789–1860* (New York: Alfred A. Knopf, 1986), chap. 4.

9. Barbara J. Berg, *The Remembered Gate: Origins of American Feminism, the Woman and the City, 1800–1860* (New York: Oxford University Press, 1978); Mary P. Ryan, "The Power of Women's Networks: A Case Study of Female Moral Reform in Antebellum America," *Feminist Studies* (Spring 1979): 66–85; Carroll Smith-Rosenberg, "Beauty, the Beast, and the Militant Woman: A Case Study of Sex Roles and Social Stress in Jacksonian America," in Nancy F. Cott and Elizabeth H. Pleck, eds., *A Heritage of Her Own: Toward a New Social History of American Women* (New York: Simon and Schuster, 1979), pp. 197–221; Nancy A. Hewitt, *Women's Activism and Social Change: Rochester, New York, 1822–1872* (Ithaca: Cornell University Press, 1984); Mary P. Ryan, *Cradle of the Middle Class: The Family in Oneida County, New York, 1790–1865* (Cambridge: Cambridge University Press, 1981); Anne M. Boylan, "Women in Groups: An Analysis of Women's Benevolent Organizations in New York and Boston, 1797–1840," *Journal of American History* (December 1984): 497–523; Stansell, *City of Women,* chap. 4.

10. Some such organizations existed before 1830. See, for example, John K. Alexander, *Render Them Submissive: Responses to Poverty in Philadelphia, 1760–1800* (Amherst, Mass.: University of Massachusetts Press, 1980), p. 135.

11. New York Female Benevolent Society, *Annual Report,* 1838, quoted in Berg, *Remembered Gate,* p. 80.

12. Berg, *Remembered Gate,* p. 232; on institution building, see Lori D. Ginzburg, " 'Moral Suasion is Moral Balderdash': Women, Politics, and Social Activism in the 1850's," *Journal of American History* (December 1986): 601–22.

13. John J. Flinn, *Chicago: A History, An Encyclopedia, and a Guide,* 2d ed. (Chicago: Standard Guide, 1892), p. 183.

14. See Mari Jo Buhle, "The Nineteenth-Century Women's Movement: Perspectives on Woman's Labor in Industrializing America," typescript, Bunting Institute of Radcliffe College, 1979; William Leach, *True Love and Perfect Union: The Feminist Reform of Sex and Society* (New York: Basic Books, 1980), chap. 7.

15. Berg, *Remembered Gate,* p. 250.

16. Mary S. Sims, *The Natural History of a Social Institution: The Young Women's Christian Association* (New York: Woman's Press, 1936), pp. 5–7.

17. Woman's Christian Association of Chicago, *First Annual Report* (1877), Constitution.

18. Ibid., p. 12; WCA of Chicago, *Second Annual Report* (1878), p. 10.

19. *Fourth Annual Report of the Commissioner of Labor, 1888: Working Women in Large Cities* (Washington, D.C.: Government Printing Office, 1889), pp. 32–57.

20. Mary S. Fergusson, "Boarding Homes and Clubs for Working Women," *Bulletin of the Department of Labor* (March 1898): 178.

21. Elizabeth Jeanne Humphreys, "Working Women in Chicago Factories and Department Stores, 1870–1895," M.A. thesis, University of Chicago, 1943, p. 50.

22. Fergusson, "Boarding Homes and Clubs," p. 178; see also Annie Marion MacLean, "Homes for Working Women in Large Cities," *Charities Review* (July 1899): 216–19; John Visher, *Handbook of Charities,* 3d ed. (Chicago: Charles H. Kerr, 1897).

23. Essie Mae Davidson, "Organized Boarding Homes for Self-Supporting Women in the City of Chicago," M.A. thesis, University of Chicago, 1914, table 2; Ann Elizabeth Trotter, *Housing of Non-Family Women in Chicago: A Survey* (Chicago: Chicago Community Trust, c. 1921), pp. 17–22.

24. Josephine J. Taylor, "Study of YWCA Room Registry," typescript, 1928, Ernest Burgess Papers 138:9, University of Chicago Manuscript Collections. I have adjusted the figures cited to discount the homes for transient women and unwed mothers. Because the 1928 YWCA report did not list the homes individually, I estimated adjustment here. The YWCA report counted seventy-one homes; I estimate that it should be reduced to around sixty-five.

25. Davidson, "Organized Boarding Homes," table 2.

26. Trotter, *Housing of Non-Family Women,* pp. 17–22; Taylor, "Study of YWCA Room Registry."

27. Handwritten minutes, Chicago YWCA, July 16, 1877, YWCA Papers, University of Illinois at Chicago Manuscript Collections.

28. On the "colored branch" home, see Henry J. McGuinn, "Recreation," in T. J. Woofter, Jr., ed., *Negro Problems in Cities* (Garden City: Doubleday, Doran, 1928), p. 246; and also YWCA of Chicago, *Annual Report* from 1915 on.

29. Davidson, "Organized Boarding Homes," table 2; Trotter, *Housing of Non-Family Women,* pp. 17–22; on Olivet Baptist Church home, see Miles Mark Fisher, "The History of the Olivet Baptist Church of Chicago," M.A. thesis, University of Chicago, 1922, p. 91; on the New First Congregational Church home, see *Social Service Directory of Chicago, 1926* (Chicago: Council of Social Agencies, 1926); on the Guardian Angel Day Nursery and Home for Working Girls, see *Poles of Chicago, 1837–1937* (Chicago: Polish Pageant, Inc., 1937), p. 119; on Jewish clubs, see Hyman L. Meites, ed., *History of the Jews of Chicago* (Chicago: Jewish Historical Society of Illinois, c. 1924); on Elam Club Home, see letter from Tillie Frankenthal, March 18, 1930, and "The Melissia Ann Elam Club Home for Girls," May 10, 1930, Julius Rosenwald Papers XIV:14, University of Chicago Manuscript Collections; on Eleanor Club, see *Chicago Tribune,* May 16, 1914.

30. Humphreys, "Working Women in Chicago Factories and Department Stores"; "The Working Girls' Clubs of Chicago," March, 1896, unknown newspaper, Hull House Scrapbook III, Hull House Association Papers. A few examples are the Wildwood Club which had a vacation home and the Chicago Woman's Club which offered working women low-cost shares in summer cottages; the Ogontz Club, the Ursula Club, and the King's Daughters which served lunches; the Girls' Friendly Society, the Industrial Arts Club, and the Aloha Club which were social and educational groups. For an overview of such groups nationally, see Lynn Y. Weiner, *From Working Girl to Working Mother: The Female Labor Force in the United States, 1820–1980* (Chapel Hill: University of North Carolina Press, 1985), pp. 61–63.

31. Dorothy Edwards Powers, "The Chicago Woman's Club," M.A. thesis, University of Chicago, 1939, p. 122; Henriette Greenebaum Frank and Amalie Hofer Jerome, comps., *Annals of the Chicago Woman's Club for the First Forty Years of Its Organization, 1876–1916* (Chicago: Chicago Woman's Club, 1916), p. 169; Chicago Relief and Aid Society, *34th Annual Report* (1891).

32. In 1908 an independent organization, the Immigrants' Protective League, was formed to continue this work. Grace Abbott directed the organization. See Immigrants' Protective League Papers, University of Illinois at Chicago Manuscript Collections.

33. Trotter, *Housing of Non-Family Women,* pp. 23–25; Ford S. Black, comp., *Black's Blue Book* (Chicago: F. S. Black, 1921), p. 80. On the Woman's Church Federation Protectorate and the Catholic Woman's League Protectorate (which ran a room registry only), see Chicago Council of Social Agencies, "Report of a Study of the Travelers' Aid Society of Chicago," May 1925, Welfare Council Papers 406, Chicago Historical Society.

34. WCA of Chicago, *Second Annual Report* (1878), p. 10; idem, *Fifth Annual Report* (1881), p. 10; idem, *Sixth Annual Report* (1882), p. 15.

35. YWCA of Chicago, *36th Annual Report* (1912), p. 20. The Woman's Christian Association of Chicago changed its name to the Young Women's Christian Association of Chicago in 1887, but it did not affiliate with the national YWCA until 1918.

36. WCA of Chicago, *Fifth Annual Report* (1881), p. 12. On reformers' concern for wage-earning women's morality, see also Alice Kessler-Harris, *Out to Work: A History of Wage-Earning Women in the United States* (New York: Oxford University Press, 1982), chap. 4.

37. WCA of Chicago, *Fifth Annual Report* (1881), bylaws.

38. YWCA of Chicago, *17th Annual Report* (1893), p. 32.

39. WCA of Chicago, *Fifth Annual Report* (1881), p. 23.

40. Ibid., p. 12.

41. YWCA of Chicago, *18th Annual Report* (1894), p. 33. On the national Travelers' Aid movement, see Weiner, *From Working Girl to Working Mother,* pp. 49–52.

42. YWCA of Chicago, *21st Annual Report* (1897), p. 36.

43. YWCA of Chicago, *28th Annual Report* (1904), p. 25.

44. Nancy F. Cott, "Passionlessness: An Interpretation of Victorian Sexual Ideology, 1790–1850," in Nancy F. Cott and Elizabeth H. Pleck, eds., *A Heritage of Her Own: Toward a New Social History of American Women* (New York: Simon and Schuster, 1979), pp. 162–81.

45. Smith-Rosenberg, "Beauty, the Beast, and the Militant Woman"; see also Berg, *Remembered Gate,* p. 172.

46. See Nancy F. Cott, *The Bonds of Womanhood: "Woman's Sphere" in New England, 1780–1830* (New Haven: Yale University Press, 1977), chap. 2; Carroll Smith-Rosenberg, "Sex as Symbol in Victorian Purity: An Ethno-historical Analysis of Jacksonian America," in John Demos and Sarane Spence Boocock, eds., *Turning Points: Historical and Sociological Essays on the Family* (Chicago: University of Chicago Press, 1978).

47. For another example of the home as remedy, see Estelle B. Freedman, *Their Sisters' Keepers: Women's Prison Reform in America, 1830–1930* (Ann Arbor, University of Michigan Press, 1981), p. 55.

48. WCA of Chicago, *Fourth Annual Report* (1880), p. 14; idem, *First Annual Report* (1877), p. 21.

49. YWCA of Chicago, *19th Annual Report* (1895), p. 26.

50. YWCA of Chicago, *22d Annual Report* (1898), p. 34.

51. WCA of Chicago, *Seventh Annual Report* (1883), p. 11.

52. Frances Willard, *How to Win: A Book for Girls* (New York: Funk and Wagnalls, 1887), p. 54.

53. On perceived threats to the family, see Christopher Lasch, *Haven in a Heartless World: The Family Besieged* (New York: Basic Books, 1977); William L. O'Neill, "Divorce in the Progressive Era," in Michael Gordon, ed., *The American Family in Social-Historical Perspective,* 2d ed. (New York: St. Martin's Press, 1978), pp. 140–51.

54. Barbara Leslie Epstein, *The Politics of Domesticity: Women, Evangelism, and Temperance in Nineteenth-Century America* (Middletown, Conn.: Wesleyan University Press, 1981), p. 128.

55. WCA of Chicago, *Fifth Annual Report* (1881), p. 20.

56. WCA of Chicago, *Seventh Annual Report* (1883), p. 10; see also idem, *Sixth Annual Report* (1882), p. 10.

57. Allan Stanley Horlick, *Country Boys and Merchant Princes: Social Control of Young Men in New York* (Lewisburg, Pa.: Bucknell University Press, 1975), p. 161; see also Smith-Rosenberg, "Sex as Symbol"; and Paul Boyer, *Urban Masses and Moral Order in America, 1820–1920* (Cambridge: Harvard University Press, 1978).

58. Elizabeth Wilson, *Fifty Years of Association Work among Young Women, 1866–1916: A History of Young Women's Christian Associations in the United States of America* (New York: National Board of YWCAs, 1916), p. 31.

59. *Social Service Directory of Chicago, 1915* (Chicago: Department of Public Welfare, 1915), St. Joseph's Home for Working Girls; Visher, *Handbook of Charities*, pp. 124, 177; Antoinette V. Wakeman, "Model Lodging House," *Gate City Catalogue*, May 16, 1895, in Hull House Scrapbook III, Hull House Association Papers; Katherine A. Jones, "The Working Girls of Chicago," *Review of Reviews* (September 1891).

60. *Social Service Directory of Chicago, 1915*, Bethany Home for Young Women.

61. See Jacqueline Jones, *Labor of Love, Labor of Sorrow: Black Women, Work, and the Family from Slavery to the Present* (New York: Basic Books, 1985), p. 146; Paula Giddings, *When and Where I Enter: The Impact of Black Women on Race and Sex in America* (Toronto: Bantam Books, 1984), p. 85.

62. Elizabeth Lindsey Davis, *The Story of the Illinois Federation of Colored Women's Clubs, 1900–1922* (n.p., 1922), pp. 16, 17.

63. Tillie S. Frankenthal, "Melissia Ann Elam Club Home for Girls," typewritten report, March 13, 1930, in Julius Rosenwald Papers XIV:14, University of Chicago Manuscript Collections.

64. Matthew Carey, "Address to the Ladies in New York Who Have Undertaken to Establish a House of Industry," in Matthew Carey, *Miscellaneous Essays* (New York: Burt Franklin, 1966; orig. 1830); Caroline H. Dall, "Lodging Houses for Young Women," *The Friend*, December 1867, pp. 376–86. I am grateful to Gary Sue Goodman for sharing the article by Caroline Dall.

65. For examples, see Harriet Fayes, "Housing of Single Women," *Municipal Affairs* (March 1899): 95–107; Clare de Graffenried, "The Needs of Self-Supporting Women," supplement to *Johns Hopkins University Studies in Historical and Political Science* (January 1890); Fergusson, "Boarding Homes and Clubs for Working Women."

66. MacLean, "Homes for Working Women in Large Cities," p. 228.

67. *Fourth Annual Report of the Commissioner of Labor*, pp. 31, 32.

68. Robert Stein, "Girls' Cooperative Boarding Homes," *The Arena*, March 1898, pp. 397–417. For a more general discussion of housing for working women and a feminist cooperative ideal, see Dolores Hayden, *The Grand Domestic Revolution: A History of Feminist Designs for American Homes, Neighborhoods, and Cities* (Cambridge: MIT Press, 1981), pp. 168–76, 254–58; see also Leach, *True Love and Perfect Union*, chap. 8.

69. Louisa May Alcott, *Work: A Story of Experience* (New York: Schocken Books, 1977), p. 128.

70. For a brief description of the "working girl" novel, see Cathy N. Davidson and Arnold E. Davidson, "Carrie's Sisters: The Popular Prototypes for Dreiser's Heroine," *Modern Fiction Studies* (Autumn 1977): 396.

71. The first fully developed American gothic romance found by literary critic Nina Baym was published in 1860. Baym distinguishes the romances from "women's fiction," such as Alcott's novels, by the lack of moral and intellectual content in romances. Nina Baym, *Woman's Fiction: A Guide to Novels by and about Women in America, 1820–1870* (Ithaca: Cornell University Press, 1978), p. 273.

In the serialized story papers, stories with the working woman as heroine boomed in the 1870s, and stories set in the cities became dominant in the 1880s; see Mary Noel, *Villains Galore: The Heyday of the Popular Story Weekly* (New York: Macmillan, 1954), pp. 277–79, 171.

Jean Carwile Masteller is writing a book-length study of working women in romance novels and melodramas. I am grateful for her generous sharing of sources and ideas.

72. Charlotte M. Stanley, "Violet, the Beautiful Street Singer; Or An Ill-Starred Betrothal," *New York Family Story Paper,* September 5, 1908.

73. Effie Adelaide Rowlands, *A Woman Scorned* (New York: Street and Smith, 1899), pt. 3, p. 7.

74. Abi S. Jackman, "Her Own Way; Or, Reaping the Harvest," *New York Family Story Paper,* December 18, 1897.

75. Ibid., January 22, 1898.

76. Ibid., December 26, 1897.

77. Ibid., April 2, 1898.

78. T. W. Hanshew, "Alone in New York: A Thrilling Portrayal of the Dangers and Pitfalls of the Metropolis," *New York Family Story Paper,* April 16, 1887.

79. Laura Jean Libbey, *Junie's Love Test* (New York: George Munro, 1883).

80. Hanshew, "Alone in New York," April 23, 1887.

81. Ibid., April 16, 1887.

82. Adah M. Howard, *Little Sunshine; Or, the Secret of the Death Chamber* (New York: Norman L. Munro, 1886), pp. 3, 8.

83. Hanshew, "Alone in New York," April 23 and 30, 1887.

84. Adah M. Howard, "Alice, the Candy Girl: Or, a Million of Money," *New York Family Story Paper,* April 26, 1880.

85. Libbey, *Junie's Love Test.*

86. "Laura Jean Libbey," in Edward T. James, ed., *Notable American Women, 1607–1950: A Biographical Dictionary* (Cambridge: Harvard University Press, 1971), vol. 2, pp. 402–3.

87. Noel, *Villains Galore,* p. 291.

88. Dorothy Richardson, *The Long Day: The Story of a New York Working Girl* (1905), in William L. O'Neill, *Women at Work* (New York: New York Times Books, 1972), p. 140.

89. Libbey, *Junie's Love Test,* p. 58.

90. Laura Jean Libbey, *Little Leafy, the Cloakmaker's Beautiful Daughter* (New York: N. L. Munro, 1891), p. 3.

91. Laura Jean Libbey, *Ione: A Broken Love Dream* (New York: Robert Bonner's Sons, 1887 and 1890), pp. 10, 23.

92. Ibid., p. 29.

93. Ibid., p. 28.

94. Libbey, *Little Leafy,* p. 20.

95. Rowlands, *A Woman Scorned,* p. 18.

96. See Mark Thomas Connelly, *The Response to Prostitution in the Progressive Era* (Chapel Hill: University of North Carolina Press, 1980); Ruth Rosen, *The Lost Sisterhood: Prostitution in America, 1900–1918* (Baltimore: Johns Hopkins University Press, 1982). See also John Burnham, "The Progressive Era Revolution in Attitudes toward Sex," *Journal of American History* (March 1973): 885–908.

97. Rosen, *Lost Sisterhood,* pp. 47–49. On early twentieth-century prostitutes and the spread of venereal disease, see Allan M. Brandt, *No Magic Bullet: A Social History of Venereal Disease in the United States Since 1880* (New York: Oxford University Press, 1985), Chap. 1.

98. *Chicago's Dark Places: Investigations by a Corps of Specially Appointed Commissioners* (Chicago: Craig Press and the Women's Temperance Publishing Association, 1891); William T. Stead, *If Christ Came to Chicago! A Plea for the Union of All Who Love in the Service of All Who Suffer* (London: Review of Reviews, 1894).

99. *Chicago's Dark Places,* p. 128.

100. Florence Mabel Dedrick, "Our Sister of the Street," in Ernest A. Bell, ed., *War on the White Slave Trade: A Book Designed to Awaken the Sleeping and to Protect the Innocent* (Chicago: n.p., 1909), p. 108.

101. Charles Bryon Chrysler, *White Slavery* (Chicago: n.p., 1909), p. 52.

102. F. M. Lehman and Rev. N. K. Clarkson, *The White Slave Hell, Or with Christ at Midnight in the Slums of Chicago* (Chicago: Christian Witness Co., 1910), p. 185.

103. Ibid., p. 150.

104. Robert O. Harland, *The Vice Bondage of a Great City or The Wickedest City in the World* (Chicago: Young People's Civic League, 1912), p. 195.

105. Leona Prall Groetzinger, *The City's Perils* (n.p., probably Chicago, c. 1910), p. 13.

106. Chrysler, *White Slavery,* p. 13.

107. Vice Commission of Chicago, *The Social Evil in Chicago: A Study of Existing Conditions with Recommendations by the Vice Commission of Chicago* (Chicago: Vice Commission of Chicago, 1911), p. 44.

108. Harland, *Vice Bondage,* p. 67.

109. Charles Washburn, *Come into My Parlor: A Biography of the Aristocratic Everleigh Sisters of Chicago* (New York: National Library Press, 1936), p. 243.

110. Virginia Brooks, *Little Lost Sister* (New York: Macaulay, 1914), pp. 362, 363.

111. Terry Ramsaye, *A Million and One Nights* (New York: Simon and Schuster, 1926), vol. 2, p. 617.

112. See Allen F. Davis, *Spearheads for Reform: The Social Settlements and the Progressive Movement, 1890–1914* (New York: Oxford University Press, 1967); on the shift from nineteenth-century female reformers to twentieth-century female social scientists, see Freedman, *Their Sisters' Keepers;* also see Rosalind Rosenberg, *Beyond Separate Spheres: Intellectual Roots of Modern Feminism* (New Haven: Yale University Press, 1982), pp. 110–11; Kathleen D. McCarthy, *Noblesse Oblige: Charity and Cultural Philanthropy in Chicago, 1849–1929* (Chicago: University of Chicago Press, 1982).

113. Some women in the Women's Trade Union League held this position. See *Chicago Record-Herald,* December 1, 1913.

114. Charles P. Neill, *Wage-Earning Women in Stores and Factories,* vol. 5 in the *Report on Condition of Woman and Child Wage-Earners in the United States* (Washington, D.C.: Government Printing Office, 1910).

115. Frances A. Kellor, "Assisted Emigration from the South—The Women," *Charities,* October 7, 1905, p. 12.

116. Bertha A. Loeb, "A Refuge for Homeless Women," *Chicago Record-Herald,* January 29, 1911.

117. On earlier literature on men, see Smith-Rosenberg, "Sex as Symbol," and Horlick, *Country Boys and Merchant Princes.*

118. "The Girl Who Comes to the City: A Symposium," *Harper's Bazaar,* January, 1908, p. 54.

119. "Non-Resident Unemployed Men in Chicago," in Chicago Bureau of Charities, *Fifth Annual Report* (1898–99), p. 32.

120. Louise Marion Bosworth, *The Living Wage of Women Workers: A Study of Incomes and Expenditures of 450 Women in the City of Boston* (New York: Longmans, Green, 1911); Edith M. Hadley, "The Housing Problem as It Affects Girls," *The Survey,* April 19, 1913, pp. 92–94; Lucile Eaves, *The Food of Working Women in Boston* (Boston: Wright and Potter, 1917).

121. Louise DeKoven Bowen, *Safeguards for City Youth at Work and at Play* (New York: Macmillan, 1914), p. 91.

122. Lawrence Veiller, *Housing Reform: A Handbook for Practical Use in American Cities* (New York: Russell Sage Foundation, 1910), p. 33.

123. Bosworth, *Living Wage,* p. 57.

124. Hadley, "Housing Problem," p. 94.

125. On environmentalism of early-twentieth-century female social scientists, see Freedman, *Their Sisters' Keepers,* chap. 6.

126. Fergusson, "Boarding Homes and Clubs," p. 142.

127. Jane Addams, *The Spirit of Youth and the City Streets* (Urbana: University of Illinois Press, 1972; orig. 1909), p. 8.

128. See, for example, Leslie Woodcock Tentler, *Wage-Earning Women: Industrial Work and Family Life in the United States, 1900–1930* (New York: Oxford University Press, 1979), p. 116.

Chapter 4: Surrogate Families

1. For similar accounts, see Sue Ainslie Clark and Edith Wyatt, *Making Both Ends Meet: The Income and Outlay of New York Working Girls* (New York: Macmillan, 1911); the works used in compiling this account include "Scant Pay for Girls," *Chicago Record-Herald,* March 16, 1907; Charles P. Neill, *Wage-Earning Women in Stores and Factories,* vol. 5 in the *Report on Condition of Woman and Child Wage-Earners in the United States* (Washington, D.C.: Government Printing Office, 1910); Louise Marion Bosworth, *The Living Wage of Women Workers: A Study of Incomes and Expenditures of 450 Women in the City of Boston,* vol. 3, Studies in Economic Relations of Women, Department of Research, Boston, Women's Educational and Industrial Union (New York: Longmans, Green, 1911); Lucile Eaves, *The Food of Working Women in Boston,* vol. 10, Studies in Economic Relations of Women, Department of Research, Boston, Women's Educational and Industrial Union (Boston: Wright and Potter, 1917).

2. Often, only size distinguished the boarding and rooming houses from private homes: investigators sometimes called a private home a commercial house when four or more lodgers lived there.

3. John Modell and Tamara K. Hareven, "Urbanization and the Malleable Household: An Examination of Boarding and Lodging in American Families," in Michael Gordon, ed., *The American Family in Social-Historical Perspective,* 2d ed. (New York: St. Martin's Press, 1978), pp. 59, 60; on caring for boarders as women's work, also see Carol Groneman, "She Earns as a Child—She Pays as a Man: Women Workers in a Mid-Nineteenth-Century New York City Community," in Richard Ehrlich, ed., *Immigrants in Industrial America* (Charlottesville: University Press of Virginia, 1977), p. 39. The landlady was not necessarily the owner of the house where she took in boarders. Landlords often charged higher rents in neighborhoods where they knew that renters took in boarders. In Chicago, this was especially true in black neighborhoods. On higher rents in black neighborhoods, see Alzada P. Comstock, "The Problem of the Negro," *American Journal of Sociology* (September 1912); and Elizabeth A. Hughes, *Living Conditions for Small-Wage Families in Chicago* (Chicago: Department of Public Welfare, City of Chicago, 1925), p. 35.

4. For a different discussion of these advantages, see Leslie Woodcock Tentler, *Wage-Earning Women in the United States, 1890–1930* (New York: Oxford University Press, 1979), p. 120.

5. Neill, *Wage-Earning Women in Stores and Factories,* p. 116.

6. Women's Trade Union League of Chicago, *Official Report of the Strike Committee, Chicago Workers' Strike, October 29, 1910–February 18, 1911,* pamphlet in National Women's Trade Union League Papers 59, Schlesinger Library, Radcliffe College, p. 20.

7. Thomas H. Russell, *The Girl's Fight for a Living: How to Protect Working Women from Dangers Due to Low Wages* (Chicago: M. A. Donahue, 1913), p. 164.

8. Virginia Brooks, *My Battles with Vice* (New York: Macauley, 1915), p. 68.

9. Census of Back of the Yards, Ethelbert Stewart Collection, Oversize Collections, Chicago Historical Society. In 26 out of 38 households with both male and female lodgers, women paid less than men. In 17 out of 38 households, women paid half or less of what men paid.

10. Interview with Philiminia P., conducted by author, October 24, 1980.

11. For single women adrift, the age difference was larger. In 1880, single women adrift were on average seventeen years younger than their households heads; in 1910, fifteen years younger. On the age difference between lodgers and household heads in Boston, see Modell and Hareven, "Urbanization and the Malleable Household," pp. 176–77.

12. For a description of several room registries, see Ann Elizabeth Trotter, *Housing of Non-Family Women in Chicago: A Survey* (Chicago: Chicago Community Trust, c. 1921), pp. 22–26.

13. See Albert B. Wolfe, "The Problem of the Roomer," *Charities*, November 2, 1907, p. 959.

14. "The Girl Who Comes to the City: A Symposium," *Harper's Bazaar*, October 1908, p. 1005.

15. Harvey W. Zorbaugh, "The Dweller in Furnished Rooms: An Urban Type," in Ernest W. Burgess, ed., *The Urban Community: Selected Papers from the Proceedings of the American Sociological Society, 1925* (Chicago: University of Chicago Press, 1926), p. 101; see also Albert Benedict Wolfe, *The Lodging House Problem in Boston* (Boston: Houghton Mifflin, 1906); and Franklin Kline Fretz, *The Furnished Room Problem in Philadelphia,* published Ph.D. dissertation, University of Pennsylvania (n.p., 1912).

16. The women adrift who were not boarders were listed as roomers, lodgers, or tenants. The sample sizes were as follows: 205 women adrift renting rooms in commercial lodgings in 1880, 248 women in commercial lodgings in 1910, 371 women in private families in 1880, 346 women in private families in 1910.

17. See, for example, *Chicago Defender,* March 30, 1918. On this day, the advertisements included sixty-eight listings for furnished rooms and only one listing for boarding.

18. See, for example, Edith Abbott, *The Tenements of Chicago, 1908–1935* (Chicago: University of Chicago Press, 1936), p. 330.

19. Newcomers here are defined as those women who had arrived in the United States after 1905.

20. In 1880, 62 percent of single women adrift over the age of thirty-five lived in private families. By 1910, only 27 percent of these women lived in private families.

21. Abbott, *Tenements of Chicago,* chap. 11.

22. Unfortunately, these data do not include breakdowns by sex. Comstock, "Problem of the Negro," pp. 241–57; Abbott, *Tenements of Chicago,* p. 361. I used Comstock, the original researcher, for the prewar data because she gives separate figures for each of the two neighborhoods while Abbott gives only

the aggregate. I did not use Abbott's figures on the "La Salle" neighborhood. Although she includes this neighborhood among the prewar canvases on p. 344, she states elsewhere, on p. 120, that the first canvas of this neighborhood was actually conducted after the war.

23. Trotter, *Housing of Non-Family Women,* p. 6.

24. Josephine J. Taylor, "Study of YWCA Room Registry," typescript, 1928, Ernest Burgess Papers 138:9, University of Chicago Manuscript Collections. Both this report and Trotter's report deal primarily with native-born white women.

The five-year decline included both a decline in the number of applicants to the room registry and, among applicants, an increase in the numbers looking for light housekeeping rooms and apartments rather than rooms in private families.

25. See Modell and Hareven, "Urbanization and the Malleable Household," p. 63. The depression decade of the 1930s may have temporarily reversed the trend of decline in boarding and lodging in private families.

26. For a somewhat different discussion of the change from boarding to lodging, see Mark Peel, "On the Margins: Lodgers and Boarders in Boston, 1860–1900," *Journal of American History* (March 1986): 820–23.

27. In Philadelphia, Franklin Kline Fretz wrote: "Many of the visitors did not care to have meals served at the homes in which they were staying." Fretz, *Furnished Room Problem in Philadelphia,* p. 30; see also Wolfe, *Lodging House Problem in Boston,* p. 48.

28. Illinois General Assembly, *Report of the Senate Vice Committee* (Chicago: n.p., 1916), p. 827.

29. See Neill, *Wage-Earning Women in Stores and Factories,* p. 62.

30. Taylor, "Study of the YWCA Room Registry," p. 2.

31. Interview with Pauline G., Oral History Archives of Chicago Polonia GOL-027, Chicago Historical Society. Interestingly, Pauline G. gave this account of boarding in response to the question, "How did you decide to marry?"

32. Abbott, *Tenements of Chicago,* pp. 309, 310, 315.

33. The term *light housekeeping* probably refers to the fact that a single-burner gas plate did not permit extensive or "heavy" cooking.

34. Homer Hoyt, *One Hundred Years of Land Values in Chicago: The Relationship of the Growth of Chicago to the Rise in Its Land Values, 1830–1933* (Chicago: University of Chicago Press, 1933), p. 231.

35. Vivien M. Palmer, "Study of the Development of Chicago's Northside," typewritten report for the United Charities, December 1932, Chicago Historical Society, p. 76.

36. Eaves, *Food of Working Women in Boston,* p. 168.

37. Taylor, "Study of YWCA Room Registry," p. 3. See also *Eleanor Record,* January 1919, p. 6.

38. Taylor, "Study of YWCA Room Registry," p. 3; Minutes of Sub-Committee on Housing of Girls' Work Section of Chicago Council of Social

Agencies, November 22, 1929, Welfare Council Papers 233, Chicago Historical Society. See also Inez Evangeline Bolin, "The Religious Adjustments of
the Newcomer Girl in Chicago," M.A. thesis, University of Chicago, 1931,
p. 20.

39. Bureau of Social Hygiene, *Housing Conditions of Employed Women
in the Borough of Manhattan* (New York: Bureau of Social Hygiene, 1922), pp. 8,
29, 11. The total number of women surveyed appears to be 1,641; the number
of black women surveyed was 509.

In Boston in 1911, Louise Marion Bosworth found similarly that women
adrift longed for their own apartments. Bosworth, *Living Wage*, pp. 19–21.

40. On the impact of another fair, the 1876 Centennial in Philadelphia,
on the shift from boarding to loading, see Fretz, *Furnished Room Problem in
Philadelphia*, p. 30; on the impact of World War I on housing in Chicago, see
Abbott, *Tenements of Chicago*, p. 317.

41. Many of these household heads were separated, divorced, or widowed women, but the increase occurred among older single women adrift as
well. Among foreign-born women (for whom the 1910 census gives year of
arrival in the United States), only 4 percent of newcomer women adrift lived
alone or headed households; in contrast, 44 percent of foreign-born women
adrift who had arrived in the United States between 1890 and 1905 lived alone
or headed households.

42. See, for examples, *Eleanor Record*, January 1917, p. 17, and January
1925, p. 12. Also see chap. 5. For a similar phenomenon in another city, see Lynn
Weiner, " 'Our Sister's Keepers': The Minneapolis Woman's Christian Association and Housing for Working Women," *Minnesota History* (Spring 1979): 200.

In 1910 the women who joined with roommates to rent flats or houses
were on average significantly older than the women who lived with private
families or in rooming houses, but they were on average significantly younger
than the women who headed households or lived alone. The average age of
these women after 1910, when this type of housing became more widespread,
is unknown.

43. David Katzman, *Seven Days a Week: Women and Domestic Service in
Industrializing America* (New York: Oxford University Press, 1978); see also
Helen Campbell, *Prisoners of Poverty: Women Wage-Workers, Their Trades and
Their Lives* (Boston: Roberts Brothers, 1887), pp. 223–31.

44. "Employment of Colored Women in Chicago," *The Crisis*, January
1911, p. 25.

45. "Anent Saleswomen: How They Live in America and Abroad,"
Chicago Inter Ocean, c. 1894, in Hull House Scrapbook I:54, Hull House.

46. On early factory housing, see Thomas Dublin, *Women at Work:
The Transformation of Work and Community in Lowell, Massachusetts, 1826–1860*
(New York: Columbia University Press, 1979).

47. Louise DeKoven Bowen, *The Girl Employed in Hotels and Restaurants* (Chicago: Juvenile Protective Association of Chicago, 1912).

48. "Home Making in the Illinois Bell Telephone Company," *Bell Telephone News*, January 1921, pp. 7–9.

49. *Social Service Directory of Chicago, 1926* (Chicago: Council of Social Agencies, 1926).

50. Edith M. Hadley, "The Housing Problem as It Affects Girls," *The Survey*, April 19, 1913, p. 94.

51. Interview with Pauline R., conducted by author, September 12, 1980.

52. YWCA of Chicago, *21st Annual Report* (1897), p. 28.

53. Case record of 7/14/91, Illinois Humane Society Papers, University of Illinois at Chicago Manuscript Collections.

54. YWCA of Chicago, *11th Annual Report* (1887), p. 23.

55. YWCA of Chicago, *33d Annual Report* (1909), p. 34.

56. Annie Marion MacLean, "Homes for Working Women in Large Cities," *Charities Review* (July 1899): 218; Trotter, *Housing of Non-Family Women*, p. 20.

57. For an example of expulsion, see Bolin, "Religious Adjustments of the Newcomer Girl," p. 36.

58. In some of the homes for black women, as in commercial housing for black lodgers, residents had kitchen privileges rather than prepared meals. The Phyllis Wheatley Home for black women did not provide meals when it first opened, nor did the Melissia Ann Elam Home for black women. Other homes for black working women, such as the Julia Johnson Home and the Indiana Avenue branch of the YWCA, did provide communal meals.

59. On outside financial support, see tables in Georgia Pearl McElroy, "Boarding Homes for Self-Supporting Women in Chicago," M.A. thesis, University of Chicago, 1913; Essie Mae Davidson, "Organized Boarding Homes for Self-Supporting Women in the City of Chicago," M.A. thesis, University of Chicago, 1914.

60. *Social Service Directory, 1915* (Chicago: City of Chicago, Department of Public Welfare, 1915).

61. Ibid.

62. Dedication of *Harriet Hammond McCormick Memorial*, December 23, 1928, privately printed.

63. Tillie S. Frankenthal, "Melissia Ann Elam Club Home for Girls," typewritten report, March 13, 1930, in Julius Rosenwald Papers XIV:14, University of Chicago Manuscript Collections.

64. See, for examples, YWCA of Chicago, *34th Annual Report* (1910), p. 34; and idem, *36th Annual Report* (1912), p. 31.

65. Mary S. Fergusson, "Boarding Homes and Clubs for Working Women," *Bulletin of the Department of Labor* (March 1898): 178; MacLean, "Homes for Working Women in Large Cities," pp. 217–19; Davidson, "Organized Boarding Homes," table 2; Taylor, "Study of YWCA Room Registry," table.

66. For figures on number of residents annually in Chicago YWCA, see annual reports.

67. *Chicago Daily Tribune*, September 28, 1873.

68. Esther Packard, *A Study of Living Conditions of Self-Supporting Women in New York City* (New York: Metropolitan Board of the YWCA, 1915), pp. 58, 59.

69. *Chicago Times,* August 12, 1888, p. 18.

70. Russell, *Girls' Fight For a Living,* p. 182.

71. Handwritten minutes, YWCA of Chicago, June 4, 1877, Chicago YWCA Papers, University of Illinois at Chicago Manuscript Collections.

72. Handwritten minutes, YWCA of Chicago, January 29, 1878, Chicago YWCA Papers, University of Illinois at Chicago Manuscript Collections.

73. Handwritten minutes, YWCA of Chicago, February 26, 1880, Chicago YWCA Papers, University of Illinois at Chicago Manuscript Collections.

74. *Sunday Inter Ocean,* November 16, 1890.

75. Abby Joan Pariser, "A History of the Early Years of the Chicago YWCA, 1879–1918," M.A. thesis, Roosevelt University, 1975.

76. YWCA of Chicago, *22d Annual Report* (1898), p. 40.

77. YWCA of Chicago, *23d Annual Report* (1899), p. 40.

78. See Fergusson, "Boarding Homes and Clubs"; Neill, *Wage-Earning Women in Stores and Factories;* Packard, *Study of Living Conditions;* McElroy, "Boarding Homes"; Davidson, "Organized Boarding Homes"; Elizabeth Beardsley Butler, *Women and the Trades, Pittsburgh, 1907–1908* (New York: Russell Sage Foundation, 1909).

79. Letter to the editor, *Life and Labor,* November 1913, p. 352.

80. Packard, *Study of Living Conditions,* p. 58.

81. Dorothy Richardson, *The Long Day: The Story of a New York Working Girl,* in William L. O'Neill, ed., *Women at Work* (New York: New York Times Books, 1972), pp. 157–59.

82. Florence Wenderoth Saunders, *Letters to a Business Girl* (Chicago: Laird and Lee, 1908), p. 15.

83. Fergusson, "Boarding Homes and Clubs," p. 146.

84. For examples of changes recommended, see Fergusson, "Boarding Homes and Clubs"; Neill, *Wage-Earning Women in Stores and Factories;* Packard, *A Study of Living Conditions;* McElroy, "Boarding Homes"; Davidson, "Organized Boarding Homes"; Butler, *Women and the Trades.*

85. Davidson, "Organized Boarding Homes," table 2; Trotter, *Housing of Non-Family Women,* pp. 17–22.

86. YWCA of Chicago, *43d Annual Report* (1919), p. 19; Trotter, *Housing of Non-Family Women,* p. 21. The six Eleanor Clubs in Chicago, which housed both college students and working women, had "house officers" who decided on "house rules"; *Chicago Tribune,* May 16, 1914.

87. Davidson, "Organized Boarding Homes," p. 19.

88. Trotter, *Housing of Non-Family Women,* p. 21.

89. Minutes of Subcommittee of Housing of Chicago Council of Social Agencies, March 18, 1925, Welfare Council Papers, Chicago Historical Society.

90. Allan Whitworth Bosch, "The Salvation Army in Chicago, 1885–1914," Ph.D. dissertation, University of Chicago, 1965, p. 261; Trotter, *Housing of Non-Family Women,* p. 21.

91. YWCA of Chicago, *39th Annual Report* (1915), p. 26, my emphasis.

92. Housing Committee of the YWCA, *Suggestions for Housing Women War Workers* (1918), p. 6.

93. YWCA of Chicago, *Report of the Emergency Bureau* (1924), p. 2.
94. YWCA of Chicago, *16th Annual Report* (1892), p. 26.
95. YWCA of Chicago, *21st Annual Report* (1897), pp. 37, 38.
96. YWCA of Chicago, *30th Annual Report* (1906), p. 27.
97. YWCA of Chicago, *51st Annual Report* (1927), p. 12.
98. YWCA of Chicago, *39th Annual Report* (1915), p. 26.
99. YWCA of Chicago, *43d Annual Report* (1919), p. 19.
100. YWCA of Chicago, *51st Annual Report* (1927), p. 12.
101. U.S. Bureau of Labor, Bureau of Industrial Housing and Transportation, *Report of the U.S. Housing Corporation* (Washington, D.C.: Government Printing Office, 1920), vol. 1, pp. 300, 301.
102. Taylor, "Study of YWCA Room Registry," p. 2.
103. Bolin, "Religious Adjustments of the Newcomer Girl," p. 29.
104. Ibid.
105. Davidson, "Organized Boarding Homes," table 2. A few of the homes also admitted students. By the 1910s, about one-half of all native-born white gainfully employed women in Chicago worked in clerical, sales, and kindred jobs (41 percent in 1910, 55 percent in 1920). See Estelle Hill Scott, *Occupational Changes among Negroes in Chicago* (Chicago: Illinois Work Projects Administration, 1939), pp. 118, 184.
106. Other historians have noted the same impulse toward independence. In her discussion of cooperative housing among self-supporting working women, Dolores Hayden writes: "The desire of women to control their own housing was expressed again and again." Dolores Hayden, *The Grand Domestic Revolution: History of Feminist Designs for American Homes, Neighborhoods and Cities* (Cambridge: MIT Press, 1981), p. 170; see also Weiner, "Our Sister's Keepers," p. 200.
107. Louise Montgomery, *The American Girl in the Stockyards District* (Chicago: University of Chicago Press, 1913), p. 59.
108. Mary E. McDowell, "The Young Girl in Industry," typescript, c. 1905, McDowell Papers 3:15, Chicago Historical Society.
109. Jane Addams, *A New Conscience and an Ancient Evil* (New York: Macmillan, 1912), p. 29.
110. See Tentler, *Wage-Earning Women,* p. 113; Elizabeth Ewen, "City Lights: Immigrant Women and the Rise of the Movies," *Signs* (Spring 1980 supplement): S57.

Chapter 5. "Friends to Help Them"

1. May Churchill Sharpe, *Chicago May: Her Story* (London: Sampson, Low, Marston, 1929), pp. 26, 28.
2. For more information on this underworld, see Harold R. Vynne, *Chicago by Day and Night: The Pleasure Seeker's Guide to the Paris of America* (Chicago: Thomas and Zimmerman, 1892), pp. 87–96, 202–3; Box-Car Bertha as told to Dr. Ben L. Reitman, *Sister of the Road: The Autobiography of Box-Car Bertha* (New York: Macauley, 1937), p. 261.

3. I use Claude Fischer's definition of subcultures: "social worlds . . . inhabited by persons who share relatively distinctive traits (like ethnicity or occupation), who tend to interact especially with one another, and who manifest a relatively distinct set of beliefs and behaviors." Claude S. Fischer, *The Urban Experience* (New York: Harcourt Brace Jovanovich, 1976), p. 36.

4. Illinois General Assembly, *Report of the Senate Vice Committee* (Chicago: n.p., 1916), p. 188.

5. On cooperation in families, see, for examples, Virginia Yans-McLaughlin, *Family and Community: Italian Immigrants in Buffalo, 1880–1930* (Ithaca: Cornell University Press, 1977); Miriam Cohen, "Italian-American Women in New York City, 1900–1950: Work and School," in Milton Cantor and Bruce Laurie, eds., *Class, Sex, and the Woman Worker* (Westport, Conn.: Greenwood Press, 1977); Leslie Woodcock Tentler, *Wage-Earning Women in the United States, 1900–1930* (New York: Oxford University Press, 1979); Tamara Hareven, *Family Time and Industrial Time: The Relationship between the Family and Work in a New England Industrial Community* (Cambridge: Cambridge University Press, 1982); Judith Smith, *Family Connections: A History of Italian and Jewish Immigrant Lives in Providence, Rhode Island, 1900–1940* (Albany: State University of New York Press, 1985). On cooperation in unions, see Meredith Tax, *The Rising of the Women: Feminist Solidarity and Class Conflict, 1880–1917* (New York: Monthly Review Press, 1980); Susan Levine, *Labor's True Woman: Carpet Weavers, Industrialization, and Labor Reform in the Gilded Age* (Philadelphia: Temple University Press, 1984); Joan M. Jensen and Sue Davidson, eds., *A Needle, A Bobbin, A Strike: Women Needleworkers in America* (Philadelphia: Temple University Press, 1984).

6. For examples of informal cooperative networks, see Barbara Melosh, *"The Physician's Hand": Work Culture and Conflict in American Nursing* (Philadelphia: Temple University Press, 1982); Susan Porter Benson, *Counter Cultures: Saleswomen, Managers, and Customers in American Department Stores, 1890–1940* (Urbana: University of Illinois Press, 1986); Ardis Cameron, "Bread and Roses Revisited: Women's Culture and Working-Class Activism in the Lawrence Strike of 1912," in Ruth Milkman, ed., *Women, Work and Protest: A Century of U.S. Women's Labor History* (Boston: Routledge and Kegan Paul, 1985).

7. Thomas Dublin, *Women at Work: The Transformation of Work and Community in Lowell, Massachusetts, 1826–1860* (New York: Columbia University Press, 1979), p. 82.

8. Louise Marion Bosworth, *The Living Wage of Women Workers: A Study of Incomes and Expenditures of 450 Women in the City of Boston*, vol. 3, Women's Educational and Industrial Union, Boston, Department of Research, Studies in Economic Relations of Women (New York: Longmans, Green, 1911), p. 52.

9. *Report of the Senate Vice Committee*, p. 827.

10. Bosworth, *Living Wage*, pp. 60, 61; Lucile Eaves, *The Food of Working Women in Boston*, vol. 10, Women's Educational and Industrial Union,

Boston, Department of Research, Studies in Economic Relations of Women (Boston: Wright and Potter, 1917), p. 78.

11. Charles P. Neill, *Wage-Earning Women in Stores and Factories,* vol. 5 in the *Report on Condition of Woman and Child Wage-Earners in the United States* (Washington, D.C.: Government Printing Office, 1910), pp. 118, 64.

12. Immigrants' Protective League, *Second Annual Report, 1910,* p. 15. Although blacks in Chicago were equally poor, studies found less crowding among black lodgers. See Chicago Commission on Race Relations, *The Negro in Chicago* (Chicago: University of Chicago Press, 1922), p. 156.

13. Clare de Graffenried, "The Needs of Self-Supporting Women," supplement to *Johns Hopkins University Studies in Historical and Political Science* (January 1890): 6.

14. Immigrants' Protective League, *Second Annual Report,* p. 15.

15. Anna Steese Richardson, *The Girl Who Earns Her Own Living* (New York: B. W. Dodge Co., 1909), p. 274; see also Inez Evangeline Bolin, "The Religious Adjustments of the Newcomer Girl in Chicago," M.A. thesis, University of Chicago, 1931, p. 29.

16. Eaves, *Food of Working Women,* p. 177.

17. "Conversation," 1/29/c. 1926, Paul Cressey notes, Ernest Burgess Papers 129:6, University of Chicago Manuscript Collections.

18. Eaves, *Food of Working Women,* pp. 78, 178.

19. YWCA of Chicago, *Annual Report of the Emergency Worker* (1921), typewritten, YWCA Papers 74-13, 28:2, University of Illinois at Chicago Manuscript Collections.

20. Bosworth, *Living Wage,* p. 56.

21. "Conversation," 1/29/c. 1926, Paul Cressey notes, Ernest Burgess Papers 129:6, University of Chicago Manuscript Collections.

22. Mary Anderson as told to Mary N. Winslow, *Woman at Work: The Autobiography of Mary Anderson* (Minneapolis: University of Minnesota Press, 1951), pp. 17, 18.

23. Ruth Shonle Cavan, *Business Girls: A Study of Their Interests and Problems* (n.p.: Religious Education Association, 1929), p. 41.

24. On middle-class women, see Carroll Smith-Rosenberg, "The Female World of Love and Ritual: Relations between Women in Nineteenth-Century America," *Signs: A Journal of Women in Culture and Society* (Autumn 1975); Judith Schwarz, "Yellow Clover: Katharine Lee Bates and Katharine Coman," *Frontiers* (Spring 1979); Lillian Faderman, *Surpassing the Love of Men: Romantic Friendship and Love between Women from the Renaissance to the Present* (New York: William Morrow, 1981), chap. 4.

25. "1914: Cora Anderson," in Jonathan Katz, ed., *Gay American History: Lesbians and Gay Men in America* (New York: Avon Books, 1976), pp. 385–90.

26. Janes Addams, *Twenty Years at Hull House* (New York: Macmillan, 1910), p. 136.

27. Mary Kenney O'Sullivan, unpublished autobiography, Schlesinger Library, Radcliffe College, p. 70.

28. Mary S. Fergusson, "Boarding Homes and Clubs for Working Women," *Bulletin of the Department of Labor* (March 1898): 145; "Fifth Anniversary of Jane Club," *Hull-House Bulletin* (June 1897): 4; *Chicago Times Herald,* June 9, 1895.

29. Constitution and by-laws of the Jane Club, Hull House Association Papers; *Chicago Herald,* August 13, 1893.

30. *Chicago Herald,* May 13, 1894.

31. "Fifth Anniversary of Jane Club," *Hull-House Bulletin* (June 1897).

32. Dolores Hayden, *The Grand Domestic Revolution: A History of Feminist Designs for American Homes, Neighborhoods and Cities* (Cambridge: MIT Press, 1981), p. 169; *Cincinnati Times-Star,* September 17, 1894.

33. *Chicago Times Herald,* June 9, 1895; Florence Kelley, "I Go to Work," *The Survey,* June 1, 1927, p. 272.

34. Mary Kenney O'Sullivan, autobiography, p. 71.

35. *Chicago Herald,* May 13, 1894; O'Sullivan, autobiography, p. 71.

36. Ann Elizabeth Trotter, *Housing of Non-Family Women in Chicago: A Survey* (Chicago: Chicago Community Trust, c. 1921), p. 16.

37. News clipping, probably *Chicago Inter Ocean,* c. 1894, Hull House Scrapbook I:48, Hull House Association Papers; Kelley, "I Go to Work," p. 272.

38. News clipping, *Chicago Inter Ocean,* c. 1894, Hull House Scrapbook I:49, Hull House Association Papers.

39. *Chicago News,* November 2, 1892, Hull House Scrapbook I:24, Hull House Association Papers. Hull House did accept a new building into which the Jane Club moved in 1899.

40. Fergusson, "Boarding Homes and Clubs," p. 146.

41. Ibid., p. 175. See also "The Working Girls' Clubs of Chicago," unknown newspaper, March 1896, Hull House Scrapbook III, Hull House Association Papers.

42. Elizabeth Jeanne Humphreys, "Working Women in Chicago Factories and Department Stores, 1870–1895," M.A. thesis, University of Chicago, 1943, p. 61.

43. S. P. Breckinridge, *New Homes for Old* (New York: Harper and Brothers, 1921), p. 210.

44. Ibid., pp. 205, 210.

45. Emmett J. Scott, *Negro Migration during the War* (New York: Arno Press, 1969; orig. 1920), p. 103; St. Clair Drake, *Churches and Voluntary Associations in the Chicago Negro Community* (Chicago: Illinois Work Projects Administration, 1940), pp. 152, 153.

46. Allan H. Spear, *Black Chicago: The Making of a Negro Ghetto, 1890–1920* (Chicago: University of Chicago Press, 1967), pp. 175–77.

47. Franklin Kline Fretz, *The Furnished Room Problem in Philadelphia* (n.p., 1912), p. 116; Dorothy Richardson, *The Long Day: The Story of a New York Working Girl,* in William L. O'Neill, ed., *Women at Work* (New York: Quadrangle Books, 1972), pp. 94, 95; see also Kathy Peiss, " 'Charity Girls' and City Pleasures: Historical Notes on Working-Class Sexuality, 1880–1920," in Ann Snitow, Christine Stansell, and Sharon Thompson, eds., *Pow-*

ers of Desire: The Politics of Sexuality (New York: Monthly Review Press, 1983), p. 77.

48. Paul G. Cressey, *The Taxi-Dance Hall: A Sociological Study in Commercialized Recreation and City Life* (Chicago: University of Chicago Press, 1932), p. 283.

49. O'Sullivan, autobiography, p. 62.

50. I have found no evidence that other major unions for women in Chicago, such as the Amalgamated Clothing Workers of America, made special efforts on behalf of women adrift.

51. One survey conducted in 1908 found that 60 percent of waitresses lived adrift; see Neill, *Wage-Earning Women in Stores and Factories,* pp. 194, 195.

52. John B. Andrews and W. D. P. Bliss, *History of Women in Trade Unions,* vol. 10 in the *Report on Condition of Woman and Child Wage Earners in the United States* (Washington, D.C.: Government Printing Office, 1911), p. 187.

53. S. M. Franklin, "Elizabeth Maloney and the High Calling of the Waitress," *Life and Labor,* February 1913, p. 38.

54. On Waitresses' Union, see Dorothy Sue Cobble, "Sisters in the Craft: Waitresses and Their Unions in the Twentieth Century," Ph.D. dissertation, Stanford University, 1986.

55. Emily Barrows, "Trade Union Organization among Women in Chicago," M.A. thesis, University of Chicago, 1927, table 8, p. 63.

56. Eliza Chester, *The Unmarried Woman* (New York: Dodd, Mead, 1892), p. 231.

57. Neill, *Wage-Earning Women in Stores and Factories,* p. 75.

58. Ibid.

59. Ibid.

60. Vice Commission of Chicago, *The Social Evil in Chicago: A Study of Existing Conditions with Recommendations by the Vice Commission of Chicago* (Chicago: Vice Commission of Chicago, 1911), p. 188.

61. *Chicago Defender,* August 20, 1921. This ordinary "pickup" became newsworthy when Gladys stole James's money.

62. See Kathy Peiss, *Cheap Amusements: Working Women and Leisure in Turn-of-the-Century New York* (Philadelphia: Temple University Press, 1986).

63. Louise DeKoven Bowen, *The Girl Employed in Hotels and Restaurants* (Chicago: Juvenile Protective Association of Chicago, 1912).

64. "Summary of the Report on Hotels," c. 1910, Juvenile Protective Association of Chicago Papers 16, University of Illinois at Chicago Manuscript Collections.

65. *Chicago Record-Herald,* December 25, 1911.

66. "Louise T——n," 2/24/26, Paul Cressey notes, Ernest Burgess Papers 129:6, University of Chicago Manuscript Collections.

67. *Chicago Tribune,* September 27, 1919.

68. Thomas H. Russell, *The Girl's Fight for a Living: How to Protect Working Women from Dangers Due to Low Wages* (Chicago: M. A. Donahue, 1913), p. 166.

69. Ibid., pp. 12, 13.

70. *Social Evil in Chicago,* p. 189.

71. Virginia Brooks, *My Battles with Vice* (New York: Macauley, 1915), p. 55.

72. *Chicago Daily Times,* January 31, 1930.

73. "Alma Nelson Z——r," c. 1926, Paul Cressey notes, Ernest Burgess Papers 129:6, University of Chicago Manuscript Collections.

74. Harvey W. Zorbaugh, "The Dweller in Furnished Rooms: An Urban Type," in Ernest W. Burgess, ed., *The Urban Community: Selected Papers from the Proceedings of the American Sociological Society, 1925* (Chicago: University of Chicago Press, 1926), p. 104.

75. "Louise T——n," 2/24/26, Paul Cressey notes, Ernest Burgess Papers 129:6, University of Chicago Manuscript Collections.

76. *Social Evil in Chicago,* p. 186.

77. Ibid., p. 213.

78. Ibid., p. 95.

79. Ibid., p. 188.

80. Ibid., p. 191.

81. Albert Benedict Wolfe, *The Lodging House Problem in Boston* (Boston: Houghton Mifflin, 1906), p. 142.

82. "Louise D——s," 1926, Paul Cressey notes, Ernest Burgess Papers 129:6, University of Chicago Manuscript Collections.

83. See, for example, "Lillian S. W——n," Paul Cressey notes, Ernest Burgess Papers 129:6, University of Chicago Manuscript Collections.

84. Joan Scott and Louise Tilly emphasize the vulnerability of migrant women in eighteenth- and nineteenth-century Europe. They suggest that high rates of bastardy among migrants resulted from the inability of these women to pressure men into marriage. Women who lived in families, they claim, could call upon family and community to exert pressure on the child's father. Louise A. Tilly and Joan W. Scott, *Women, Work, and Family* (New York: Holt, Rinehart and Winston, 1978), chap. 2.

85. Almost all of the 419 cases involved wage-earning women. Thirty-two percent of the cases involved women who boarded or lived alone. Likely, this high figure includes domestic servants who lived in the homes of their employers. It also includes women adrift, though, as seen in the case studies presented in the report. Louise De Koven Bowen, *A Study of Bastardy Cases* (Chicago: Juvenile Protective Agency of Chicago, 1914), p. 13. I have found no evidence suggesting that women adrift bore more (or fewer) children out of wedlock than other wage-earning women.

86. E. Franklin Frazier, *The Negro Family in Chicago* (Chicago: University of Chicago Press), p. 76.

87. Anderson, "Life History of a Rooming House Keeper," c. 1925, Ernest Burgess Papers 127:2, University of Chicago Manuscript Collection, pp. 16, 17.

88. See, for examples, Dublin, *Women at Work,* p. 82; Christine Stansell, *City of Women: Sex and Class in New York, 1789–1860* (New York: Alfred A. Knopf, 1986).

89. See Susan Porter Benson, " 'The Customers Ain't God': The Work Culture of Department-Store Saleswomen, 1890–1940," in Michael H. Frisch and Daniel J. Walkowitz, eds., *Working-Class America: Essays on Labor, Community, and American Society* (Urbana: University of Illinois Press, 1983); Peiss, " 'Charity Girls' and City Pleasures." On the growth of working-class leisure-time industries, see also Roy Rosenzweig, *Eight Hours for What We Will: Workers and Leisure in an Industrial City, 1870–1920* (Cambridge: Cambridge University Press, 1983).

90. Leslie Woodcock Tentler claims that working women who lived apart from family "lacked the resources to experiment with new styles of life." In contrast, I argue that women adrift did indeed experiment and in part because they lacked the resources for independent living. In this case, a lack of resources encouraged women to experiment with substitutes for family support. See Tentler, *Wage-Earning Women,* p. 135.

91. Similar subcultures most likely existed among women workers in Chicago factories, laundries, and other workplaces as well. For evidence of factory subcultures in New York, see Dorothy Richardson, *The Long Day: The Story of a New York Working Girl* (1905), in William O'Neill, ed., *Women at Work* (New York: New York Times Books, 1972).

92. Donovan, *Woman Who Waits,* pp. 94, 101, 81, 145, 220, 138, 145.

93. In closed dance halls, the customers were exclusively male; the female dancers were hired by the hall. In public dance halls, both men and women were customers.

94. Cressey, *Taxi-Dance Hall,* p. 32.

95. Ibid., p. 255. "Fishing" refers to the practice of suckering men into giving gifts and money.

96. In 1880 many women adrift lived in the heart of downtown Chicago, but by 1910 virtually no women adrift lived in this area.

97. In 1920, for example, only 16 percent of the population of Chicago's North Side furnished room district was under the age of twenty-one; in contrast, in Chicago as a whole, 37 percent of the population was under twenty-one. These figures are derived from Ernest W. Burgess and Charles W. Newcomb, eds., *Census Data of the City of Chicago, 1920* (Chicago: University of Chicago Press, 1931).

98. Edith Abbott, *The Tenements of Chicago, 1908–1935* (Chicago: University of Chicago Press, 1936), chap. 10.

99. In the 1910s, the South Side district ran from Sixteenth to Thirty-third streets and from Clark Street to Prairie Avenue; the West Side district ran from Washington to Harrison streets and from Ashland Boulevard to Halsted Street; the North Side district went from Division Street to the Chicago River and from Wells to Rush streets. By the 1920s, the districts had expanded. The South Side covered the area from Sixteenth to Sixty-fifth streets and from Wentworth Avenue irregularly to Lake Michigan; the West Side district ran from Randolph to Harrison streets and from Damen Avenue to Halsted Street and further west along Madison Street; the North Side included the area from North Avenue to the Chicago River and from Wells to Rush streets. These

boundaries are from Abbott, *Tenements of Chicago*. Other studies of the furnished room districts give slightly different boundaries.

On the furnished room districts of Chicago, see Abbott, *Tenements of Chicago*, chap. 10; T. W. Allison, "Population Movements in Chicago," *Journal of Social Forces* (May 1924): 529–33; Ann Elizabeth Trotter, *Housing of Non-Family Women in Chicago: A Survey* (Chicago: Chicago Community Trust, 1921); Vivien M. Palmer, "Study of the Development of Chicago's Northside," typewritten report for the United Charities, 1932, Chicago Historical Society; Harvey Warren Zorbaugh, *The Gold Coast and the Slum: A Sociological Study of Chicago's Near North Side* (Chicago: University of Chicago Press, 1929).

Information on the population of the furnished room districts was also derived from the Federal Manuscript Census, Chicago samples of women adrift, 1880 and 1910, and the tract-by-tract census data found in Burgess and Newcomb, *Census Data of the City of Chicago, 1920*; and Ernest W. Burgess and Charles Newcomb, eds., *Census Data of the City of Chicago, 1930* (Chicago: University of Chicago Press, 1933).

100. On growth of districts, see Abbott, *Tenements of Chicago*, chap. 10; Kimball Young, "Sociological Study of a Disintegrated Neighborhood," M.A. thesis, University of Chicago, 1918; on number of lodgers, see Allison, "Population Movements in Chicago." The lodging houses included in the 1923 register were only those with over ten roomers.

101. Zorbaugh, *Gold Coast and the Slum*, p. 72.

102. See Wolfe, *Lodging House Problem in Boston;* for examples of permissive landladies in Chicago, see Louise DeKoven Bowen, *The Straight Girl on the Crooked Path: A True Story* (Chicago: Juvenile Protective Association of Chicago, 1916).

103. In 1920 the sex ratio in the North Side district was 1.4, and in the West Side district it was 1.6. In 1930 the ratio in the North Side district was 1.3 and in the West Side district 2.0. In both 1920 and 1930 the South Side district, which was more dispersed over a larger area, had a sex ratio of 1.0. These sex ratios were derived from tract-by-tract census data found in Burgess and Newcomb, *Census Data of the City of Chicago, 1920* and *Census Data of the City of Chicago, 1930*.

104. *Social Evil in Chicago*, pp. 87–91.

105. Ibid., pp. 73, 74, 92–94.

106. Ibid., p. 92.

107. Case record, 6/7/17, Chicago Committee of Fifteen Papers 7:206, MS1028, University of Chicago Manuscript Collections.

108. "Investigation of Commercialized Prostitution," December 1922, Juvenile Protective Association of Chicago Papers 5:92, University of Illinois at Chicago Manuscript Collections.

109. Young, "Sociological Study of a Disintegrated Neighborhood," p. 52.

110. Ibid., p. 42.

111. Abbott, *Tenements of Chicago*, p. 322.

112. James R. Grossman, "A Dream Deferred: Black Migration to Chicago, 1916–1921," Ph.D. dissertation, University of California at Berkeley, 1982, p. 48; Frazier, *Negro Family in Chicago,* p. 103.

113. Frazier, *Negro Family in Chicago,* p. 103. See also Carroll Binder, "Negro Active in Business World," *Chicago Daily News,* August 5, 1927; Junius B. Wood, *The Negro in Chicago,* reprint of articles in *Chicago Daily News,* December 11–27, 1916, p. 25.

114. See especially Zorbaugh, *Gold Coast and the Slum.*

115. Young, "Sociological Study of a Disintegrated Neighborhood," p. 54.

116. Ibid., p. 79.

117. Case record, from Chicago Vice Study File, cited in Walter C. Reckless, *Vice in Chicago* (Chicago: University of Chicago Press, 1933), pp. 53, 54.

118. *Report of the Senate Vice Committee,* pp. 423, 429; see also *Chicago Examiner,* April 12, 1913.

119. Zorbaugh, *Gold Coast and the Slum,* pp. 77–81.

120. Box-Car Bertha, *Sister of the Road,* pp. 68, 70, 62, 29.

121. There is some evidence of a lesbian community in Paris as early as the 1880s, and also evidence suggesting that some lesbians in New York participated in the male homosexual subculture there by the 1890s. In general, though, American lesbian communities were not visible until the 1920s, perhaps because the majority of women had fewer opportunities than men to leave family life, fewer chances for economic independence. Moreover, romantic attachments between women were not usually labeled deviant in America until the early twentieth century. Middle- and upper-class women who lived together as couples in "Boston marriages," for example, were not segregated as outcasts from heterosexual family and friends. On early male homosexual subcultures in American cities, see Jonathan Katz, ed., *Gay American History: Lesbians and Gay Men in the U.S.A.* (New York: Avon Books, 1976), pp. 61–81; and idem, *Gay/Lesbian Almanac: A New Documentary* (New York: Harper and Row, 1983), pp. 157, 218–20. See also John D'Emilio, "Capitalism and Gay Identity," in Carole S. Vance, ed., *Pleasure and Danger: Exploring Female Sexuality* (Boston: Routledge and Kegan Paul, 1984). On the lesbian prostitutes in Paris and on the late-nineteenth- and early-twentieth-century tolerance for lesbianism, see Faderman, *Surpassing the Love of Men,* pp. 282, 298.

122. Paul Oliver, *Screening the Blues: Aspects of the Blues Tradition* (London: Cassell, 1968), pp. 225, 226.

123. Box-Car Bertha, *Sister of the Road,* p. 65.

124. Zorbaugh, *Gold Coast and the Slum,* p. 100.

125. Box-Car Bertha, *Sister of the Road,* pp. 65, 223, 66, 69, 288.

126. Frazier, *Negro Family in Chicago,* p. 103; interview with Eulalia B., conducted by author, 10/16/80.

127. Zorbaugh, *Gold Coast and the Slum,* p. 91.

128. Interview with Eulalia B., conducted by author, 10/16/80.

129. Walter Reckless, "The Natural History of Vice Areas in Chicago," Ph.D. dissertation, University of Chicago, 1925, pp. 374, 375. For a similar

rejection of social background found in the taxi dancers' subculture, see the story of Christina Stranski (a.k.a. DeLoris Glenn) in Cressey, *Taxi-Dance Hall,* p. 56.

130. Reckless, "Natural History of Vice Areas," p. 381.

131. E. H. Wilson, "Chicago Families in Furnished Rooms," M.A. thesis, University of Chicago, 1929, p. 100.

132. On middle-class sexual mores, see Paula S. Fass, *The Damned and the Beautiful: American Youth in the 1920s* (New York: Oxford University Press, 1977); John Modell, "Dating Becomes the Way of American Youth," in Leslie Page Moch and Gary Stark, eds., *Essays on the Family and Historical Change* (College Station: Texas A&M University Press, 1983); James McGovern, "The American Woman's Pre-World War I Freedom in Manners and Morals," *Journal of American History* (September 1968); Kenneth Yellis, "Prosperity's Child: Some Thoughts on the Flapper," *American Quarterly* (Spring 1969): 44–64.

133. On bohemians as a vanguard of sex radicalism, see Henry F. May, *The End of American Innocence: A Study of the First Years of Our Time, 1912–1917* (New York: Alfred A. Knopf, 1959); Linda Gordon, *Woman's Body, Woman's Right: A Social History of Birth Control in America* (New York: Penguin Books, 1977), pp. 190–202.

134. Ellen Carol DuBois and Linda Gordon, "Seeking Ecstasy on the Battlefield: Danger and Pleasure in Nineteenth-Century Feminist Sexual Thought," in Carole S. Vance, ed., *Pleasure and Danger: Exploring Female Sexuality* (Boston: Routledge and Kegan Paul, 1984).

135. On working-class sexuality, see Peiss, *Cheap Amusements.* For earlier suggestions of a working-class vanguard of changing sexual mores, see Nathan G. Hale, *Freud and the Americans: The Beginnings of Psychoanalysis in the United States, 1876–1917* (New York: Oxford University Press, 1971), p. 477. Also, Lewis Erenberg discusses the influence of working-class recreation institutions on middle-class behavior; Lewis A. Erenberg, *Steppin' Out: New York Nightlife and the Transformation of American Culture, 1890–1930* (Westport, Conn.: Greenwood Press, 1981). Daniel Scott Smith argues that less educated women changed their sexual behavior earlier than did college-educated women; Daniel Scott Smith, "The Dating of the American Sexual Revolution: Evidence and Interpretation," in Michael Gordon, ed., *The American Family in Social-Historical Perspective* (New York: St. Martin's Press, 1973).

136. See Fass, *Damned and the Beautiful*; Modell, "Dating Becomes the Way of American Youth."

Chapter 6. Urban Pioneers

1. Willard Thorp, "Afterword," in Theodore Dreiser, *Sister Carrie* (New York: New American Library, 1961), pp. 470–72.

2. See chap. 3, and see also letter to the editor, *Chicago Times,* August 5, 1888.

3. Quoted in *Chicago's Dark Places: Investigations by a Corps of Specially Appointed Commissioners,* 5th ed. (Chicago: Craig Press and the Women's Temperance Publishing Association, 1891), p. 75.

4. Frances Donovan, *The Woman Who Waits* (New York: Arno Press, 1974; orig. 1920), p. 9.

5. Leona Prall Groetzinger, *The City's Perils* (n.p., c. 1910), p. 109.

6. Mary S. Fergusson, "Boarding Homes and Clubs for Working Women," *Bulletin of the Department of Labor* (March 1898): 150.

7. Anna Steese Richardson, *The Girl Who Earns Her Own Living* (New York: B. W. Dodge and Co., 1909), p. 274.

8. Grace H. Dodge, *A Bundle of Letters to Busy Girls on Practical Matters,* in *Grace H. Dodge: Her Life and Work* (New York: Arno Press, 1974; orig. 1887), pp. 103, 104.

9. See, for example, Florence Wenderoth Saunders, *Letters to a Business Girl* (Chicago: Laird and Lee, 1908), pp. 131–35.

10. League for the Protection of Immigrants, *Annual Report, 1909–1910,* p. 21.

11. See Louise DeKoven Bowen, *Safeguards of City Youth at Work and at Play* (New York: Macmillan, 1914), p. 23; Clara E. Laughlin, *The Work-a-Day Girl* (New York: Arno Press, 1974; orig. 1913), p. 51.

12. Groetzinger, *City's Perils,* p. 110.

13. Laughlin, *Work-a-Day Girl,* pp. 107, 108.

14. Ibid., p. 276.

15. On NLPCW, see Nancy J. Weiss, *The National Urban League, 1910–1940* (New York: Oxford University Press, 1974), pp. 18, 19.

16. Immigrants' Protective League, handwritten minutes, c. 1909, Travelers' Aid Society Papers 73-17, 44:4, University of Illinois at Chicago Manuscript Collections.

17. "History," Travelers' Aid Society Papers 73-17, 27:1, University of Illinois at Chicago Manuscript Collections.

18. YWCA of Chicago, *42d Annual Report* (1918), p. 15.

19. Bureau of Social Hygiene, *Housing Conditions of Employed Women in the Borough of Manhattan* (New York: Bureau of Social Hygiene, 1922), p. 25.

20. Subcommittee on Housing of the Chicago Council of Social Agencies, Welfare Council Papers 233, Chicago Historical Society.

21. YWCA of Chicago, *44th Annual Report* (1920), p. 20.

22. "A Warning for Country Girls," *Literary Digest,* December 13, 1924, p. 33.

23. See chap. 3.

24. O. Latham Hatcher, *Rural Girls in the City for Work: A Study Made for the Southern Women's Educational Alliance* (Richmond, Va.: Garrett and Massie, 1930), p. 83.

25. YWCA of Chicago, *52d Annual Report* (1928), p. 10.

26. Subcommittee on Housing Minutes, October 28, 1929, and November 22, 1929, Welfare Council Papers 233, Chicago Historical Society.

27. See chap. 4.

28. Mary Conyngton, *Relation between Occupation and Criminality of Women,* vol. 15 in the *Report on Condition of Woman and Child Wage-Earners in the United States* (Washington, D.C.: Government Printing Office, 1911), pp. 102, 103.

29. Ibid., p. 95.

30. Charles Bryon Chrysler, *White Slavery* (Chicago: n.p., 1909), p. 49.

31. Conyngton, *Relation between Occupation and Criminality,* p. 94.

32. See James R. McGovern, "The American Woman's Pre-World War One Freedom in Manners and Morals," *Journal of American History* (September 1968): 315–33; Mary P. Ryan, *Womanhood in America: From Colonial Times to the Present* (New York: New Viewpoints, 1975), pp. 251–303.

33. Alyse Gregory, "The Changing Morality of Women," *Current History* (November 1923): 298, 299.

34. Theresa Wolfson, *The Woman Worker and the Trade Unions* (New York: International Publishers, 1926), p. 43.

35. Mark Thomas Connelly, *The Response to Prostitution in the Progressive Era* (Chapel Hill: University of North Carolina Press, 1980), p. 145; see also Estelle B. Freedman, *Their Sisters' Keepers: Women's Prison Reform in America, 1830–1930* (Ann Arbor: University of Michigan Press, 1981), pp. 146, 147. For an extended account of the government programs against prostitution and venereal disease during World War I, see Allan M. Brandt, *No Magic Bullet: A Social History of Venereal Disease in the United States Since 1880* (New York: Oxford University Press, 1985), Chaps. 2 and 3. Brandt describes a shift in federal programs from the protection of young women to the detention and punishment of prostitutes.

36. See chap. 2.

37. Clarke A. Chambers, *Seedtime of Reform: American Social Service and Social Action, 1918–1933* (Minneapolis: University of Minnesota, 1963), p. 89.

38. Lewis A. Erenberg, *Steppin' Out: New York Nightlife and the Transformation of American Culture, 1890–1930* (Westport, Conn.: Greenwood Press, 1981), p. 223.

39. On Thaw trial, see ibid., p. 53; and Lary May, *Screening Out the Past: The Birth of Mass Culture and the Motion Picture Industry* (New York: Oxford University Press, 1980), pp. 34, 43.

40. May, *Screening Out the Past,* p. 108.

41. Ibid., p. 119.

42. Ibid., p. 142, 143.

43. Ibid., p. 122, 123.

44. "The Outcast," *Picture-Play Weekly,* April 24, 1915, pp. 12–15.

45. "June Friday," *Picture-Play Weekly,* September 18, 1915, pp. 17–24.

46. Kenneth Munden, ed., *The American Film Institute Catalog, Feature Films, 1921–1930* (New York: R. R. Bowker, 1971), p. 29.

47. May, *Screening Out the Past,* chap. 8; Marjorie Rosen, *Popcorn Venus: Women, Movies and the American Dream* (New York: Coward, McCann and Geoghegan, 1973), pp. 78–82.

48. "The Model; Or, Women and Wine," *Picture-Play Weekly*, June 12, 1915, pp. 12–16.

49. Mary P. Ryan, "The Projection of a New Womanhood: The Movie Moderns in the 1920s," in Jean E. Friedman and William G. Shade, eds., *Our American Sisters: Women in American Life and Thought,* 2d ed. (Boston: Allyn and Bacon, 1976), p. 376.

50. See Sumiko Higashi, *Virgins, Vamps, and Flappers: The American Silent Movie Heroine* (Montreal: Eden Press Women's Publications, 1978).

51. Eugene Walter, *The Easiest Way* (n.p., 1908), p. 9; see also Elizabeth Ewen, "City Lights: Immigrant Women and the Rise of the Movies," *Signs* (Spring 1980 supplement): S59.

52. Anita Loos, *Gentlemen Prefer Blondes: The Illuminating Diary of a Professional Lady* (New York: Boni and Liveright, 1925), p. 77.

53. Erenberg, *Steppin' Out*, p. 210.

54. Ibid., p. 223.

55. While some stories were probably based on real events, the veracity of most stories is doubtful. In one "true story," for example, a man travels to Jupiter. I am grateful to Elliot Meyerowitz for advice on this subject.

56. *True Story Magazine, True Romances,* and *Dream World* were all published by MacFadden Publications. *Real Love Magazine,* known first as *Live Girl Stories,* was published by Street and Smith.

57. "Forget the Past," *Dream World*, January 1925, p. 50.

58. Montanye Perry, "The Girl Who Couldn't Pretend," *Dream World,* November 1924, p. 70.

59. "A Girl Athlete's Romance: What a Western Girl Learned in New York," *True Story Magazine,* April 1920, p. 67.

60. "She Who Laughs Last Laughs Best: When a Woman Scorned Turned the Tables," *True Story Magazine,* January 1920, p. 53.

61. "Marcia Makes Good," *True Story Magazine,* July 1922, p. 95.

62. "The Face with the Three Crosses," *True Romances,* October 1923, p. 85.

63. Laura Jean Libbey, *A Forbidden Marriage: Or, In Love with a Handsome Spendthrift* (New York: American News, 1888), p. 121.

64. "The Road of No Returning," *True Story Magazine,* April 1920, p. 38.

65. "Such a Slip of a Girl," *True Romances,* November 1924, p. 90.

66. "Love Is Not a Plaything," *Dream World,* August 1924, p. 32.

67. "Would You Marry for Money?" *Dream World,* October 1924, p. 40.

68. Ibid., p. 93.

69. Lewis Allen Browne, "Be My Husband," *Dream World,* August 1924.

70. "The Confessions of a Beautiful Model," *True Romances,* December 1923, p. 18.

71. "Small Town Morals," *Dream World,* September 1924, p. 15.

72. See chap. 1.

73. *American Newspaper Annual and Directory, 1924* (Philadelphia: N. W. Ayer and Sons, 1924), p. 741; *American Newspaper Annual and Directory, 1929* (Philadelphia: N. W. Ayer and Sons, 1929), p. 760.

74. May, *Screening Out the Past,* p. 165.

75. In an attempt to court respectability, the MacFadden magazines (*True Story Magazine, True Romances,* and *Dream World*) carried letters from clergymen who said the stories were educational.

76. Anzia Yezierska, *Bread Givers: A Struggle between a Father of the Old World and a Daughter of the New* (New York: Persea Books, 1975; orig. 1925), pp. 157, 159.

77. Theodore Dreiser, *An American Tragedy* (New York: New American Library, 1961; orig. 1925).

78. Carl Van Vechten, *Firecrackers: A Realistic Novel* (New York: Alfred A. Knopf, 1925), pp. 195, 196.

79. On the influence of German social theorists, see Richard Sennett, "Introduction," in Richard Sennett, ed., *Classic Essays on the Culture of Cities* (New York: Meredith Corporation, 1969).

80. Robert E. L. Faris, *Chicago Sociology, 1920–1932* (Chicago: University of Chicago Press, 1979; orig. 1967), p. 35.

81. Robert Park, "Introduction," in Harvey Warren Zorbaugh, *The Gold Coast and the Slum: A Sociological Study of Chicago's North Side* (Chicago: University of Chicago Press, 1929), p. viii.

82. Zorbaugh, *Gold Coast and the Slum,* p. 86.

83. Ruth Shonle Cavan, *Suicide* (Chicago: University of Chicago Press, 1928), p. 81; Faris, *Chicago Sociology,* p. 86.

84. Cavan, *Suicide,* p. 93.

85. Paul G. Cressey, *The Taxi-Dance Hall: A Sociological Study in Commercialized Recreation and City Life* (Chicago: University of Chicago Press, 1932), p. 293.

86. Ernest Mowrer, *Family Disorganization: An Introduction to Sociological Analysis* (Chicago: University of Chicago Press, 1927), p. 111.

87. E. Franklin Frazier, *The Negro Family in Chicago* (Chicago: University of Chicago Press, 1932), pp. 80, 73.

88. Faris, *Chicago Sociology,* p. 79.

89. Park, "Introduction," p. viii; Zorbaugh, *Gold Coast and the Slum,* pp. 91, 99.

90. Frazier, *Negro Family in Chicago,* p. 103.

91. Ruth Shonle Cavan, *Business Girls: A Study of Their Interests and Problems* (Religious Education Association, 1929), p. 51.

92. Robert E. Park, "Community Organization and Juvenile Delinquency," in Robert E. Park, Ernest W. Burgess, and Roderick D. McKenzie, eds., *The City* (Chicago: University of Chicago Press, 1925), p. 108.

93. Walter C. Reckless, "The Natural History of Vice Areas in Chicago," Ph.D. dissertation, University of Chicago, 1925, p. 209.

94. Ibid., p. 211.

95. Zorbaugh, *Gold Coast and the Slum,* p. 199.

96. Donovan, *Woman Who Waits,* p. 220.

97. Walter C. Reckless, *Vice in Chicago* (Chicago: University of Chicago Press, 1933), pp. 44–48.

98. W. I. Thomas, *The Unadjusted Girl, with Cases and Standpoint for Behavioral Analysis* (Boston: Little, Brown, 1923), p. 150.

99. Frances R. Donovan, *The Saleslady* (Chicago: University of Chicago Press, 1929), p. 177.

100. Ernest R. Groves, "Psychic Causes of Rural Migration," *American Journal of Sociology* (March 1916): 627.

101. Thomas, *Unadjusted Girl,* p. 119.

102. Cressey, *Taxi-Dance Hall,* p. 47.

Conclusion

1. See, for examples, Meredith Tax, *The Rising of the Women: Feminist Solidarity and Class Conflict, 1880–1917* (New York: Monthly Review Press, 1980); Susan Porter Benson, *Counter Cultures: Saleswomen, Managers, and Customers in American Department Stores, 1890–1940* (Urbana: University of Illinois Press, 1986); Joan M. Jensen and Sue Davidson, eds., *A Needle, A Bobbin, A Strike: Women Needleworkers in America* (Philadelphia: Temple University Press, 1984); Ruth Milkman, ed., *Women, Work and Protest: A Century of U.S. Women's Labor History* (Boston: Routledge and Kegan Paul, 1985).

2. U.S. Department of Agriculture, Economic Research Service, *Farm Population: Estimates for 1910–1962* (Washington, D.C.: Government Printing Office, 1963), p. 23.

3. Christine Stansell, *City of Women: Sex and Class in New York, 1789–1960* (New York: Alfred A. Knopf, 1986), pp. 83–101, 171–92; Linda Gordon, *Woman's Body, Woman's Right: A Social History of Birth Control in America* (New York: Penguin Books, 1977), pp. 203–4; Barbara Ehrenreich, Elizabeth Hess, and Gloria Jacobs, *Re-Making Love: The Feminization of Sex* (Garden City, N.Y.: Anchor Press/Doubleday, 1986), pp. 39–42, 54–62.

4. The literature on self-supporting women in third world nations is large and growing. Good introductory sources include *International Migration Review* (Winter 1984); James T. Fawcett, Siew-ean Khoo, and Peter C. Smith, *Women in the Cities of Asia: Migration and Urban Adaptation* (Boulder, Colo.: Westview Press, 1984); Gavin W. Jones, ed., *Women in the Urban and Industrial Workforce: Southeast and East Asia* (Canberra: Australian National University, 1984); Annette Fuentes and Barbara Ehrenreich, *Women in the Global Factory* (Boston: South End Press, 1983); International Labour Office, *Women Workers in Multinational Enterprises in Developing Countries* (Geneva: International Labour Organization, 1985).

5. Siew-ean Khoo, Peter C. Smith, and James T. Fawcett, "Migration of Women to Cities: The Asian Situation in Comparative Perspective," *International Migration Review* (Winter 1984): 1251; Renée Pittin, "Migration of Women in Nigeria: The Hausa Case," *International Migration Review* (Winter 1984): 1306; John Connell, "Status or Subjugation? Women, Migration, and

Development in the South Pacific," *International Migration Review* (Winter 1984): 966; Fuentes and Ehrenreich, *Women in the Global Factory,* p. 25; Sharon Stichter, *Migrant Laborers* (Cambridge: Cambridge University Press, 1985), p. 154.

6. Fuentes and Ehrenreich, *Women in the Global Factory,* p. 12; Noeleen Heyzer, "From Rural Subsistence to Industrial Peripheral Work Force: An Examination of Female Malaysian Migrants and Capital Accumulation in Singapore," in Lourdes Beneria, ed., *Women and Development: The Sexual Division of Labor in Rural Societies* (New York: Praeger, 1982), p. 185.

7. Khoo, Smith, and Fawcett, "Migration of Women," p. 1252; Pittin, "Migration of Women in Nigeria," p. 1303; Fuentes and Ehrenreich, *Women in the Global Factory,* pp. 25, 33; International Labour Office, *Women Workers in Multinational Enterprises,* pp. 83, 87; Lim Lin Lean, "Towards Meeting the Needs of Urban Female Factory Workers in Peninsular Malaysia," in Jones, *Women in the Urban and Industrial Workforce,* pp. 138–39.

8. Pittin, "Migration of Women in Nigeria," p. 1302; Fuentes and Ehrenreich, *Women in the Global Factory,* p. 26; "Softness and Docility Sought: West German Traffic in Thai Women," in *Second Class, Working Class: An International Woman's Reader* (Oakland, Calif.: People's Translation Service, 1979), p. 52.

9. Fuentes and Ehrenreich, *Women in the Global Factory,* p. 25; Heyzer, "From Rural Subsistence to Industrial Peripheral Work Force," pp. 191, 196; Connell, "Status or Subjugation?" p. 966; Khoo, Smith, and Fawcett, "Migration of Women to Cities," p. 1252.

10. Jamilah Ariffin, "Migration of Women Workers in Peninsular Malaysia: Impact and Implications," in Fawcett, Khoo, and Smith, eds., *Women in the Cities of Asia,* p. 221; Fuentes and Ehrenreich, *Women in the Global Factory,* p. 25; Connell, "Status or Subjugation?" p. 966; Lean, "Towards Meeting the Needs," p. 138.

11. Ilsa Schuster, "Marginal Lives: Conflict and Contradiction in the Position of Female Traders in Lusaka, Zambia," in Edna G. Bay, ed., *Women and Work in Africa* (Boulder, Colo.: Westview Press, 1982), p. 107; Michael B. Whiteford, "Women, Migration, and Social Change: A Colombian Case Study," *International Migration Review* (Summer 1978): 245; Stichter, *Migrant Laborers,* pp. 154, 166; Fuentes and Ehrenreich, *Women in the Global Factory,* p. 26.

Bibliography

Manuscript Collections

Chicago Historical Society, Chicago, Illinois
    Louise DeKoven Bowen Scrapbooks
    Mary McDowell Papers
    Oral History Archives of Chicago Polonia
    Ethelbert Stewart Collection
    Welfare Council of Chicago Papers
Hull House, Chicago, Illinois
    Hull House Association Papers
Library of Congress, Manuscript Division, Washington, D.C.
    National Consumers' League Papers
Arthur and Elizabeth Schlesinger Library on the History of Women in America,
Radcliffe College, Cambridge, Massachusetts
    Ellen Martin Henrotin Papers
    Harriet Burton Laidlaw Papers
    National Women's Trade Union League Papers
    Leonora O'Reilly Papers
    Mary Kenney O'Sullivan Autobiography
University of Chicago, Joseph Regenstein Library, Chicago, Illinois
    Grace and Edith Abbott Papers
    Ernest Burgess Papers
    Chicago Committee of Fifteen Papers
    Julius Rosenwald Papers
University of Illinois at Chicago, Manuscript Collections, Chicago, Illinois
    Chicago and Illinois Charitable Institution Papers
    Illinois Humane Society Papers
    Immigrants' Protective League Papers
    Juvenile Protective Association of Chicago Papers
    Phyllis Wheatley Home Association Papers
    Travelers' Aid Society of Chicago and Illinois Papers
    Women's Trade Union League of Chicago Papers
    Young Women's Christian Association of Chicago Papers

Newspapers and Periodicals

Chicago Daily News, 1892, 1916, 1927
Chicago Defender, 1910, 1918, 1921
Chicago Evening Post, 1890, 1911, 1922
Chicago Examiner, 1913
The Chicago Girl, 1929–30
Chicago Herald, 1893, 1894
Chicago Herald and Examiner, 1921
Chicago Inter Ocean, 1890, 1894
Chicago Record, 1894
Chicago Record-Herald, 1904–13
Chicago Times, 1888, 1890
Chicago Times Herald, 1873, 1877, 1911, 1913–15, 1919
Chicago Whip, 1922
The Day Book, 1913
Dream World, 1924, 1925, 1927, 1928, 1930, 1931
The Eleanor Record, 1917–30
Life and Labor, 1911–21
Life and Labor Bulletin, 1922–32
Picture Play Magazine, 1915–19
Real Love Magazine, 1928–30
True Romances, 1923–24
True Story, 1920, 1922

Unpublished Papers and Dissertations

Barrows, Emily. "Trade Union Organization among Women in Chicago." M.A. thesis, University of Chicago, 1927.

Beckner, Earl Rucker. "History of Illinois Labor Legislation." Ph.D. dissertation, University of Chicago, 1927.

Bolin, Inez Evangeline. "Religious Adjustments of the Newcomer Girl in Chicago." M.A. thesis, University of Chicago, 1931.

Bosch, Allan Whitworth. "The Salvation Army in Chicago, 1885–1914." Ph.D. dissertation, University of Chicago, 1965.

Buhle, Mari Jo. "The Nineteenth Century Woman's Movement: Perspectives on Women's Labor in Industrializing America." Bunting Institute of Radcliffe College, 1979.

Cavan, Ruth Shonle. "Suicide: A Study of Personal Disorganization." Ph.D. dissertation, University of Chicago, 1926.

Cobble, Dorothy Sue. "Sisters in the Craft: Waitresses and Their Unions in the Twentieth Century." Ph.D. dissertation, Stanford University, 1986.

Davidson, Essie Mae. "Organized Boarding Homes for Self-Supporting Women in the City of Chicago." M.A. thesis, University of Chicago, 1914.

Faragher, John Mack. "Sister Carrie's Sisters: White Country Girls in the City of Chicago, 1880–1930." Typescript, 1983.

Fisher, Miles M. "History of the Olivet Baptist Church of Chicago." M.A. thesis, University of Chicago, 1922.

Gottlieb, Peter. "Making Their Own Way: Southern Blacks' Migration to Pittsburgh, 1916–1930." Ph.D. dissertation, University of Pittsburgh, 1977.

Grossman, James R. "A Dream Deferred: Black Migration to Chicago, 1916–1921." Ph.D. dissertation, University of California at Berkeley, 1982.

Helmbold, Lois Rita. "Making Choices, Making Do: Black and White Working-Class Women's Lives and Work during the Great Depression." Ph.D. dissertation, Stanford University, 1983.

Humphreys, Elizabeth Jeanne. "Working Women in Chicago Factories and Department Stores, 1870–1895." M.A. thesis, University of Chicago, 1943.

McElroy, Georgia Pearl. "Boarding Homes for Self-Supporting Women in Chicago." M.A. thesis, University of Chicago, 1913.

Miller, Alice Mae. "Rents and Housing Conditions in the Stock Yards District of Chicago, 1923." M.A. thesis, University of Chicago, 1923.

Palmer, Vivien M. "Study of the Development of Chicago's Northside." Prepared for the United Charities of Chicago, 1932. Chicago Historical Society.

Pariser, Abby Joan. "A History of the Early Years of the Chicago YWCA, 1879–1918." M.A. thesis, Roosevelt University, 1975.

Perry, Joseph Samuel. "Rents and Housing Conditions among the Lithuanians in Chicago." M.A. thesis, University of Chicago, 1925.

Powers, Dorothy Edwards. "The Chicago Woman's Club." M.A. thesis, University of Chicago, 1939.

Quaintance, Esther Crockett. "Rents and Housing Conditions in the Italian District of the Lower North Side of Chicago, 1924." M.A. thesis, University of Chicago, 1925.

Reckless, Walter. "The Natural History of Vice Areas in Chicago." Ph.D. dissertation, University of Chicago, 1925.

Rood, Alice Quan. "Social Conditions among the Negroes on Federal Street between 45th Street and 53rd Street." M.A. thesis, University of Chicago, 1924.

Stansell, Mary Christine. "Women of the Laboring Poor in New York City, 1820–1860." Ph.D. dissertation, Yale University, 1979.

Weiner, Lynn. "Protecting the City from Sister Carrie: Women Transients and Travelers' Aid in Minneapolis, 1893–1935." Paper presented at Berkshire Conference on the History of Women, August 1978.

Wright, Richard R., Jr. "The Industrial Condition of Negroes in Chicago." Bachelor of Divinity dissertation, University of Chicago, 1901.

Young, Kimball. "Sociological Study of a Disintegrated Neighborhood." M.A. thesis, University of Chicago, 1918.

Books, Pamphlets, Serials, and Articles

Abbott, Edith. *The Tenements of Chicago, 1908–1935.* Chicago: University of Chicago Press, 1936.

Abbott, Edith, and S. P. Breckinridge. "Women in Industry: The Chicago Stockyards." *Journal of Political Economy* (October 1911): 632–54.

Abbott, Grace. "The Chicago Employment Agency and the Immigrant Worker." *American Journal of Sociology* (November 1908): 289–305.

Addams, Jane. *A New Conscience and an Ancient Evil*. New York: Macmillan, 1912.

————. *The Spirit of Youth and the City Streets*. 1909. Reprint. Urbana, Illinois: University of Illinois Press, 1972.

————. *Twenty Years at Hull House*. New York: Macmillan, 1910.

Alcott, Louisa May. *Work: A Story of Experience*. 1873. Reprint. New York: Schocken Books. 1977.

Alexander, John K. *Render Them Submissive: Responses to Poverty in Philadelphia, 1760–1800*. Amherst: University of Massachusetts Press, 1980.

Allen, Frederick Lewis. *Only Yesterday*. New York: Harper and Brothers, 1931.

Allison, T. W. "Population Movements in Chicago." *Journal of Social Forces* (May 1924): 529–33.

American Newspaper Annual and Directory, 1924. Philadelphia: N. W. Ayer and Sons, 1924.

American Newspaper Annual and Directory, 1929. Philadelphia: N. W. Ayer and Sons, 1929.

Anderson, Margaret. *My Thirty Years' War: The Autobiography, Beginnings and Battles to 1930*. 1929. Reprint. New York: Horizon Press, 1969.

Anderson, Michael. *Family Structure in Nineteenth Century Lancashire*. Cambridge: University of Cambridge Press, 1971.

Andrews, John B. and W. D. P. Bliss. *History of Women in Trade Unions*. Vol. 10 of the *Report on Condition of Woman and Child Wage-Earners in the United States*. Washington, D.C.: Government Printing Office, 1911.

Ankarloo, Bengt. "Agriculture and Women's Work: Directions of Change in the West, 1700–1900. *Journal of Family History* (Summer 1979): 111–20.

Aronovici, Carol. *Unmarried Girls with Sex Experience*. N.p.: Bureau for Social Research of the Seybert Institution, c. 1914.

Baer, Judith A. *The Chains of Protection: The Judicial Response to Women's Labor Legislation*. Westport, Conn.: Greenwood Press, 1978.

Baym, Nina. *Women's Fiction: A Guide to Novels by and about Women in America, 1820–1870*. Ithaca: Cornell University Press, 1978.

Beard, Mary Ritter. *Women's Work in Municipalities*. New York: D. Appleton, 1915.

Beneria, Lourdes, ed. *Women and Development: The Sexual Division of Labor in Rural Societies*. New York: Praeger, 1982.

Benson, Susan Porter. *Counter Cultures: Saleswomen, Managers, and Customers in American Department Stores, 1890–1940*. Urbana: University of Illinois Press, 1986.

————. " 'The Customers Ain't God': The Work Culture of Department-Store Saleswomen, 1890–1940." In Michael H. Frisch and Daniel J. Walkowitz, eds., *Working-Class America: Essays on Labor, Community, and American Society*. Urbana: University of Illinois Press, 1983.

Berg, Barbara J. *The Remembered Gate: Origins of American Feminism, the Woman and the City, 1800–1860*. New York: Oxford University Press, 1978.

Bethel, Elizabeth Rauh. *Promisedland: A Century of Life in a Negro Community*. Philadelphia: Temple University Press, 1981.

Black, Ford S., comp. *Black's Blue Book*. Chicago: F. S. Black, 1921.

Bliss, Mrs. N. S. *A Glimpse of Shadowed Lives in a Great City, and an Autobiographical Sketch of the Author*. Chicago: n.p., 1913.

Bogue, Donald J. *Principles of Demography*. New York: John Wiley, 1969.

Boone, Gladys. *The Women's Trade Union League in Great Britain and the United States of America*. 1942. Reprint. New York: AMS Press, 1968.

Boserup, Ester. *Woman's Role in Economic Development*. New York: St. Martin's Press, 1970.

Bosworth, Louise Marion. *The Living Wage of Women Workers: A Study of Incomes and Expenditures of 450 Women in the City of Boston*. Vol. 3, Studies in Economic Relations of Women, Women's Educational and Industrial Union, Boston, Department of Research. New York: Longmans, Green, 1911.

Bowen, Louise DeKoven. *The Colored People of Chicago: An Investigation Made for the Juvenile Protective Association*. Chicago: Juvenile Protective Association of Chicago, 1913.

———. *The Department Store Girl: Based upon Interviews with 200 Girls*. Chicago: Juvenile Protective Association of Chicago, 1911.

———. *The Girl Employed in Hotels and Restaurants*. Chicago: Juvenile Protective Association of Chicago, 1912.

———. *Our Most Popular Recreation Controlled by the Liquor Interests: A Study of Public Dance Halls*. Chicago: Juvenile Protective Association of Chicago, 1911.

———. *The Road to Destruction Made Easy in Chicago*. Chicago: Juvenile Protective Association of Chicago, 1916.

———. *Safeguards for City Youth at Work and at Play*. New York: Macmillan, 1914.

———. *The Straight Girl on the Crooked Path: A True Story*. Chicago: Juvenile Protective Association of Chicago, 1916.

———. *A Study of Bastardy Cases*. Chicago: Juvenile Protective Association of Chicago, 1914.

Boyer, Paul. *Urban Masses and Moral Order in America, 1820–1920*. Cambridge: Harvard University Press, 1978.

Boylan, Anne M. "Women in Groups: An Analysis of Women's Benevolent Organizations in New York and Boston, 1797–1840." *Journal of American History* (December 1984): 497–523.

Brandt, Allan M. *No Magic Bullet: A Social History of Venereal Disease in the United States Since 1880*. New York: Oxford University Press, 1985.

Breckinridge, Sophinisba P. *Family Welfare Work in a Metropolitan Community: Selected Case Records.* Chicago: University of Chicago Press, 1924.

———. *New Homes for Old.* New York: Harper and Brothers, 1921.

Breckinridge, Sophinisba, and Edith Abbott. "Families in Furnished Rooms." *American Journal of Sociology* (November 1910): 289–308.

———. "The Twenty-ninth Ward Back of the Yards." *American Journal of Sociology* (January 1911): 433–68.

Brooks, Virginia. *Little Lost Sister.* New York: Macauley, 1914.

———. *My Battles with Vice.* New York: Macauley, 1915.

Bureau of Social Hygiene. *Housing Conditions of Employed Women in the Borough of Manhattan.* New York: Bureau of Social Hygiene, 1922.

Burgess, Ernest W., and Charles W. Newcomb, eds. *Census Data of the City of Chicago, 1920.* Chicago: University of Chicago Press, 1931.

———. *Census Data of the City of Chicago, 1930.* Chicago: University of Chicago Press, 1933.

Burnham, John. "The Progressive Era Revolution in American Attitudes toward Sex." *Journal of American History* (March 1973): 885–908.

Butler, Elizabeth Beardsley. *Women and the Trades, Pittsburgh, 1907–1908.* New York: Russell Sage Foundation, 1909.

Cameron, Ardis. "Bread and Roses Revisited: Women's Culture and Working-Class Activism in the Lawrence Strike of 1912." In Ruth Milkman, ed., *Women, Work and Protest: A Century of U.S. Women's Labor History.* Boston: Routledge and Kegan Paul, 1985.

Campbell, Helen. *Prisoners of Poverty: Women Wage-Workers, Their Trades and Their Lives.* Boston: Roberts Brothers, 1887.

Carbaugh, Harvey C. *Human Welfare Work in Chicago.* Chicago: A. C. McClurg, 1917.

Carey, Matthew. "Address to the Ladies in New York Who Have Undertaken to Establish a House of Industry." In Matthew Carey, *Miscellaneous Essays.* 1830. Reprint. New York: Burt Franklin, 1966.

Cavan, Ruth Shonle. *Business Girls: A Study of Their Interests and Problems.* Chicago: Religious Education Association, 1929.

———. *Suicide.* Chicago: University of Chicago Press, 1928.

Chafe, William H. *The American Woman: Her Changing Social, Economic and Political Roles, 1920–1970.* New York: Oxford University Press, 1972.

Chambers, Clarke A. *Seedtime of Reform: American Social Service and Social Action, 1918–1933.* Minneapolis: University of Minnesota Press, 1963.

Chambers-Schiller, Lee Virginia. *Liberty, A Better Husband, Single Women in America: The Generations of 1780–1840.* New Haven: Yale University Press, 1984.

Chester, Eliza. *The Unmarried Woman.* New York: Dodd, Mead, 1892.

Chicago Bureau of Charities. "Non-Resident Unemployed Men in Chicago." In *Fifth Annual Report.* 1898–99.

Chicago Commission on Race Relations. *The Negro in Chicago.* Chicago: University of Chicago Press, 1922.

Chicago Committee of Fifteen. *Annual Report.* 1913–18, 1920, 1922, 1923, 1925.

Chicago Exchange for Women's Work. *Annual Report.* 1880.

Chicago Home for the Friendless. *Annual Report.* 1867, 1877.

Chicago Protective Agency for Women and Children. *Annual Report.* 1888.

Chicago Relief and Aid Society. *Annual Report.* 1891.

Chicago Urban League. *Annual Report.* 1917–19.

―――. *Two Decades of Service, 1916–1936.* N.p., n.d.

Chicago Women's Church Federation Protectorate. *Annual Report.* 1922.

Chicago's Dark Places: Investigations by a Corps of Specially Appointed Commissioners. Chicago: Craig Press and the Women's Temperance Publishing Association, 1891.

Chrysler, Charles Bryon. *White Slavery.* Chicago: n.p., 1909.

Clark, Sue Ainslie, and Edith Wyatt. *Making Both Ends Meet: The Income and Outlay of New York Working Girls.* New York: Macmillan, 1911.

Cohen, Miriam. "Italian-American Women in New York City, 1900–1950: Work and School." In Milton Cantor and Bruce Laurie, eds., *Class, Sex and the Woman Worker.* Westport, Conn.: Greenwood Press, 1977.

Comstock, Alzada P. "The Problem of the Negro." *American Journal of Sociology* (September 1912): 241–57.

Connell, John. "Status or Subjugation? Women, Migration and Development in the South Pacific." *International Migration Review* (Winter 1984): 964–83.

Connelly, Mark Thomas. *The Response to Prostitution in the Progressive Era.* Chapel Hill: University of North Carolina Press, 1980.

"Convention of the National Women's Trade Union League: The Chicago Conference." *Union Labor Advocate,* December 1908, 43.

Conyngton, Mary. *Relation between Occupation and Criminality of Women.* Vol. 15 in the *Report on Condition of Woman and Child Wage-Earners in the United States.* Washington, D.C.: Government Printing Office, 1911.

"Cost of Living." *Monthly Labor Review* (February 1930): 241–68.

Costello, Cynthia B. " 'WEA're Worth It!' Work Culture and Conflict at the Wisconsin Education Association Insurance Trust." *Feminist Studies* (Fall 1985): 497–518.

Cott, Nancy F. *The Bonds of Womanhood: "Woman's Sphere" in New England, 1780–1835.* New Haven: Yale University Press, 1977.

―――. "Passionlessness: An Interpretation of Victorian Sexual Ideology, 1790–1850." In Nancy F. Cott and Elizabeth H. Pleck, eds., *A Heritage of Her Own: Toward a New Social History of American Women.* New York: Simon and Schuster, 1979.

Coulter House, Home for Girls. *Annual Report.* 1913.

Cressey, Paul G. *The Taxi-Dance Hall: A Sociological Study in Commercialized Recreation and City Life.* Chicago: University of Chicago Press, 1932.

Critoph, Gerald. "The Flapper and Her Critics." In Carol V. R. George, ed., *"Remember the Ladies": New Perspectives on Women in American History.* Syracuse: Syracuse University Press, 1975.

Dall, Caroline H. "Lodging-Houses for Young Women." *The Friend,* December 1867, 376–86.

Davidson, Cathy N., and Arnold E. Davidson. "Carrie's Sisters: The Popular Prototypes for Dreiser's Heroines." *Modern Fiction Studies* (Autumn 1977): 395–407.

Davis, Allen F. *Spearheads for Reform: The Social Settlements and the Progressive Movement, 1890–1914.* New York: Oxford University Press, 1967.

Davis, Elizabeth Lindsay. *Lifting as They Climb.* Washington, D.C.: National Association of Colored Women, 1933.

———. *The Story of the Illinois Federation of Colored Women's Clubs, 1900–1922.* Chicago: n.p., 1922.

Davis, Michael M., Jr. *The Exploitation of Pleasure: A Study of Commercial Recreations in New York City.* New York: Russell Sage Foundation, 1911.

Davis, Samuel M. "Women and the Wages Question." *American Journal of Politics* (January 1894): 63–70.

Dedrick, Florence Mabel. "Our Sister of the Street." In Ernest A. Bell, ed., *War on the White Slave Trade: A Book Designed to Awaken the Sleeping and to Protect the Innocent.* Chicago: Charles C. Thompson, 1909.

Degler, Carl N. *At Odds: Women and the Family in America from the Revolution to the Present.* New York: Oxford University Press, 1980.

De Graffenried, Clare. "The Condition of Wage-Earning Women." *Forum*, March 1893, 68–82.

———. "The Needs of Self-Supporting Women." Supplement to *Johns Hopkins University Studies in Historical and Political Science* (January 1890).

D'Emilio, John. "Capitalism and Gay Identity." In Ann Snitow, Christine Stansell, and Sharon Thompson, eds., *Powers of Desire: The Politics of Sexuality.* New York: Monthly Review Press, 1983.

———. *Sexual Politics, Sexual Communities: The Making of a Homosexual Minority in the United States, 1940–1970.* Chicago: University of Chicago Press, 1983.

Di Leonardo, Micaela. "Women's Work, Work Culture, and Consciousness (An Introduction)." *Feminist Studies* (Fall 1985): 491–95.

Diner, Hasia. *Erin's Daughters in America: Irish Immigrant Women in the Nineteenth Century.* Baltimore: Johns Hopkins University Press, 1983.

Divers, Vivia H. *The "Black Hole" or the Missionary Experience of a Young Girl in the Slums of Chicago, 1891–1892.* N.p., 1893.

"Do Working Women Want a 'Hotel'?" *Public Opinion*, January 19, 1899, 78–79.

Dodge, Grace H. *A Bundle of Letters to Busy Girls on Practical Matters.* 1897. Reprinted in *Grace H. Dodge: Her Life and Work.* New York: Arno Press, 1974.

Donovan, Frances R. *The Saleslady.* Chicago: University of Chicago Press, 1929.

———. *The Woman Who Waits.* 1920. Reprint. New York: Arno Press, 1974.

Douglas, Dorothy. "The Cost of Living for Working Women: A Criticism of Current Theories." *Quarterly Journal of Economics* (February 1920): 225–59.

Drake, St. Clair. *Churches and Voluntary Associations in the Chicago Negro Community.* Chicago: Illinois Work Projects Administration, 1940.

Dreiser, Theodore. *An American Tragedy.* 1925. Reprint. New York: New American Library, 1964.

———. *Sister Carrie.* 1900. Reprint. New York: New American Library, 1961.

Dublin, Thomas. "Rural-Urban Migrants in Industrial New England: The Case of Lynn, Massachusetts, in the Mid-Nineteenth Century." *Journal of American History* (December 1986): 623–44.

———. *Women at Work: The Transformation of Work and Community in Lowell, Massachusetts, 1826–1860.* New York: Columbia University Press, 1979.

DuBois, Ellen Carol, and Linda Gordon. "Seeking Ecstasy on the Battlefield: Danger and Pleasure in Nineteenth-Century Feminist Sexual Thought." In Carole S. Vance, ed., *Pleasure and Danger: Exploring Female Sexuality.* Boston: Routledge and Kegan Paul, 1984.

Dudden, Faye. *Serving Women: Household Service in Nineteenth-Century America.* Middletown, Conn.: Wesleyan University Press, 1983.

Dye, Nancy Schrom. *As Equals and as Sisters: Feminism, the Labor Movement and the Women's Trade Union League of New York.* Columbia: University of Missouri Press, 1980.

Eaves, Lucile. *The Food of Working Women in Boston.* Vol. 10, Studies in Economic Relations of Women, Women's Educational and Industrial Union, Boston, Department of Research. Boston: Wright and Potter, 1917.

Edholm, Charlton. *Traffic in Girls and Florence Crittenton Missions.* Chicago: Women's Temperance Publishing Association, 1893.

Edwards' Directory of Chicago. 1870.

Ehrenreich, Barbara, Elizabeth Hess, and Gloria Jacobs. *Re-Making Love: The Feminization of Sex.* Garden City, N.Y.: Anchor Press/Doubleday, 1986.

Eisenstein, Sarah. *Give Us Bread but Give Us Roses: Working Women's Consciousness in the United States, 1890 to the First World War.* London: Routledge and Kegan Paul, 1983.

Elder, Glen H., Jr. "History and the Family: The Discovery of Complexity." *Journal of Marriage and the Family* (August 1981): 489–519.

"Employment of Colored Women in Chicago." *The Crisis,* January 1911, 24–25.

England, W. P. "The Lodging House." *Survey,* December 2, 1911, 1313–17.

Epstein, Barbara Leslie. *The Politics of Domesticity: Women, Evangelism, and Temperance in Nineteenth-Century America.* Middletown, Conn.: Wesleyan University Press, 1981.

Erenberg, Lewis A. *Steppin' Out: New York Nightlife and the Transformation of American Culture, 1890–1930.* Westport, Conn.: Greenwood Press, 1981.

Ewen, Elizabeth. "City Lights: Immigrant Women and the Rise of the Movies." *Signs: Journal of Women in Culture and Society* (Spring 1980 supplement): S45–65.

———. *Immigrant Women in the Land of Dollars: Life and Culture on the Lower East Side, 1890–1925.* New York: Monthly Review Press, 1985.

Faderman, Lillian. *Surpassing the Love of Men: Romantic Friendship and Love between Women from the Renaissance to the Present.* New York: William Morrow, 1981.

Faris, Robert E. *Chicago Sociology, 1920–1932.* 1967. Reprint. Chicago: University of Chicago Press, 1979.

Fass, Paula. *The Damned and the Beautiful: American Youth in the 1920's.* New York: Oxford University Press, 1977.

Fawcett, James T., Siew-ean Khoo, and Peter C. Smith, eds. *Women in the Cities of Asia: Migration and Urban Adaptation.* Boulder, Colo.: Westview Press, 1984.

Fayes, Harriet. "Housing of Single Women." *Municipal Affairs* (March 1899): 95–107.

Fergusson, Mary S. "Boarding Homes and Clubs for Working Women." *Bulletin of the Department of Labor* (March 1898): 141–96.

Fischer, Claude S. "Toward a Subcultural Theory of Urbanism." *American Journal of Sociology* (May 1975): 1319–41.

———. *The Urban Experience.* New York: Harcourt Brace Jovanovich, 1976.

Flinn, John J. *Chicago: A History, An Encyclopedia, and a Guide.* 2d ed. Chicago: Standard Guide, 1892.

Flower, B. O. "Social Conditions as Feeders of Immorality." *Arena,* February 1895, 399–412.

Frank, Henriette Greenbaum, and Amalie Hofer Jerome. *Annals of the Chicago Woman's Club for the First Forty Years of Its Organization, 1876–1916.* Chicago: Chicago Woman's Club, 1916.

Frazier, E. Franklin. *The Negro Family in Chicago.* Chicago: University of Chicago Press, 1932.

Freedman, Estelle B. *Their Sisters' Keepers: Women's Prison Reform in America, 1830–1930.* Ann Arbor: University of Michigan Press, 1981.

Fretz, Franklin Kline. *The Furnished Room Problem in Philadelphia.* N.p., 1912.

Fuentes, Annette, and Barbara Ehrenreich. *Women in the Global Factory.* Boston: South End Press, 1983.

Giddings, Paula. *When and Where I Enter: The Impact of Black Women on Race and Sex in America.* Toronto: Bantam Books, 1984.

Gilman, Charlotte Perkins. *Women and Economics: A Study of the Economic Relations between Men and Women as a Factor in Social Evolution.* 1898. Reprint. New York: Harper and Row, 1966.

Ginzburg, Lori D. " 'Moral Suasion Is Moral Balderdash': Women, Politics, and Social Activism in the 1850's." *Journal of American History* (December 1986): 601–22.

"The Girl Who Comes to the City: A Symposium." *Harper's Bazaar,* January 1908–November 1908.

Glasco, Laurence A. "The Life Cycles and Household Structure of American Ethnic Groups: Irish, Germans, and Native-born Whites in Buffalo, New York, 1855." *Journal of Urban History* (May 1975): 339–64.

Gordon, Linda. *Woman's Body, Woman's Right: A Social History of Birth Control in America.* New York: Penguin Books, 1977.

Greenwald, Maurine Weiner. *Women, War, and Work: The Impact of World War I on Women Workers in the United States.* Westport, Conn.: Greenwood Press, 1980.

Gregory, Alyse. "The Changing Morality of Woman." *Current History* (November 1923): 295–99.

Groetzinger, Leona Prall. *The City's Perils.* N.p., c. 1910.

Groneman, Carol. "She Earns as a Child; She Pays as a Man." In Milton Cantor and Bruce Laurie, eds., *Class, Sex and the Woman Worker.* Westport, Conn.: Greenwood Press, 1977.

Groves, Ernest R. "Psychic Causes of Rural Migration." *American Journal of Sociology* (March 1916): 623–27.

Groves, Ernest R., and William F. Ogburn. *American Marriages and Family Relationships.* New York: Henry Holt, 1928.

Gutman, Herbert G. *The Black Family in Slavery and Freedom, 1750–1925.* New York: Pantheon Books, 1976.

Hadley, Edith M. "The Housing Problem as It Affects Girls." *Survey,* April 19, 1913, 92–94.

Hale, Nathan G., Jr. *Freud and the Americans: The Beginnings of Psychoanalysis in the United States, 1876–1917.* New York: Oxford University Press, 1971.

Hanshaw, T. W. "Alone in New York: A Thrilling Portrayal of the Dangers and Pitfalls of the Metropolis." *New York Family Story Paper,* April 16, 1887–August 27, 1887.

Hareven, Tamara. "Family Time and Industrial Time: Family and Work in a Planned Corporation Town, 1900–1924." In Tamara Hareven, ed., *Family and Kin in Urban Communities, 1700–1922.* New York: Franklin Watts, 1977.

———. *Family Time and Industrial Time: The Relationship between the Family and Work in a New England Industrial Community.* Cambridge: Cambridge University Press, 1982.

Harland, Marion. "The Passing of the Home Daughter." *The Independent,* July 13, 1911, 88–91.

Harland, Robert O. *The Vice Bondage of a Great City or the Wickedest City in the World.* Chicago: Young People's Civic League, 1912.

Harper, Ida Husted. "Women Ought to Work." *The Independent,* May 16, 1901, 1123–27.

Hartmann, Heidi I. "The Family as the Locus of Gender, Class, and Political Struggle: The Example of Housework." *Signs: Journal of Women in Culture and Society* (Spring 1981): 366–94.

Hatcher, O. Latham. *Rural Girls in the City for Work: A Study Made for the Southern Women's Educational Alliance.* Richmond, Va.: Garrett and Massie, 1930.

Hayden, Dolores. *The Grand Domestic Revolution: A History of Feminist Designs for American Homes, Neighborhoods and Cities.* Cambridge: MIT Press, 1981.

Henri, Florette. *Black Migration: Movement North, 1900–1920.* Garden City, N.Y.: Anchor Press, 1975.

Henry, Alice. *Women and the Labor Movement*. New York: George H. Doran
    Co., 1923.
Herbst, Alma. *The Negro in the Slaughtering and Meat-Packing Industry in
    Chicago*. Boston: Houghton Mifflin, 1932.
Hewitt, Nancy A. *Women's Activism and Social Change: Rochester, New York,
    1822–1872*. Ithaca: Cornell University Press, 1984.
Higashi, Sumiko. *Virgins, Vamps, and Flappers: The American Silent Movie Her-
    oine*. Montreal: Eden Press Women's Publications, 1978.
Hill, Joseph A. *Women in Gainful Occupations, 1870 to 1920*. U.S. Bureau of the
    Census. Washington, D.C.: Government Printing Office, 1929.
Historic City: The Settlement of Chicago. Chicago: Department of Development
    and Planning, 1976.
Holt, Glen E., and Dominic A. Pacyga. *Chicago: A Historical Guide to the Neigh-
    borhoods, the Loop and South Side*. Chicago: Chicago Historical Society,
    1979.
"Home Making in the Illinois Bell Telephone Company." *Bell Telephone News*,
    January 1921, 7–9.
Horlick, Allan Stanley. *Country Boys and Merchant Princes: Social Control of
    Young Men in New York*. Lewisburg, Pa.: Bucknell University Press, 1975.
Horowitz, Helen Lefkowitz. *Culture and the City: Cultural Philanthropy in
    Chicago from the 1880s to 1917*. Lexington: University Press of Kentucky,
    1976.
Howard, Adah M. *Little Sunshine: Or, the Secret of the Death Chamber*. New
    York: Norman L. Munro, 1886.
Howe, Jane Sheldrick. *All Work and No Play: A Plea for Saturday Afternoon—
    Stories Told by Two Hundred Department Store Girls*. Chicago: Juvenile
    Protective Association, 1910.
Hoyt, Homer. *One Hundred Years of Land Values in Chicago: The Relationship
    of the Growth of Chicago to the Rise in Its Land Values, 1830–1933*. Chicago:
    University of Chicago Press, 1933.
Hughes, Elizabeth A. *Living Conditions for Small-Wage Families in Chicago*. Chi-
    cago: Department of Public Welfare, 1925.
Hull House. *Hull House Bulletin*. 1896, 1897, 1898, 1900, 1902, 1904.
Hull House Maps and Papers. New York: Thomas Y. Crowell and Co., 1895.
Illinois Bureau of Labor Statistics. *Biennial Report*. 1892, 1906, 1908.
Illinois General Assembly. Senate Vice Committee. *Report of the Senate Vice
    Committee*. Chicago: n.p., 1916.
Illinois Writers' Project. Work Projects Administration. *Annals of Labor and
    Industry in Illinois: Volume I, January, February, March, 1890*. Chicago:
    n.p., 1939.
Immigrants' Protective League. *Annual Report*. 1909–18.
International Labour Office. *Women Workers in Multinational Enterprises in
    Developing Countries*. Geneva: International Labour Organisation, 1985.
Israels, Bell Linder. "The Way of the Girl." *Survey*, July 3, 1909, 486–97.
Jackman, Abi S. "Her Own Way: Or, Reaping the Harvest." *New York Family
    Story Paper*, December 18, 1897–September 2, 1898.

Jackson, Pauline. "Women in Nineteenth-Century Irish Emigration." *International Migration Review* (Winter 1984): 1004–20.

Janiewski, Dolores. *Sisterhood Denied: Race, Gender, and Class in a New South Community.* Philadelphia: Temple University Press, 1985.

Jelin, Elizabeth. "Migration and Labor Force Participation of Latin American Women: The Domestic Servants in the Cities." *Signs: Journal of Women in Culture and Society* (Fall 1977): 129–41.

Jensen, Joan M. *With These Hands: Women Working on the Land.* Old Westbury, N.Y.: Feminist Press, 1981.

Jensen, Joan M., and Sue Davidson, eds. *A Needle, a Bobbin, a Strike: Women Needleworkers in America.* Philadelphia: Temple University Press, 1984.

Jones, Gavin W., ed. *Women in the Urban and Industrial Workforce: Southeast and East Asia.* Canberra: Australian National University, 1984.

Jones, Jacqueline. *Labor of Love, Labor of Sorrow: Black Women, Work, and the Family from Slavery to the Present.* New York: Basic Books, 1985.

Jones, Katharine A. "The Working Girls of Chicago." *Review of Reviews* (September 1891).

Katz, Jonathan, ed. *Gay American History: Lesbians and Gay Men in America.* New York: Avon Books, 1976.

———. *Gay/Lesbian Almanac: A New Documentary.* New York: Harper and Row, 1983.

Katz, Michael B. *The People of Hamilton, Canada West: Family and Class in a Mid-Nineteenth-Century City.* Cambridge: Harvard University Press, 1975.

Katz, Michael B., and Ian E. Davey. "Youth and Early Industrialization in a Canadian City." In John Demos and Sarane Spence Boocock, eds., *Turning Points: Historical and Sociological Essays on the Family.* Chicago: University of Chicago Press, 1978.

Katzman, David M. *Seven Days a Week: Women and Domestic Service in Industrializing America.* New York: Oxford University Press, 1978.

Kelley, Florence. "I Go to Work." *Survey,* June 1, 1927, 271–74, 301.

Kellor, Frances A. "Assisted Emigration from the South—The Women." *Charities,* October 7, 1905, 11–14.

———. "Immigrant Woman." *Atlantic,* September 1907, 401–7.

———. "Southern Colored Girls in the North: The Problem of Their Protection." *Charities,* March 18, 1905, 584–85.

Kennedy, Louise Venable. *The Negro Peasant Turns Cityward: Effects of Recent Migrations to Northern Cities.* New York: Columbia University Press, 1930.

Kessler-Harris, Alice. "Independence and Virtue in the Lives of Wage-Earning Women: The United States, 1870–1930." In Judith Friedlander, Blanche Wiesen Cook, Alice Kessler-Harris, and Carroll Smith-Rosenberg, eds., *Women in Culture and Politics: A Century of Change.* Bloomington: Indiana University Press, 1986.

———. *Out to Work: A History of Wage-Earning Women in the United States.* New York: Oxford University Press, 1982.

Kett, Joseph F. *Rites of Passage: Adolescence in America, 1790 to the Present.* New York: Basic Books, 1977.

Khoo, Siew-ean, Peter C. Smith, and James T. Fawcett. "Migration of Women to Cities: The Asian Situation in Comparative Perspective." *International Migration Review* (Winter 1984): 1247–63.

Kiser, Clyde Vernon. *Sea Island to City: A Study of St. Helena Islanders in Harlem and Other Urban Centers*. New York: Columbia University Press, 1932.

Klaczynska, Barbara. "Why Women Work: A Comparison of Various Groups— Philadelphia, 1910–1930." *Labor History* (Winter 1976): 73–87.

Kobrin, Frances E. "The Fall in Household Size and the Rise of the Primary Individual in the United States." In Michael Gordon, ed., *The American Family in Social-Historical Perspective*. 2d ed. New York: St. Martin's Press, 1978.

Kolko, Gabriel. *The Triumph of Conservatism*. New York: Macmillan, 1963.

Lakeside Annual Directory of the City of Chicago. 1880–1917.

Lamphere, Louise. "Bringing the Family to Work: Women's Culture on the Shop Floor." *Feminist Studies* (Fall 1985): 519–40.

Lasch, Christopher. *Haven in a Heartless World: The Family Besieged*. New York: Basic Books, 1977.

Laughlin, Clara E., *The Work-a-Day Girl*. 1913. Reprint. New York: Arno Press, 1974.

Leach, William. *True Love and Perfect Union: The Feminist Reform of Sex and Society*. New York: Basic Books, 1980.

Lebsock, Suzanne. *The Free Women of Petersburg: Status and Culture in a Southern Town, 1784–1860*. New York: W. W. Norton, 1984.

Lehman, F. M., and Rev. N. K. Clarkson. *The White Slave Hell, Or with Christ at Midnight in the Slums of Chicago*. Chicago: Christian Witness, 1910.

Leuchtenburg, William. *The Perils of Prosperity, 1914–32*. Chicago: University of Chicago Press, 1958.

Levine, Susan. *Labor's True Woman: Carpet Weavers, Industrialization, and Labor Reform in the Gilded Age*. Philadelphia: Temple University Press, 1984.

Lewis, Lloyd, and Henry Justin Smith. *Chicago: The History of Its Reputation*. New York: Harcourt, Brace, 1929.

Libbey, Laura Jean. *A Forbidden Marriage: Or, in Love with a Handsome Spendthrift*. New York: American News, 1888.

———. *Ione: A Broken Love Dream*. New York: Robert Bonner's Sons, 1887 and 1890.

———. *Junie's Love Test*. New York: George Munro, 1883.

———. *Little Leafy, the Cloakmaker's Beautiful Daughter*. New York: N. L. Munro, 1891.

"Libbey, Laura Jean." In Edward T. James, ed., *Notable American Women, 1607–1950: A Biographical Dictionary*. Vol. 2. Cambridge: Harvard University Press, 1971.

Lippmann, Walter. *A Preface to Politics*. New York: Mitchell Kennerly, 1913.

Livermore, Mary. *What Shall We Do with Our Daughters? Superfluous Women and Other Lectures*. Boston: Lee and Shepherd, 1883.

Loos, Anita. *Gentlemen Prefer Blondes: The Illuminating Diary of a Professional Lady*. New York: Boni and Liveright, 1925.

McCarthy, Kathleen. *Noblesse Oblige: Charity and Cultural Philanthropy in Chicago, 1849–1929*. Chicago: University of Chicago Press, 1982.

McDermott, Valeria D., and Annie Elizabeth Trotter. *Chicago Social Service Directory*. Chicago: Department of Public Welfare, 1918.

McGovern, James. "The American Woman's Pre–World War I Freedom in Manners and Morals." *Journal of American History* (September 1968): 315–33.

McGuinn, Henry J. "Recreation." In T. J. Woofter, Jr., ed., *Negro Problems in Cities*. Garden City, N.Y.: Doubleday, Doran, 1928.

McKeever, William A. *Farm Boys and Girls*. New York: Macmillan, 1912.

MacLean, Annie Marion. "Homes for Working Women in Large Cities." *Charities Review* (July 1899): 215–28.

————. *Wage-Earning Women*. New York: Macmillan, 1910.

Manning, Caroline. *The Immigrant Woman and Her Job*. U.S. Women's Bureau. Bulletin 74. Washington, D.C.: Government Printing Office, 1930.

Matthaei, Julie A. *An Economic History of Women in America: Women's Work, the Sexual Division of Labor, and the Development of Capitalism*. New York: Schocken Books, 1982.

May, Henry. *The End of American Innocence: A Study of the First Years of Our Own Time, 1912–1917*. New York: Alfred A. Knopf, 1959.

May, Lary. *Screening Out the Past: The Birth of Mass Culture and the Motion Picture Industry*. New York: Oxford University Press, 1980.

Meites, Hyman L. *History of the Jews in Chicago*. Chicago: Jewish Historical Society of Illinois, c. 1924.

Melosh, Barbara. *"The Physician's Hand": Work, Culture, and Conflict in American Nursing*. Philadelphia: Temple University Press, 1982.

Milkman, Ruth, ed. *Women, Work and Protest: A Century of U.S. Women's Labor History*. Boston: Routledge and Kegan Paul, 1985.

Moch, Leslie Page. "Adolescence and Migration, Nimes, France, 1906." *Social Science History* (Winter 1981): 25–51.

Modell, John. "Dating Becomes the Way of American Youth." In Leslie Page Moch and Gary Stark, eds., *Essays on the Family and Historical Change*. College Station: Texas A&M University Press, 1983.

Modell, John, Frank F. Furstenberg, and Theodore Hershberg. "Social Change and Transitions to Adulthood in Historical Perspective." *Journal of Family History* (August 1973): 7–32.

Modell, John, and Tamara Hareven. "Urbanization and the Malleable Household: An Examination of Boarding and Lodging in American Families." *Journal of Marriage and the Family* (August 1973): 467–79.

Monroe, Day. *Chicago Families: A Study of Unpublished Census Data*. Chicago: University of Chicago Press, 1932.

Montgomery, Louise. *The American Girl in the Stockyards District*. Chicago: University of Chicago Press, 1913.

Morgan, Anne. *The American Girl*. New York: Harper and Brothers, 1914.

Morrison, Peter A. "The Functions and Dynamics of the Migration Process." In Alan A. Brown and Egon Neuberger, eds., *Internal Migration: A Comparative Perspective*. New York: Academic Press, 1977.

Mowrer, Ernest. *Family Disorganization: An Introduction to Sociological Analysis*. Chicago: University of Chicago Press, 1927.

Mowry, George E. *The Urban Nation, 1920–1960*. New York: Hill and Wang, 1965.

Munden, Kenneth, ed. *The American Film Institute Catalog, Feature Films, 1921– 1930*. New York: R. R. Bowker, 1971.

Nash, June, and Maria Patricia Fernandez-Kelly. *Women, Men, and the International Division of Labor*. Albany: State University of New York Press, 1983.

Nathan, Maud. "Women Who Work and Women Who Spend." *Annals of American Academy of Political and Social Science* (May 1906): 184–88.

National Consumers' League. *Annual Report*. 1900–6, 1909–13.

National Industrial Conference Board. Wages in the United States, 1914–1930. New York: National Industrial Conference Board, 1931.

National Urban League for Social Service among Negroes. *Twenty-fifth Anniversary Souvenir Booklet: "Not Alms; But Opportunity."* New York: n.p., 1935.

Neill, Charles P. *Wage-Earning Women in Stores and Factories*. Vol. 5 in the *Report on Condition of Woman and Child Wage-Earners in the United States*. Washington, D.C.: Government Printing Office, 1910.

Newton, Esther. "The Mythic Mannish Lesbian: Radclyffe Hall and the New Woman." *Signs: Journal of Women in Culture and Society* (Summer 1984): 557–75.

Nichols, Anne E. "Woman and Trade Unions." *The Commons*, June 1904, 268– 73.

Noel, Mary. *Villains Galore: The Heyday of the Popular Story Weekly*. New York: Macmillan, 1954.

Norton, Mary Beth. *Liberty's Daughters: The Revolutionary Experience of American Women, 1750–1800*. Boston: Little, Brown, 1980.

"Objects of Charity." *New Republic*, January 23, 1914, 10.

O'Brien, David J., and Mary Joan Roach. "Recent Developments in Urban Sociology." *Journal of Urban History* (February 1984): 145–70.

Oliver, Paul. *Screening the Blues: Aspects of the Blues Tradition*. London: Cassell, 1968.

O'Neill, William. "Divorce in the Progressive Era." In Michael Gordon, ed., *The American Family in Social-Historical Perspective*. 2d ed. New York: St. Martin's Press, 1978.

Ovington, Mary White. *Half a Man: The Status of the Negro in New York*. New York: Longmans, Green, 1911.

Packard, Esther. *A Study of Living Conditions of Self-Supporting Women in New York City*. New York: Metropolitan Board of the YWCA, 1915.

Park, Robert E. "The City as a Social Laboratory." In T. V. Smith and Leonard D. White, eds., *Chicago: An Experiment in Social Science Research*. Chicago: University of Chicago Press, 1929.

_____."Community Organization and Juvenile Delinquency." In Robert E. Park, Ernest W. Burgess, and Roderick D. McKenzie, eds., *The City*. Chicago: University of Chicago Press, 1925.

Patterson, Orlando. "Migration in Caribbean Societies: Socioeconomic and Symbolic Resource." In William H. McNeill and Ruth S. Adams, eds., *Human Migration: Patterns and Policies*. Bloomington: Indiana University Press, 1978.

Peel, Mark. "On the Margins: Lodgers and Boarders in Boston, 1860–1900." *Journal of American History* (March 1986): 813–34.

Peiss, Kathy. " 'Charity Girls' and City Pleasures: Historical Notes on Working-Class Sexuality, 1880–1920." In Ann Snitow, Christine Stansell, and Sharon Thompson, eds., *Powers of Desire: The Politics of Sexuality*. New York: Monthly Review Press, 1983.

_____. *Cheap Amusements: Working Women and Leisure in Turn-of-the-Century New York*. Philadelphia: Temple University Press, 1986.

Penny, Virginia. *The Employment of Women: A Cyclopedia of Woman's Work*. Boston: Walker, Wise, 1863.

Persons, C. D. "Women's Work and Wages in the United States." *Quarterly Journal of Economics* (February 1915): 201–34.

Pidgeon, Mary Elizabeth. *Women in Five-and-Ten-Cent Stores and Limited-Price Chain Department Stores*. U.S. Women's Bureau. Bulletin 76. Washington, D.C.: Government Printing Office, 1930.

Pierce, Bessie Louise. *A History of Chicago. Vol. III, The Rise of a Modern City, 1871–1893*. New York: Alfred A. Knopf, 1957.

Pittin, Renée. "Migration of Women in Nigeria: The Hausa Case." *International Migration Review* (Winter 1984): 1293–1314.

Pivar, David J. *Purity Crusade: Sexual Morality and Social Control, 1868–1900*. Westport, Conn.: Greenwood Press, 1973.

Pleck, Elizabeth. "A Mother's Wages: Income Earning among Married Italian and Black Women, 1896–1911." In Michael Gordon, ed., *The American Family in Social-Historical Perspective*. 2d. ed. New York: St. Martin's Press, 1978.

_____. "Two Worlds in One: Work and Family." *Journal of Social History* (Winter 1976): 178–95.

Poles of Chicago, 1837–1937. Chicago: Polish Pageant, Inc., 1937.

President's Research Committee on Social Trends. *Recent Social Trends*. New York: Whittlesey House, McGraw-Hill, 1934.

"Quantity-Cost Budget Necessary to Maintain Single Man or Woman in Washington, D.C." *Monthly Labor Review* (January 1920): 35–44.

Ramsaye, Terry. *A Million and One Nights*. Vol. 1. New York: Simon and Schuster, 1926.

Ravenstein, E. G. "The Laws of Migration." *Journal of the Statistical Society* (June 1885): 199.

Reckless, Walter C. *Vice in Chicago*. Chicago: University of Chicago Press, 1933.

Rees, Seth Cook. *Miracle in the Slums, or Thrilling Stories of Those Rescued from the Cesspools of Iniquity, and Touching Incidents in the Lives of the Unfortunate*. Chicago: Seth Cook Rees, 1905.

Regan, John. *Crimes of White Slavers and the Results*. Chicago: J. Regan and Co., 1912.

Reitman, Ben Lewis. *Sister of the Road: The Autobiography of Box-Car Bertha as Told to Dr. Ben L. Reitman*. New York: Macauley, 1937.

Richardson, Anna Steese. *The Girl Who Earns Her Own Living*. New York: B. W. Dodge and Co., 1909.

Richardson, Dorothy. "The Difficulties and Dangers Confronting the Working Woman." *Annals of American Academy of Political and Social Science* (May 1906): 162–64.

———. *The Long Day: The Story of a New York Working Girl*. 1905. Reprinted in William O'Neill, ed., *Woman at Work*. New York: New York Times Books, 1972.

Rose, Arnold M. "Interest in the Living Arrangements of the Urban Unattached." *American Journal of Sociology* (May 1948): 483–93.

———. "Living Arrangements of Unattached Persons." *American Sociological Review* (August 1947): 429–35.

Rosen, Marjorie. *Popcorn Venus: Women, Movies and the American Dream*. New York: Coward, McCann and Geoghegan, 1973.

Rosen, Ruth. *The Lost Sisterhood: Prostitution in America, 1900–1918*. Baltimore: Johns Hopkins University Press, 1982.

Rosenberg, Rosalind. *Beyond Separate Spheres: Intellectual Roots of Modern Feminism*. New Haven: Yale University Press, 1982.

Rosenzweig, Roy. *Eight Hours for What We Will: Workers and Leisure in an Industrial City, 1870–1920*. Cambridge: Cambridge University Press, 1983.

Rotella, Elyce J. *From Home to Office: U.S. Women and Work, 1870–1930*. Ann Arbor: University Microfilms International Research Press, 1981.

Rothman, Ellen. *Hands and Hearts: A History of Courtship in America*. New York: Basic Books, 1984.

Rothman, Sheila M. *Woman's Proper Place: A History of Changing Ideals and Practices, 1870 to the Present*. New York: Basic Books, 1978.

Rowlands, Effie Adelaide. *A Woman Scorned*. Pt. 3. New York: Street and Smith, 1899.

Russell, Thomas H. *The Girl's Fight for a Living: How to Protect Working Women from Dangers Due to Low Wages*. Chicago: M. A. Donahue and Co., 1913.

Ryan, Mary P. *Cradle of the Middle Class: The Family in Oneida County, New York, 1790–1865*. Cambridge: Cambridge University Press, 1981.

———. "The Power of Women's Networks: A Case Study of Female Moral Reform in Antebellum America." *Feminist Studies* (Spring 1979): 66–85.

———. "The Projection of a New Womanhood: The Movie Moderns in the 1920s." In Jean E. Friedman and William G. Shade, eds., *Our American*

Sisters: Women in American Life and Thought. 2d ed. Boston: Allyn and Bacon, 1976.

―――. *Womanhood in America: From Colonial Times to the Present.* 2d ed. New York: New Viewpoints, 1979.

Saunders, Florence Wenderoth. *Letters to a Business Girl.* Chicago: Laird and Lee, 1908.

Schwarz, Judith. "Yellow Clover: Katherine Lee Bates and Katharine Coman." *Frontiers* (Spring 1979): 59–67.

Scott, Emmett J. "Additional Letters of Negro Migrants of 1916–1918." *Journal of Negro History* (October 1919): 412–65.

―――. "Letters of Negro Migrants of 1916–1918." *Journal of Negro History* (July 1919): 290–334.

―――. *Negro Migration during the War.* 1920. Reprint. New York: Arno Press, 1969.

Scott, Estelle Hill. *Occupational Changes among Negroes in Chicago.* Chicago: Illinois Work Projects Administration, 1939.

Second Class, Working Class: An International Women's Reader. Oakland, Calif.: Peoples Translation Service, 1979.

Sennett, Richard, ed. *Classic Essays on the Culture of Cities.* New York: Meredith Corporation, 1969.

Sharpe, May Churchill. *Chicago May: Her Story.* London: Sampson, Low, Marston, 1929.

Shorter, Edward. *The Making of the Modern Family.* New York: Basic Books, 1975.

Showalter, Elaine. "Introduction." In Elaine Showalter, ed., *These Modern Women: Autobiographical Essays from the Twenties.* Old Westbury, N.Y.: Feminist Press, 1978.

Sims, Mary S. *The Natural History of a Social Institution: The Young Women's Christian Association.* New York: Woman's Press, 1936.

Smith, Daniel Scott. "The Dating of the American Sexual Revolution: Evidence and Interpretation." In Michael Gordon, ed., *The American Family in Socio-Historical Perspective.* 2d ed. New York: St. Martin's Press, 1978.

Smith, Judith E. *Family Connections: A History of Italian and Jewish Immigrant Lives in Providence, Rhode Island, 1900–1940.* Albany: State University of New York Press, 1985.

Smith-Rosenberg, Carroll. "Beauty, the Beast, and the Militant Woman: A Case Study in Sex Roles and Social Stress in Jacksonian America." In Nancy F. Cott and Elizabeth H. Pleck, eds., *A Heritage of Her Own: Toward a New Social History of American Women.* New York: Simon and Schuster, 1979.

―――. *Disorderly Conduct: Visions of Gender in Victorian America.* New York: Alfred A. Knopf, 1985.

―――. "The Female World of Love and Ritual: Relations between Women in Nineteenth-Century America." *Signs: Journal of Women in Culture and Society* (Autumn 1975): 1–29.

―――. "Sex as Symbol in Victorian Purity: An Ethnological Analysis of Jacksonian America." In John Demos and Sarane Spence Boocock, eds.,

Turning Points: Historical and Sociological Essays on the Family. Chicago: University of Chicago Press, 1978.

Sochen, June. *The New Woman: Feminism in Greenwich Village, 1910–1920.* New York: Quadrangle Books, 1972.

Social Service Directory, 1915. Chicago: Department of Public Welfare, 1915.

Social Service Directory Chicago, 1923. Chicago: Council of Social Agencies, 1923.

Social Service Directory of Chicago, 1926. Chicago: Council of Social Agencies, 1926.

Social Service Directory of Chicago, 1930. Chicago: Council of Social Agencies, 1930.

Sonneborn, Ida, ed. *Chicago Charities Directory, 1906.* Chicago: Chicago Charity Directory Association, 1906.

Spear, Allan H. *Black Chicago: The Making of a Negro Ghetto, 1890–1920.* Chicago: University of Chicago Press, 1967.

The Sporting and Club House Directory. Chicago: Rose and St. Clair, 1889.

Stanley, Charlotte M. "Violet, the Beautiful Street Singer: Or, an Ill-Starred Betrothal." *New York Family Story Paper,* August 22, 1908–October 11, 1908.

Stansell, Christine. *City of Women: Sex and Class in New York, 1789–1860.* New York: Alfred A. Knopf, 1986.

Stead, William T. *If Christ Came to Chicago! A Plea for the Union of All Who Love in the Service of All Who Suffer.* London: Review of Reviews, 1894.

Stein, Robert. "Girls' Cooperative Boarding Homes." *The Arena,* March 1898, 397–418.

Stichter, Sharon. *Migrant Laborers.* Cambridge: Cambridge University Press, 1985.

Strickland, Arvarh E. *History of the Chicago Urban League.* Urbana: University of Illinois Press, 1966.

Sumner, Helen L. *History of Women in Industry in the United States.* Vol. 9 in the *Report on Condition of Woman and Child Wage-Earners in the United States.* Washington, D.C.: Government Printing Office, 1910.

Taueber, Irene, and Conrad Taueber. *People in the U.S. in the Twentieth Century.* U.S. Bureau of the Census. Washington, D.C.: Government Printing Office, 1971.

Taussig, F. W. "Minimum Wages for Women." *Quarterly Journal of Economics* (May 1916): 411–42.

Tax, Meredith. *The Rising of the Women: Feminist Solidarity and Class Conflict, 1880–1917.* New York: Monthly Review Press, 1980.

Tentler, Leslie Woodcock. *Wage-Earning Women: Industrial Work and Family Life in the United States, 1900–1930.* New York: Oxford University Press, 1979.

Thomas, W. I. *The Unadjusted Girl, with Cases and Standpoint for Behavior Analysis.* Boston: Little, Brown, 1923.

Thornthwaite, C. Warren. *Internal Migration in the United States.* Philadelphia: University of Pennsylvania Press, 1934.

Tilly, Louise A. "Paths of Proletarianization: Organization of Production, Sexual Division of Labor and Women's Collective Action." *Signs: Journal of Women in Culture and Society* (Winter 1981): 400–417.

Tilly, Louise A., and Joan W. Scott. *Women, Work, and Family.* New York: Holt, Rinehard and Winston, 1978.

Tilly, Louise A., Joan W. Scott, and Miriam Cohen. "Women's Work and European Fertility Patterns." *Journal of Interdisciplinary History* (Winter 1976): 447–76.

Travelers' Aid Society of Chicago and Illinois. *Annual Report.* 1916, 1919, 1920, 1923.

Trotter, Ann Elizabeth. *Housing of Non-Family Women in Chicago: A Survey.* Chicago: Chicago Community Trust, c. 1921.

True, Ruth S. *The Neglected Girl.* New York: Russell Sage, 1914.

U.S. Bureau of the Census. Decennial Census. *Metropolitan Districts.* 1930.

————. Decennial Census. *Occupations.* 1900, 1920, 1930.

————. Decennial Census. *Population.* 1870, 1880, 1890, 1900, 1910, 1920, 1930.

————. Decennial Census. *Social Statistics of Cities.* 1880.

————. *Historical Statistics of the United States: Colonial Times to 1970.* Washington, D.C.: Government Printing Office, 1975.

————. *Negroes in the U.S., 1920–1932.* Washington, D.C.: Government Printing Office, 1935.

————. *Negro Population, 1790–1915.* Washington, D.C.: Government Printing Office, 1918.

————. *Statistics of Women at Work.* Washington, D.C.: Government Printing Office, 1907.

U.S. Bureau of Labor. Bureau of Industrial Housing and Transportation. *Report of the U.S. Housing Corporation.* Washington, D.C.: Government Printing Office, 1920.

————. *Standards Recommended for Permanent Industrial Housing Developments.* Washington, D.C.: Government Printing Office, 1918.

U.S. Commissioner of Labor. *Fourth Annual Report, 1888: Working Women in Large Cities.* Washington, D.C.: Government Printing Office, 1889.

U.S. Department of Agriculture. Economic Research Service. *Farm Population: Estimates for 1910–62.* Washington, D.C.: Government Printing Office, 1963.

U.S. Department of Labor. Bureau of Labor Statistics. *History of Wages in the U.S. from Colonial Times to 1928.* Washington, D.C.: Government Printing Office, 1934.

————. Division of Negro Economics. *Negro Migration in 1916–17.* Washington, D.C.: Government Printing Office, 1919.

————. Women's Bureau. *The Development of Minimum-Wage Laws in the United States, 1912 to 1927.* Bulletin 62. Washington, D.C.: Government Printing Office, 1928.

————. *The Family Status of Breadwinning Women: A Study of Material in the Census Schedules of a Selected Locality.* Bulletin 23. Washington, D.C.: Government Printing Office, 1922.

―――. *The Family Status of Breadwinning Women in Four Selected Cities: Revision and Extension of Bulletin 23.* Bulletin 41. Washington, D.C.: Government Printing Office, 1925.

―――. *Negro Women in Industry.* Bulletin 20. Washington, D.C.: Government Printing Office, 1922.

―――. *Wages of Candy Makers in Philadelphia in 1919.* Bulletin 4. Washington, D.C.: Government Printing Office, 1919.

―――. *Women in the Candy Industry in Chicago and St. Louis: A Study of Hours, Wages and Working Conditions in 1920–1921.* Bulletin 25, Washington, D.C.: Government Printing Office, 1923.

―――. *Women in Illinois Industries: A Study of Hours and Working Conditions.* Bulletin 51. Washington, D.C.: Government Printing Office, 1926.

Van Vechten, Carl. *Firecrackers: A Realistic Novel.* New York: Alfred A. Knopf, 1925.

Van Vorst, Mrs. John, and Marie Van Vorst. *The Woman Who Toils: Being the Experiences of Two Ladies as Factory Girls.* New York: Doubleday, Page, 1903.

Veiller, Lawrence. *Housing Reform: A Handbook for Practical Use in American Cities.* New York: Russell Sage, 1910.

Vice Commission of Chicago. *The Social Evil in Chicago: A Study of Existing Conditions with Recommendations by the Vice Commission of Chicago.* Chicago: Vice Commission of Chicago, 1911.

Vicinus, Martha. *Independent Women: Work and Community for Single Women, 1850–1920.* Chicago: University of Chicago Press, 1985.

Visher, John. *Handbook of Charities.* Chicago: Charles H. Kerr, 1897.

Vynne, Harold R. *Chicago by Day and Night: The Pleasure Seeker's Guide to the Paris of America.* Chicago: Thomas and Zimmerman, 1892.

Walter, Eugene. *The Easiest Way.* New York: n.p., 1908.

"A Warning for Country Girls." *Literary Digest,* December 13, 1924, 33.

Washburn, Charles. *Come into My Parlor: A Biography of the Aristocratic Everleigh Sisters of Chicago.* New York: National Library Press, 1936.

Weatherly, U. G. "How Does the Access of Women to Industrial Occupations React on the Family?" *American Journal of Sociology* (May 1909): 740–65.

Weber, Adna Ferrin. *The Growth of Cities in the Nineteenth Century: A Study in Statistics.* New York: Macmillan, 1899.

Weeks, Jeffrey. *Coming Out: Homosexual Politics in Britain, from the Nineteenth Century to the Present.* London: Quartet Books, 1977.

Weiner, Lynn. *From Working Girl to Working Mother: The Female Labor Force in the United States, 1820–1980.* Chapel Hill: University of North Carolina Press, 1985.

―――. " 'Our Sister's Keepers': Minneapolis Woman's Christian Association and Housing for Working Women." *Minnesota History* (Spring 1979): 189–200.

Weiss, Nancy J. *The National Urban League, 1910–1940.* New York: Oxford University Press, 1974.

Welter, Barbara. "The Cult of True Womanhood: 1820–1860." *American Quarterly* (Summer 1966): 151–74.

Wertheimer, Barbara Mayer. *We Were There: The Story of Working Women in America*. New York: Pantheon Books, 1977.

Wheeler, Adade Mitchell, with Marlene Stein Wortman. *The Roads They Made: Women in Illinois History*. Chicago: Charles H. Kerr, 1977.

Whiteford, Michael B. "Women, Migration, and Social Change: A Columbian Case Study." *International Migration Review* (Summer 1978): 236–47.

Wiebe, Robert H. *The Search for Order, 1877–1920*. New York: Hill and Wang, 1967.

Wilkie, Jane Riblett. "The Black Urban Population of the Pre–Civil War South." *Phylon* (September 1976): 250–62.

Willard, Frances. *How to Win: A Book for Girls*. New York: Funk and Wagnalls, 1887.

Williams, Fannie Barrier. "The Club Movement among Colored Women of America." In J. E. MacBrady, ed., *A New Negro for a New Century*. Chicago: American Publishing House, c. 1900.

Wilson, Elizabeth. *Fifty Years of Association Work among Young Women, 1866–1916: A History of Young Women's Christian Associations in the United States of America*. New York: National Board of YWCA, 1916.

Wilson, Harriet E. *Our Nig; Or, Sketches from the Life of a Free Black*. New York: Vintage Books, 1983.

Wilson, Samuel Paynter. *Chicago and Its Cess-Pools of Infamy*. Chicago: n.p., 1909.

Wolfe, Albert Benedict. *The Lodging House Problem in Boston*. Boston: Houghton Mifflin, 1906.

———. "The Problem of the Roomer." *Charities*, November 2, 1907, 957–62.

Wolfson, Theresa. *The Woman Worker and the Trade Unions*. New York: International Publishers, 1926.

Women's Trade Union League of Chicago. *Annual Report*. 1907–8.

———. *Official Report of the Strike Committee, Chicago Workers' Strike, October 29, 1910–February 18, 1911*. Chicago: Women's Trade Union League of Chicago, 1911.

———. *Report of the Immigration Committee of the Women's Trade Union League of Chicago*. 1908.

Wright, Carroll D. *The Slums of Baltimore, Chicago, New York, and Philadelphia*. U.S. Bureau of Labor. Washington, D.C.: Government Printing Office, 1894.

Yans-McLaughlin, Virginia. *Family and Community: Italian Immigrants in Buffalo, 1880–1930*. Ithaca: Cornell University Press, 1977.

———. "Italian Women and Work: Experience and Perception." In Milton Cantor and Bruce Laurie, eds., *Class, Sex and the Woman Worker*. Westport, Conn.: Greenwood Press, 1977.

Yellis, Kenneth. "Prosperity's Child: Some Thoughts on the Flapper." *American Quarterly* (Spring 1969). 44–64.

Yezierska, Anzia. *Bread Givers: A Struggle between a Father of the Old World and a Daughter of the New.* 1925. Reprint. New York: Persea Books, 1975.

Young, E. C. *The Movement of Farm Population.* Ithaca: Cornell University Agricultural Experiment Station, 1924.

Young Women's Christian Association, U.S. National Board, War Work Council. *Housing for Women in War Work.* New York: n.p., 1918.

Young Women's Christian Association of Chicago. *Annual Report.* 1877, 1878, 1880–1901, 1903–28.

———. *Dedication of Harriet Hammond McCormick Memorial.* Chicago: n.p., 1928.

———. *Report of the Emergency Bureau.* 1921, 1923, 1924.

Zavella, Patricia. " 'Abnormal Intimacy': The Varying Work Networks of Chicana Cannery Workers." *Feminist Studies* (Fall 1985): 541–57.

Zimmerman, Carle C. "The Migration to Towns and Cities." *American Journal of Sociology* (November 1926): 450–55.

———. "The Migration to Towns and Cities, II." *American Journal of Sociology* (July 1927): 105–9.

Zimmerman, Mrs. Jean Turner. *Chicago's Black Traffic in White Girls.* N.p., 1912.

Zorbaugh, Harvey W. "The Dweller in Furnished Rooms: An Urban Type." In Ernest W. Burgess, ed., *The Urban Community: Selected Papers from the Proceedings of the American Sociological Society, 1925.* Chicago: University of Chicago Press, 1926.

———. *The Gold Coast and the Slum: A Sociological Study of Chicago's Near North Side.* Chicago: University of Chicago Press, 1929.

Index